ORIGEN'S DOCTRINE OF TRADITION

ORIGEN'S DOCTRINE OF TRADITION

BY

R. P. C. HANSON, D.D.

Lecturer in Theology in the University of Nottingham

LONDON

S · P · C · K

1954

CAMBRIDGE
UNIVERSITY PRESS

University Printing House, Cambridge CB2 8BS, United Kingdom

Cambridge University Press is part of the University of Cambridge.

It furthers the University's mission by disseminating knowledge in the pursuit of
education, learning and research at the highest international levels of excellence.

www.cambridge.org
Information on this title: www.cambridge.org/9781107586017

© Cambridge University Press 1954

First published 1954
First paperback edition 2015

A catalogue record for this publication is available from the British Library

ISBN 978-1-107-58601-7 Paperback

ALEXANDRO R. VIDLER
PRAECLARI INGENII AUCTORI
STUDIORUM IUVENTUTIS INSTIGATORI
CONSTANTI AMICO

CONTENTS

ACKNOWLEDGEMENTS

Acknowledgements are due to the following for permission to quote from the works indicated:

The Editor of *The Eastern Churches Quarterly* (*E.C.Q.*, Vol. VII, Supplementary Issue).

The Epworth Press (J. Lawson, *The Biblical Theology of Saint Irenaeus*).

Methuen and Co., Ltd. (J. F. Bethune-Baker, *An Introduction to the Early History of Christian Doctrine*, 5th ed.).

Revue d'Histoire Ecclésiastique, Louvain (*R.H.E.*, tom. 19 and tom. 20).

Williams and Norgate, Ltd. (R. B. Tollinton, *Clement of Alexandria*, Vol. II).

PREFACE

IT is no doubt incumbent upon anybody who produces a work upon Origen's doctrine of tradition to begin by giving some reasons why he should have chosen such a subject, and, as I have spent a good deal of time spared from parochial work and work in a Theological College over eight years in dealing as well as I can with this subject, I have every reason for prefacing the result of this labour with a short justification of my choice.

This study is part of a much larger examination which I hope some day to complete of Origen's interpretation of Scripture. Origen was one of the great Biblical scholars of the early Christian Church, and it should be of interest and indeed of profit to many students and scholars to know how far modern Biblical scholarship has anything in common with one of the best representatives of ancient scholarship, or whether—as some have concluded—the gulf between the Fathers' interpretation of the Bible and ours is unbridgable. But an examination of Origen's interpretation of the Bible cannot be properly undertaken until his attitude to tradition, in its broadest sense, has been fully explored. This study may therefore be considered as a necessary preliminary to a full study of Origen's attitude to the Bible, an establishing of basic assumptions, a pegging-out of positions, so to speak, from which the wider study can proceed. This is the reason why this work is so little concerned with those parts of Origen's theology which usually hold so much interest for those who read him—his doctrine of the pre-existence of souls, his belief in universal salvation, his speculation concerning a pre-mundane fall, his subordination of the Son to the Father, his treatment of the resurrection of the body, and so on. We have been concerned merely to assemble the materials which Origen used in order to build his daring edifice of doctrine, without feeling it necessary ourselves to sketch more than the foundations of that edifice. If the reader finds us much concerned with historical fact and little with theological synthesis, let him think of us as toiling obscurely at a task which is humble but necessary if Origen's theology is to be properly articulated and understood.

We call the task necessary, because, for various reasons, nobody has yet attempted it at all fully. Indeed, as far as English scholarship is concerned, Origen is almost unexplored territory. On the Continent the situation is better, because several articles in French and German have appeared dealing partly or entirely with aspects of Origen's doctrine of tradition, and French and German scholars have devoted full-length works to expounding Origen's theology as a whole. But nobody has ever written a book in any language on Origen's doctrine of tradition, and until his doctrine on this point is fairly understood no study of his theology as a whole can be quite complete.

On one point in particular perhaps this study will be of some use, in that I call attention in it, as strongly as I can, to the necessity of using a carefully critical judgement in assessing the value of the Latin translations of Origen's works. This is a point which has been entirely ignored by some scholars, not very highly accounted of by many, and properly appreciated by—I venture to say—very few. And yet it is of indispensable importance for our setting out of the evidence for almost any doctrine in Origen, and not least for his doctrine of tradition.

The question of the development of the doctrine of tradition in the early Church generally is a most interesting one, though it necessarily touches upon several controversial points. As far as I know—but I confess my knowledge does not go very far—it has not attracted the attention of many scholars. Perhaps this study may serve as an introduction, even in its defects, to the study of a Christian Father who has been too long neglected by English scholarship and to a subject which should attract our attention more strongly than it has in the past.

I wish to express my gratitude to the authorities of those libraries which have granted me facilities and shown me kindness and courtesy during the compilation of this work: of the Library of Trinity College, Dublin; of the Library of the Queen's University, Belfast; of the Library of Handsworth Theological College, Birmingham; of the

Library of the British Museum; of the Library of the University of Birmingham; and of the National Library, Dublin. I also owe thanks to the Queen's College, Birmingham, and to the Seabury-Western Theological Seminary, Evanston, Illinois, for enabling and encouraging me to give lectures on the Christian Platonists of Alexandria, and thereby giving me the incentive and opportunity to put into shape the material I had collected. Finally I should like to thank the readers of the Cambridge University Press and of S.P.C.K. for many valuable suggestions, and my wife for considerable help in compiling the Indices.

R. P. C. HANSON

ABBREVIATIONS

E.C.Q.   *The Eastern Churches Quarterly*, Vol. VII, Supplementary Issue.

G.C.S.   *Die Griechischen Christlichen Schriftsteller der ersten drei Jahrhunderte.*

H.E.   Eusebius, *Ecclesiastical History.*

J.T.S.   *Journal of Theological Studies.*

P.G.   Migne, *Patrologia Graeca.*

P.L.   Migne, *Patrologia Latina.*

Throughout this work I have referred to that part of Origen's *Commentary on Matthew* which is extant (with the exception of a few fragments) only in Latin, and is usually known as the *Commentariorum Series*, as *Commentary on Matthew*, Part II.

On several occasions I have referred in footnotes to books by the names of their authors instead of by their titles, but on each occasion it is perfectly obvious which book is intended.

INTRODUCTION

THE DATE AND ORDER OF ORIGEN'S WORKS

IN order to determine as far as we can the date and order of Origen's works, we must first establish the dates of the main events of his life. Eusebius tells us (*H.E.* VI. 2) that Origen's father Leonidas was martyred when Laetus was governing Alexandria under Severus, and that at that time Origen was seventeen. This would mean that Origen must have been born in 186[1] and his father martyred in 203.[2] By 204 he was presiding over the Catechetical School. Daniélou has some interesting remarks on this school.[3] The school-teaching which Origen took on when he sold, as Eusebius tells us (*H.E.* VI. 3), his secular books was not that of a general school of the liberal arts, such as Gregory describes him as keeping later in Caesarea, uniting the study of philosophy and of Scripture, nor was it delivered to a group of disciples imbibing and spreading outwards the influence of their master, such as he probably conducted while he was in Athens much later, and such as was probably conducted by Clement of Alexandria and by Pantaenus, his master, before him. But it was with a Catechetical School in the strict sense, for the instructing of catechumens before baptism, that Origen, young as he was, must have been entrusted, in default, perhaps, of any other through persecution. He was probably the first to be thus officially the head of a Catechetical School in Alexandria.[4] Eusebius tells us (*H.E.* VI. 19) that Origen, some time before he left Alexandria, handed the teaching of the catechumens over to Heraclas, and confined his teaching to the more advanced pupils.

---

[1] Halévy puts Origen's birth at 186 ('L'Origine de la Transcription', etc., pp. 335–41). Daniélou puts it at 185, and Leonidas' martyrdom at 202 (*Origène*, p. 22).

[2] So Lawlor and Oulton, Vol. II, p. 192. We can disregard, with Eusebius, Porphyry's statement that Origen was brought up a pagan. See *H.E.* VI. 19.

[3] *Origène*, pp. 25–6, 29; he is relying mainly on an article by Bardy in the *Revue Biblique* (2e série, pp. 84 ff.).

[4] Bishops entrusted learned laymen with such an office, and thence developed the order of *lector*; there is some reference to this in Hippolytus' *Apostolic Tradition* (12).

A letter of Origen quoted in *H.E.* VI. 19 and Eusebius' comments on it make it clear that what Origen then ran was a sort of Christian University, where the teaching included references to pagan philosophy and to the doctrines of heretics.

Not long after 204 Origen must have performed his act of self-castration,[1] and at about the same time he converted from heresy Ambrosius, who was to become his life-long friend and patron.[2] He visited Rome with Ambrosius,[3] probably in 212, though Cadiou would date this visit 210–11.[4] Cadiou also quotes S. Jerome as saying, in his *De Viris Illustribus* LXI, that at Rome Hippolytus greeted Origen among his hearers during a lecture.[5] He wants to place Ambrosius' conversion during this visit.[6] Bardy, however, agrees with Lawlor and Oulton in dating the visit 212.[7] A visit to Arabia shortly after this (*H.E.* VI. 14) may be dated 214.[8] Further we are told (*H.E.* VI. 16) that Origen found a copy of the 'Sixth' or 'Seventh' versions of the Psalms in a jar in Jericho in the time of Antoninus, the son of Severus, which suggests 215 as the date of Origen's first visit to Palestine, and to Caesarea in particular (mentioned in *H.E.* VI. 19).[9] Then in 232[10] Origen left Alexandria finally, was ordained presbyter in Palestine, visited Athens for the first time, and later Asia Minor, and settled at Caesarea in Palestine. The authority for this is *H.E.* VI. 23, which dates Origen's ordination by the accession of Pontianus to the see of Rome, and of Zebinus to that of Antioch. There is also *H.E.* VI. 26, which, speaking of Origen's move to Caesarea, says ἔτος δ' ἦν τοῦτο δέκατον τῆς δηλουμένης ἡγεμονίας (i.e. Alexander Severus'), which brings us to 232. This is confirmed by the statement, also in *H.E.* VI.

---

[1] Lawlor and Oulton, p. 194, place this in 210 at latest.

[2] *H.E.* VI. 23. See Lawlor and Oulton, pp. 213–14.

[3] *H.E.* VI. 14, 16. See Lawlor and Oulton, pp. 201, 203–4.

[4] *La Jeunesse d'Origène*, p. 62.   [5] Ibid. p. 63.   [6] Ibid. p. 84.

[7] G. Bardy, 'La Règle de Foi d'Origène', p. 167.

[8] Lawlor and Oulton, p. 201. Cadiou would date this 214 or 215 (*La Jeunesse d'Origène*, p. 107).

[9] Lawlor and Oulton are ambiguous here. On p. 201 of their work they date this first visit to Palestine as '*c.* 216', yet on pp. 203 and 206 they date it as 215. Rauer apparently dates it 216 (Introduction to his edition of the *Commentary* and *Homilies on Luke*, pp. xiii–xv).

[10] So Lawlor and Oulton and Field (*Origenis Hexaplorum Quae Supersunt, Praefatio et Prolegomena*, p. 1). Denis (*De la Philosophie d'Origène*, p. 390) dates it 231, Cadiou (*La Jeunesse d'Origène*, p. 392) 230–1.

26, that 'not long after' Demetrius was succeeded by Heraclas as Bishop of Alexandria, having been bishop for forty-three years. Now *H.E.* v. 22 tells us that Demetrius became bishop in 190, so this would put his death, very appropriately to this scheme of dating, at 233. Lawlor and Oulton point out[1] that the only evidence for Origen's return to Alexandria after his visit to Greece mentioned in *H.E.* VI. 23 (a return assumed by several scholars)[2] is the statement of Photius, apparently based on Rufinus' translation of Pamphilus' *Apology for Origen*, that Origen was ordered to depart from Alexandria. Jerome merely says *damnatus*, not 'banished' (*Epistle* xxxiii).[3] It is much easier to reconcile what we know of his journey with the assumption that when Origen left Alexandria for this journey he left it for good, having appointed Heraclas as his successor in the Catechetical School. He cannot have left Alexandria earlier than 230, the date of Pontianus' accession (*H.E.* VI. 23); he was ordained presbyter in Caesarea (ibid.); he held a debate with a heretic in Athens, staying in Athens long enough for a garbled account of the debate to have reached Alexandria before he returned to Palestine,[4] and with another heretic in Antioch. Moreover the news of his ordination must have had time to reach Alexandria, and to cause Demetrius to write a new series of letters to bishops against him (in addition to a former series mentioned in *H.E.* VI. 19). All this would hardly leave time for Origen to return to Alexandria and be expelled by 232. Anyway, Eusebius nowhere says that Origen was *expelled*, only that he left; and Origen's own reference in the *Commentary on John* says 'we were rescued from Egypt' (ἐξειλκύσθημεν: VI. 2). Again, it was probably on his journey to or from Athens that Origen had an interview with the Empress Mammaea at Antioch (*H.E.* VI. 21). This interview took place in the reign of Alexander Severus (which is all that the ἐν τούτῳ of *H.E.* VI. 21 implies). Some scholars would place it in 218, but Mammaea was not then the Emperor's mother, as Eusebius calls her, but his aunt, because Elagabalus was then on the throne.[5] Now, it is known that Mammaea was at Antioch in the

---

[1] Op. cit. pp. 218–19.   [2] E.g. Cadiou, *La Jeunesse d'Origène*, p. 372.

[3] But a later council under Demetrius degraded Origen from the priesthood. See Cadiou, op. cit. p. 392.

[4] Fragment of a letter of Origen quoted in Rufinus' Epistle prefixed to Pamphilus' *Apology for Origen* (*P.G.* XVII, 624–5).

[5] Cadiou (op. cit. pp. 334–8) suggests 224–5 as the best date for this interview, for he thinks that it coincides with the commencement of the *Commentary on*

winter of 232 with her son. Eusebius does not say that Origen went to the interview from Alexandria or returned to Alexandria from it. He may have gone there from Caesarea, or on his journey back from Greece.[1]

It is probable that between the years 235 and 237, during the persecution of Maximin, Origen was staying in Caesarea in Cappadocia with (for at least part of his stay there) Firmilian its bishop (see *H.E.* VI. 27). Eusebius tells us that Origen gained some of Symmachus' writings (ὑπομνήματα) from a certain Juliana, who had received them from the hands of Symmachus himself (*H.E.* VI. 17). Lawlor and Oulton believe[2] that these writings could not have been Symmachus' translation of the Old Testament. They argue thus: Palladius in his Lausiac History says that Origen received these writings from Juliana in Cappadocian Caesarea when he was in hiding 'from the hostility of the Greeks', and he quotes a note by Origen himself found in a very old book. 'The hostility of the Greeks' is an ambiguous phrase, but it may well have been from the hostility of pagan persecutors that Origen was hiding, and if we assume that it was, we can best date this residence in Cappadocia as 235–7. This makes it impossible that the writings of Symmachus gained from Juliana should have been his version of the Old Testament, because Origen uses that version in a note on Psalm 4. 1,[3] and we know that his *Commentary on Psalms 1–25* was written before he quitted Alexandria (see below). The five years' residence with Origen at Caesarea of Theodorus, also called Gregory (by others, not Eusebius, called Thaumaturgus), is best placed after the persecution of Maximin, as we know that Gregory was born in 218 and visited Caesarea when he was about twenty. Lawlor and Oulton[4] date this visit 238–43 (see *H.E.* VI. 30).

In the years 243 and 244 must be placed Origen's second visit to Athens,[5] which must have been a fairly long one, considering the amount of work Origen did there (see below, p. 15).[6] And during this

---

John, on the strength of a reference in that work to an absence of Origen from Ambrosius and a return: μετὰ τὸ κατὰ τὸ σῶμα κεχωρίσθαι ἡμᾶς ἀλλήλων (1. 2). Daniélou (p. 34) apparently puts it in 218.

[1] See Lawlor and Oulton, pp. 219–20.

[2] Op. cit. pp. 204, 230.   [3] *P.G.* XII, 1132–3.

[4] Op. cit. pp. 221–2.   [5] Lawlor and Oulton, p. 224.

[6] Koetschau for some reason dates this visit 240. See the Introduction to his edition of the *Concerning Prayer*, p. lxxvii. But if we accept Lawlor and Oulton's suggestion concerning Gregory's residence with Origen, this date is an unlikely one.

period we can with probability place Origen's contact with two eminent pagan scholars, Plotinus and Longinus. The relation between Origen and these two is one of the thorny questions of Origenistic scholarship, and we must set out here some of the evidence. It almost all derives from Porphyry's *Life of Plotinus*. In this *Life* Porphyry tells us[1] that Plotinus was in Persia with the imperial armies when the younger Gordian was murdered there. This took place in 244. Plotinus thereupon made his way to Rome. Then Porphyry has a paragraph which mentions Origen: Ἐρεννίῳ δὲ καὶ Ὠριγένει καὶ Πλωτίνῳ συνθηκῶν γεγονυιῶν, μηδὲν ἐκκαλύπτειν τῶν Ἀμμωνίου δογμάτων, ἃ δὴ ἐν ταῖς ἀκροάσεσιν αὐτοῖς ἀνεκεκάθαρτο, ἔμενε καὶ ὁ Πλωτῖνος συνὼν μέν τισι τῶν προσιόντων, τηρῶν δὲ ἀνέκπυστα τὰ παρὰ τοῦ Ἀμμωνίου δόγματα. Ἐρεννίου δὲ πρώτου τὰς συνθήκας παραβάντος Ὠριγένης μὲν ἠκολούθει τῷ φθάσαντι Ἐρεννίῳ, ἔγραψε δὲ οὐδὲν πλὴν τὸ περὶ τῶν δαιμόνων σύγγραμμα, καὶ ἐπὶ Γαλλιήνου ὅτι μόνος ποιητὴς ὁ βασιλεύς. There is of course in this no actual statement that it was in Rome that Origen met Plotinus. Rather the assumption is that they both studied under Ammonius in Alexandria (as indeed we know that at least Plotinus did earlier), and there made this agreement not to divulge Ammonius' teaching. Then, considerably later in the *Life*,[2] during a description of Plotinus' life in Rome, Porphyry mentions Origen again: Ὠριγένους δὲ ἀπαντήσαντός ποτε εἰς τὴν συνουσίαν πληρωθεὶς ἐρυθήματος ἀνίστασθαι μὲν ἐβούλετο, λέγειν δὲ ὑπὸ Ὠριγένους ἀξιούμενος ἔφη ἀνίλλεσθαι τὰς προθυμίας, ὅταν εἰδῇ ὁ λέγων ὅτι πρὸς εἰδότας ἐρεῖ ἃ αὐτὸς μέλλει λέγειν· καὶ οὕτως ὀλίγα διαλεχθεὶς ἐξανέστη. Though this again does not actually say that Origen met Plotinus on this occasion in Rome, the inference is strong. It is, however, very difficult indeed to imagine when the two could have met in Rome, as Plotinus did not go there till 244 or 245, and Origen, as far as we know, did not go there after 211. It should be remembered that Porphyry (as he tells us himself)[3] did not meet Plotinus till long after Plotinus came to Rome—to be precise, in the tenth year of Gallienus (263), when Porphyry was thirty, by which time Origen must have been dead for nearly ten years. The memory of the incident of Origen's meeting Plotinus, as related to Porphyry, presumably by Plotinus himself, might well have become blurred.

Later still in his *Life* Porphyry quotes from a Preface of one of the

---

[1] Sect. 3, p. 8. [2] Sect. 14, p. 14. [3] Sect. 4, p. 7.

books of Longinus, in which the author mentions among contemporary philosophers Πλατωνικοὶ μὲν Ἀμμώνιος καὶ Ὡριγένης, οἷς ἡμεῖς τὸ πλεῖστον τοῦ χρόνου προσεφοιτήσαμεν, ἀνδράσι οὐκ ὀλίγῳ τῶν καθ' ἑαυτοὺς εἰς σύνεσιν διενεγκοῦσιν.[1] Longinus lived from *c.* 213 to 273. He studied at Alexandria and taught for thirty years at Athens before going further east for a more adventurous life which was to end with his execution after the fall of Zenobia.[2] Where could he have for some considerable time sat at the feet of Ammonius and Origen, as he tells us he did? Ammonius no doubt he attended in Alexandria, and conceivably that is where he frequented Origen's school too. But this is not a very likely conjecture, because Longinus must have been at the most nineteen when Origen left Alexandria for good. Athens is a much more probable place for the meeting of Longinus and Origen, either in the year 232, when Origen first visited it, or, much more probably, in 244 and 245. We know from the letter already referred to[3] that on his first visit to Athens Origen gave lectures attended by, among others, heretics, and that he was treated as something of a celebrity there. It is easy to imagine that Origen gave lectures which non-Christians could attend, of a philosophical nature, during his second stay at Athens, and that Longinus attended them. We may also with some confidence conjecture that it was at Athens and at this period (244-5) that there occurred this meeting between Plotinus and Origen described by Porphyry. The route from Persia to Rome would almost certainly lie through Athens for a man such as Porphyry, and he may well have spent some time lecturing there before going on to Rome. The question of the philosophical treatises ascribed by Porphyry and Longinus[4] to Origen will be discussed later. It is perhaps enough to claim at the moment that an encounter of Origen with Plotinus in Athens in 244 or 245 would put the final nail into the coffin of the legend of 'Origen the pagan'.

Somewhere towards the end of the reign of Gordian,[5] Origen paid

---

[1] Sect. 20, p. 19.

[2] See the article 'Longinus, Cassius' in the *Encyclopaedia Britannica*, 1937 ed. The author apparently believes in the myth of 'Origen the pagan'.

[3] See p. 3, n. 4.

[4] Later in this same Preface (Sect. 20, p. 19) Longinus has the phrase, referring to Origen and the philosophers of his class, καὶ γὰρ εἴ τι τούτων γέγραπταί τισιν, ὥσπερ Ὡριγένει μὲν τὸ περὶ Δαιμόνων.

[5] Lawlor and Oulton, p. 224, suggest 244.

his second visit to Arabia, mentioned in *H.E.* VI. 33, to recover Berullus, Bishop of Bostra, from heresy. Gordian reigned from 238 to 244, so we shall have to place this visit before the second visit to Athens, and therefore in 243 or 244. About 248 Origen paid his third visit to Arabia, mentioned in *H.E.* VI. 37, in order to bring back to the faith some heretics who were erring concerning the fate of the soul after death.[1] In 249–50 Origen suffered as a Confessor during Decius' persecution (*H.E.* VI. 39). By 254 he was being attacked, according to Denis,[2] by Eustathius of Antioch for his tendency to allegorize. We are told by Eusebius that Origen died some time during the reign of Gallus (251–3), aged sixty-nine. Photius, on the other hand,[3] alleges that Pamphilus, in his *Apology for Origen*, said that Origen died in Caesarea during the Decian persecution, but that others said that he survived 'till the reign of Gallus and Volusianus', and died in his sixty-ninth year in Tyre. Migne points out in a footnote[4] that Eusebius (*H.E.* VI. 37) says that Origen survived Decius' persecution, as his letters written after it testify. Photius mentions these letters, but is not sure of their authenticity. Eusebius collaborated with Pamphilus in the *Apology*, and yet says nothing of the story of Origen's death during the persecution, so that, even though the relevant part of the *Apology* does not survive, we may dismiss Photius' statement as a wrong reading of Eusebius. But his other tradition, placing Origen's death in Tyre, may be right, for we have independent evidence that he was there at the end of his life. Eusebius (*H.E.* VI. 19) quotes quite a long passage from Porphyry about Origen (and there can be no question whatever about this being Origen the Christian) in the course of which he says: ὁ δὲ τρόπος τῆς ἀτοπίας ἐξ ἀνδρὸς ᾧ κἀγὼ κομιδῇ νέος ὢν ἔτι ἐντετύχηκα, σφόδρα εὐδοκιμήσαντος καὶ ἔτι δι' ὧν καταλέλοιπεν συγγραμμάτων εὐδοκιμοῦντος, παρειλήφθω, Ὠριγένους, οὗ κλέος παρὰ τοῖς διδασκάλοις τούτων τῶν λόγων μέγα διαδέδοται. The place where Porphyry is most likely to have met Origen is in Porphyry's native town of Tyre[5] and the most likely date is about 253, when Porphyry would have been about twenty or twenty-one, which answers well to his

---

[1] See below, pp. 17, 18.   [2] *De la Philosophie d'Origène*, p. 408.

[3] Quoted by Migne, Preface to Rufinus' translation of Pamphilus' *Apology for Origen* (*P.G.* XVII, 536–7), from *Biblioth.*, codex cviii.

[4] *P.G.* XVII, 535.

[5] That Porphyry came from Tyre we know from his *Life of Plotinus*; see, for instance, Sect. 21, p. 21.

description of himself as κομιδῇ νέος.[1] We may therefore with fair probability say that Origen moved to Tyre before his death and died there. But we cannot adopt Eusebius' dating, 'the reign of Gallus', if we are to put Origen's birth at 186 and maintain that he died at the age of sixty-nine, or if we are to take seriously Porphyry's statement that he wrote his treatise *That the King Alone is Creator* during the reign of Gallienus.[2] One cannot read Porphyry's *Life of Plotinus* without being struck by the fact that the author is taking great care with his chronology, greater care than one could ever imagine Eusebius taking. I believe, therefore, that we can on this occasion trust Porphyry rather than Eusebius, especially since Porphyry actually met Origen at the end of his life, and assume that Eusebius made a mistake and for 'Gallus' should have written 'Gallienus', and that Photius in his 'till the reign of Gallus and Volusianus' is simply reproducing what he found in Eusebius.[3] It is reasonable, then, to place Origen's death at Tyre, not in 253, but about 255.[4]

Eusebius (*H.E.* VI. 24) gives us a list of Origen's works which were written before he left Alexandria for Caesarea. This includes the first five books of his *Commentary on John*, the first eight books of his *Commentary on Genesis*, a *Commentary on Psalms 1–25*, the *Concerning First Principles*, the *Commentary on Lamentations*, and his *Stromateis*. This last Jerome describes as Origen's first work in point of time, and he adds that *On the Resurrection*,[5] which is not mentioned by Eusebius, was his second.[6] Contrary to the statements of several scholars, Eusebius gives no direct information concerning the order of Origen's early works. He merely says ἐξ ἐκείνου δὲ καὶ Ὠριγένει τῶν εἰς τὰς θείας γραφὰς ὑπομνημάτων ἐγίνετο ἀρχή (*H.E.* VI. 23), and goes on to

---

[1] The *Life*, Sect. 4, pp. 6–7, tells us that in 263, when he met Plotinus, Porphyry was 30.

[2] See above, p. 5.

[3] Incidentally, Porphyry could not be calculating Gallienus' reign from the moment that he gained sole power (260), but from his association in power with Valerian (263), for he tells us that he met Plotinus in Rome in the tenth year of Gallienus. Gallienus only reigned alone for eight years.

[4] Cadiou (*La Jeunesse d'Origène*, p. 257n.) says that, '*selon l'opinion la plus commune*', Origen died about 252, and that this was the view of Valois. Redepenning gave the date as 254, Baronius as 256.

[5] Parts of this work can be recovered from Methodius' attack on Origen and Pamphilus' *Apology for Origen*.

[6] See Denis, p. 390.

describe how Ambrosius urged Origen to this task and supplied him with labour. The ἐξ ἐκείνου is a very vague indication of date, and must not be pressed too closely. Most scholars agree that it means about 218, but nobody can be sure.[1] Then, a little later (VI. 24), Eusebius gives us the list, already mentioned, of Origen's works which were certainly written before he left Alexandria to reside in Caesarea. But he does not give us any further indication of their date or order, except that he says of the *Stromateis*: κατὰ τὴν Ἀλεξάνδρου συντάττει βασιλείαν, ὡς καὶ τοῦτο ὁλόγραφοι δηλοῦσιν αὐτοῦ πρὸ τῶν τόμων ἐπισημειώσεις.[2] This means of course that if we accept the date 218 as that intended by the phrase ἐξ ἐκείνου, Jerome's statement that the *Stromateis* was Origen's first work cannot be accurate, as Alexander Severus did not begin his reign till 222.

Cadiou places *On the Resurrection* about 215, and he would assign the same date to Origen's *Commentary on Lamentations*, because of the resemblance of its theology to that of the *Commentary on Psalms*, and its appropriateness to a period when Origen had just seen Jerusalem for the first time.[3] Neither point, of course, supplies a very accurate indication of date. Koetschau agrees with Cadiou in so far as he places *On the Resurrection* (which he calls 'eine Art von Vorarbeit zu de Principiis') before 218. With this, he argues, are consonant both the close connection between the *Concerning First Principles* and *On the Resurrection* and the fact that Origen seems to have left off studying Hebrew under a Jewish master some little time before writing this work; Eusebius tells us that it was in the reign of Caracalla (who died in 217) that Origen studied thus.[4] Of the *Commentary on Lamentations*, Klostermann, its editor, can say no more than that it was written before 231.[5] Cadiou places the *Commentary on Genesis* next after *On the Resurrection*, and the *Stromateis* (a work putting theological and

[1] Daniélou's statement (p. 36), 'À partir de ce temps, nous dit Eusèbe, Origène lui aussi (comme Hippolyte) commençait les commentaires sur les saintes Écritures', is too confident.

[2] Koetschau has pointed out that the chronological indication can apply only to the *Stromateis* and not to the other works mentioned in this passage. See his Introduction to the edition of the *Concerning First Principles*, p. x.

[3] *La Jeunesse d'Origène*, pp. 115–16, 119.

[4] See Koetschau's Introduction, p. xi; *H.E.* VI. 16; *Concerning First Principles* I. 3. 4 and IV. 3. 14.

[5] Introduction to his edition of the remains of this work, pp. xxxviii, xxxix.

philosophical ideas side by side without strict order, in imitation, perhaps, of Clement of Alexandria's *Stromateis*) about 222.[1]

Next in order Cadiou places the two philosophical treatises mentioned by Plotinus and Longinus,[2] *That the King Alone is Creator* and *Concerning Demons*, on the grounds that this is the only time, shortly after the completion of the philosophical *Stromateis*, that Origen is likely to have written purely philosophical treatises. The difficulty is that, as we have seen, Porphyry says that the former of these was written during the reign of Gallienus. A further difficulty is created by the fact that Longinus in the Preface already referred to classes Origen among the philosophers who preferred teaching their disciples orally to writing, and seems to imply that the work on demons was his only published one. Porphyry appears to support this when he says in the passage from the *Life of Plotinus* quoted earlier:[3] 'But he wrote nothing except the *Concerning Demons* and, in the reign of Gallienus, *That the King Alone is Creator*.' It is difficulties such as these which have given rise to the desperate theory of 'Origen the pagan'. Porphyry, however, could not possibly have thought that Origen wrote nothing more than these two philosophical works, as his references to Origen in the earlier part of the passage quoted by Eusebius in *H.E.* VI. 19 show, and his very evident dislike, observable in the same passage, of Origen's habit of allegorizing. It is not, I think, too strange an hypothesis to assume that where Plotinus and Longinus refer to Origen's works as if he only wrote one or two, they intend his *purely philosophical* works, and do not mean their words to apply to his specifically Christian and theological works. We have no really sound reason for doubting that Origen did write these two philosophical works, or that the second of them must be placed in the reign of Gallienus, about 253. We might allow Cadiou the *Concerning Demons* as a work of Origen's earlier days as a writer, or we might place it late in Origen's life with the other. We can certainly heartily agree with him in exploding 'Origen the pagan'.[4]

The *Commentary on Psalms 1–25* Cadiou places between 214 and 218, making it Origen's first work. With Harnack, Cadiou imagines that Eusebius (in *H.E.* VI. 23, 24) implies that the *Commentary on John* was the first of Origen's commentaries, and that in this Eusebius was

---

[1] *La Jeunesse d'Origène*, pp. 248, 249. [2] See above, pp. 5, 6 (n. 4).
[3] See above, p. 5. [4] See *La Jeunesse d'Origène*, pp. 252–6.

mistaken. Origen, in a passage in this commentary already referred to (1. 4), calls it an ἀπαρχή of his work, but, Cadiou contends, only an ἀπαρχή after his return to Alexandria, not an ἀπαρχή of all his labours on the Bible.[1] In fact we have seen that Eusebius does not imply anything certain about the date or order of Origen's works before 231, except for the placing of his *Stromateis* in the reign of Alexander Severus. Koetschau believes that the *Commentaries on John, on Genesis, and on Psalms 1–25* were all begun about the same time, and that the *Commentary on Psalms* was not finished by 231–2. He quotes references in the *Concerning First Principles* to a *Commentary on Psalms* which includes Psalm 2, and to a *Commentary on Genesis* which is still only begun. The beginning of these three big commentaries he dates about 218, relying on the passage in Eusebius *H.E.* vi. 23 already referred to.[2] He believes that the *Commentary on John* was finished by 233, and the *Commentary on Genesis* (which even when complete covered no more than the first few chapters of Genesis) by 231. Cadiou places the beginning of the *Commentary on John* in 224–5, arguing that its reference, to which we have already referred, to Origen's absence from and return to Ambrosius must be connected with his visit to the Empress Mammaea in Antioch, and that this visit is best placed at this time. Four volumes, he thinks, were complete by 229, the fifth was written between 230 and 231, and the sixth between 231 and 232. His source for these conclusions is of course Eusebius (*H.E.* vi. 24).[3]

It seems to me quite likely that Origen began his three big commentaries, *on the Psalms, on Genesis,* and *on John,* at about the same time, but I cannot believe that he began any of them as early as 218. One of the most remarkable and most demonstrable points about Origen is the speed with which he could work. We have only to observe how quickly he must have completed such large undertakings as the *Commentary on Matthew* (probably 246) and *Against Celsus* (248) to see how much is demanded of us when scholars ask us to believe that commentaries begun in 218 were not completed by 230. Again, we must rid ourselves of the idea that Eusebius' ἐξ ἐκείνου compels us to put the beginning of these works in 218 or thereabouts. It *may* refer to the date of Origen's visit to Mammaea, and that visit *may* have taken place in 218, or it *may*

---

[1] See ibid. pp. 87–9.

[2] Introduction to his edition of the *Concerning First Principles,* pp. ix, x.

[3] *La Jeunesse d'Origène,* pp. 334–8.

refer to Origen's contact with Hippolytus, but none of these inferences are certain and some not even probable. Moreover, immediately after his description of the undertaking of these labours (*H.E.* VI. 23), Eusebius refers to events which we know to have taken place as late as 231–2, with only a τούτων δὲ οὕτως ἐχόντων for connection. Far less are we justified in putting the date of the *Commentary on Psalms 1–25* or of the *Commentary on Lamentations* as early as 215, as Cadiou does. I do not believe that Eusebius, when he wrote the phrase ἐξ ἐκείνου, knew exactly when any of these commentaries or works mentioned shortly afterwards in his account were written, or in what order, except that they were all begun before Origen left Alexandria, and that the *Stromateis* was written in the reign of Alexander Severus (and this he learnt from inscriptions in the work itself).

We are free, therefore, to surmise that the *Commentary on John* may have been begun about 225, and we agree with Koetschau in placing the *Commentaries on Genesis* and *on Psalms* a little before it.[1] We may agree with both Cadiou and Koetschau in putting *On the Resurrection* early (and thereby making it, against Jerome's statement, Origen's first work), though we need not put it earlier than 218 if we no longer hold that Eusebius' ἐξ ἐκείνου must refer to 218. We must place the *Stromateis*, with Cadiou, as early as possible in the reign of Alexander Severus, in 222, and follow it perhaps by one of the Platonic works, *Concerning Demons*, in 223. Of the *Commentary on Lamentations* all we can say is that it was written some time between 220 and 230.

The *Concerning First Principles* Harnack[2] placed some time between 220 and 230; Cadiou, between 220 and 225;[3] Koetschau, nearer 220 than 230.[4] Eusebius also quotes (*H.E.* VI. 19) part of a letter of Origen defending his habit of studying the works of heretical and pagan

---

[1] When this last Commentary was finished is a very uncertain point. It undoubtedly was carried on beyond Psalm 25, as the fragments which survive of Origen's work on the Psalms testify. Cadiou (*Commentaires Inédits des Psaumes*, pp. 49–50), arguing from a remark in these fragments which he has edited (a comment on Ps. 142. 5, justifying flight during a persecution), holds that the completion of the work should be placed after Maximin's persecution. There is much to be said for this view.

[2] Quoted by Molland, *The Conception of the Gospel*, p. 164.

[3] And nearer the end of that period than the beginning; see *La Jeunesse d'Origène*, p. 267.

[4] Introduction to his edition of the *Concerning First Principles*, p. xi.

writers, which Lawlor and Oulton put at about 232.[1] One more work we must place in this period before 232, and fairly early in it, and that is Origen's 'Little Commentary' on the Song of Songs, mentioned in *Philocalia* VII. 1,[2] where an extract from it is given, headed ἐκ τοῦ εἰς τὸ ᾆσμα μικροῦ τόμου ὃν τῇ νεότητι ἔγραψεν. We might place it about 225.

The work *Concerning Prayer* Cadiou places in 232,[3] but Koetschau, with more careful calculation, in 233 or 234. A passage in this work (xxviii. 10), concerning people who unjustifiably take upon themselves the power of forgiving mortal sins by priestly authority, Koetschau interprets (following Döllinger, Harnack, and others) as referring to Pope Callistus (217–22) and his policy of moderation towards the *lapsi*, and Origen seems here to be taking the side of Hippolytus. Koetschau also thinks that this denunciation includes Pope Urbanus (222–30) and Pope Pontianus (230–5), under whom Hippolytus' schism persisted. Again, in another passage in this work, Origen uses the phrase ἐξετάζοντες τὰ εἰς τὴν Γένεσιν, obviously having finished the *Commentary on Genesis* (see *Concerning Prayer* xxiii. 4). Now this commentary was not finished, as we have seen, till Origen came to live at Caesarea, at the earliest by 231. Koetschau also sees in *Concerning Prayer* xv. 1 a reference to a passage in the *Commentary on John* (I. 21), which suggests that *Concerning Prayer* must have been written after, and soon after, this work. So he puts it at 233 or 234 at the earliest. He thinks that we can make 240 a *terminus ante quem* for this work, because in it (iii. 3) Origen refers to a *Commentary on Exodus* yet to be composed. Now this commentary is referred to as finished in the *Commentary on the Song of Songs*, and we know that this latter work was begun in Athens during Origen's second visit there. Koetschau places this second visit in 240. Finally, because there is no mention of persecution in the work, Koetschau concludes that the book must have been written before Maximin's persecution in 235, and this confirms his dating the book 233–4.[4] We may well agree with this date for the work,

---

[1] Op. cit. p. 206.

[2] J. Armitage Robinson's edition, p. 50. It is strange that Harnack and Koetschau and Cadiou have ignored this work. It is the 'Little' one in comparison with the longer one, written much later. See below, p. 15.

[3] *La Jeunesse d'Origène*, p. 24.

[4] See Koetschau's Introduction to his edition of *Concerning Prayer*, pp. lxxv–lxxvii.

without, however, excluding the possibility of placing it rather later, if other evidence seems to suggest such a change. The fact that the book does not mention persecution cannot be taken as a serious argument for placing it before Maximin's persecution, and, as we have seen, it is better to place Origen's second visit to Athens in 243–4 rather than in 240. Somewhere in the period 233–40 we should probably place the *Commentary on Revelation*. Klostermann and Benz[1] say that it came after the *Commentary on Romans*. But the surviving fragments of the work on Revelation do not refer to the *Commentary on Romans*, and suggest rather that it was written not long after the *Commentary on John* (234–) and well before the *Commentary on Ezekiel* (243 +).[2]

It is easier to date the *Exhortation to Martyrdom* accurately. This work makes it obvious that Origen's friends, Ambrosius and Protoctetus, for whom the work was written, expect to be taken to Germania and there executed. We can therefore with certainty date the work 235, when the Emperor Maximin, having ordered a persecution of the Christians, set out for Pannonia.[3] It is difficult to understand why Denis will go no further than to place the work some time after Severus' persecution.[4] In the year 243 we may place Origen's *Letter to Gregory*. In it Origen urges Gregory to devote himself to Christianity rather than to making himself a Roman lawyer, and his closing remarks have a valedictory ring, as if he were saying goodbye to a favourite pupil whom he has known for some time, so that the letter probably was written at the end of Gregory's stay with Origen.[5] The

---

[1] *Zur Überlieferung der Matthäusklärung des Origenes*, p. 1.

[2] These fragments have been edited by Diobouniotis and Harnack (*Die Scholien-Kommentar des Origenes zur Apokalypse Johannis*, Leipzig, 1911). The proximity to the *Comm. on John* is suggested by a reference (p. 28, XVII) to the theory that Jezebel had a 'nature destined for perdition', a type of theory frequently referred to in Origen's work on the Fourth Gospel, but seldom elsewhere. The fact that his *Comm. on Revelation* must have appeared well before his *Comm. on Ezekiel* is indicated by his quotation in the former (p. 37, XXXI) of Ezekiel 9. 5, 6 (in connection with Rev. 7. 3) without making any attempt to answer the question, what was the sign? or why was it a *tau*? This question he discusses fully in his work on Ezekiel. I infer that when he wrote the *Comm. on Revelation* he had not learnt as much Hebrew nor come into as close contact with Rabbinic scholarship as he had when he wrote the *Comm. on Ezekiel*, perhaps as long as nine years later.

[3] See Eusebius, *H.E.* VI. 28; *Exhortation to Martyrdom* xli; Koetschau's Introduction to his edition of this work, p. ix; Daniélou, p. 13.

[4] Denis, p. 390.   [5] See the *Letter to Gregory*, *P.G.* XI, 88, 92.

Letter to Africanus Lawlor and Oulton[1] put in the year 243, because its mention of the Hexapla as completed puts it long after Origen's retreat from Alexandria, and Origen is, as he writes it, passing through Nicomedia on his way to Athens. This would best fit in with Origen's second visit to Athens in 243 or 244.[2] Incidentally, this means that the Hexapla must have been finished by 243.[3] In a sense this was Origen's first work, because he must have been working on it when he discovered one version of the Greek Old Testament in Nicopolis in Epirus, presumably on his way to Rome as early as 212, and another in a jar in Jericho during his first visit to Palestine in 215. But Eusebius hardly counted this among the written works of Origen. A letter by Origen to his friends at Alexandria survives in part in Rufinus' Epilogue to his translation of Pamphilus' *Apology for Origen*.[4] Lawlor and Oulton place it during his first visit to Athens, 231–2.

Later Eusebius gives us (*H.E.* VI. 32) a list of Origen's works which were composed while he was in Caesarea in Palestine—the *Commentary on Isaiah*, the *Commentary on Ezekiel*, and the *Commentary on the Song of Songs*. He tells us that of the last two the first was finished in Athens and the second begun in Athens, so that we can date them respectively about 243 and 244.[5] Later still (*H.E.* VI. 36) Eusebius tells us that when he was over the age of sixty (i.e. some time after 246) Origen first allowed his Homilies to be taken down in shorthand and published. This apparently means that we cannot date any of his Homilies before 246.[6] Eusebius adds that ἐν τούτῳ ('about that time', a very vague

---

[1] Op. cit. p. 223.   [2] See *H.E.* VI. 31.

[3] Halévy, for reasons which it is hard to conjecture, puts the composition of the Hexapla at 235–54 ('L'Origine de la Transcription', p. 335). We cannot possibly put the *Letter to Africanus* as late as 254; indeed by 254 Origen was probably in Tyre and possibly dead. We know that the Hexapla was preserved in 'Pamphilus' Library' in Palestinian Caesarea. Swete thinks that it was after his first visit to Caesarea that Origen began compiling the Hexapla, or 'perhaps from the moment that he began to read the Old Testament in the original'. It was finished in his view by 240 or 245, and the Tetrapla (that is, a reproduction of the Hexapla without the columns presenting the Hebrew and the Hebrew transliterated) by the end of Origen's life, perhaps in Tyre. See *An Introduction to the Old Testament in Greek*, pp. 60, 73, 74. Daniélou (p. 12) follows Swete.

[4] See Migne, *P.G.* XVII. 624–5. It has already been referred to. See p. 3.

[5] Koetschau, of course, 240 or 241.

[6] Some scholars seem to hold that this is not what Eusebius meant. I do not see how we can otherwise interpret his plain words, though we shall have to allow some exceptions. See below, pp. 20–2.

indication) he composed the *Against Celsus*, the *Commentary on Matthew*, and the *Commentary on the Twelve Prophets*. He is also said to have composed a *Letter to the Emperor Philip*, and another to a relation of the Emperor called Severa, and one to Fabian, Bishop of Rome. This last must be placed between 236 and 249, and the other two between 244 and 249. *Against Celsus* we can date quite accurately. Koetschau[1] says that Neumann has shown conclusively that no other year than 248 can be allotted to it, between the persecutions of Maximin and Decius. Neumann's clinching proof is the phrase in III. 15: ἡ ἐπὶ τοσοῦτο νῦν στάσις, which is only consistent with the year 248, in which three pretenders to the Empire were rising against Philip the Arab. The year 248 also saw the festival of the millenium of Roman rule, and Origen may have wanted to produce a manifesto against pagan religion for that year particularly.

Koetschau places the *Commentary on Romans* (to which Eusebius does not refer) in 244. Harnack, according to Molland,[2] placed it some time after 244. Klostermann and Benz[3] put it immediately after 244. It is referred to in the *Commentary on Matthew* and in *Against Celsus*. In the same context Klostermann and Benz tell us that the *Commentary on Matthew* came after the *Commentary on Daniel*, the *Homilies on Luke*, and the *Commentary on John*; and they interpret Eusebius' reference to the *Commentary on Matthew* to mean that he placed it in the year 244. But none of this information is of much value, because Eusebius' ἐν τούτῳ is sufficient to assure us anyway that this work came after the *Commentary on John*, but it is not nearly precise enough for us to be sure that he intended it for the year 244; indeed it is fairly clear that he did not know the exact year of the composition of this commentary. We do not know anything about the *Commentary on Daniel*, which has not survived, and we shall see that it is impossible to place with confidence the *Homilies on Luke*, as we do other Homilies, after the limiting date for Homilies given us by Eusebius. We do know, however, that the *Commentary on Matthew* refers to the Hexapla (which suggests a date after 243) and is referred to in a *Homily on Psalm 38* (Homily I. 2),[4] which suggests a date before the year 247-8—the most likely date (as we shall see) for the *Homilies on Psalms*. We have therefore to choose

---

[1] Introduction to his edition of *Against Celsus*, Sect. I.
[2] *The Conception of the Gospel*, p. 164.
[3] Op. cit. p. I. [4] *P.G.* XII, 1375.

a date between 245 (*Commentary on Romans*) and 247–8 (*Homilies on Psalms*). We can with fair probability place the *Commentary on Matthew* in 246.

Towards the end of his account of Origen, Eusebius mentions him (*H.E.* VI. 38) as contending against the sect of the Helcesaites, an Ebionite heresy, which had originated some time before in Apamea in Syria, claiming a new revelation and a new forgiveness of sins. Eusebius quotes from Origen's *Homily on Psalm 82*, which mentions the heresy. Lawlor and Oulton[1] give details of the heresy, and they think that this reference dates Origen's *Homilies on the Psalms* between 244 and 249. As we shall see, there are no references to these Homilies in other works of Origen which can give us any sure indication of date. We must, of course, put them after 246. *Homily* I *on Psalm 38*[2] refers to the *Commentary on Matthew*, which we have tentatively placed in 246. Again in a *Homily on Psalm 37*[3] Origen refers to a ruler who was cast down after flourishing, just thirty years before the time of the composition of the Homily. Migne believes that the ruler was Severus and the date of the Homily 241; but, quite apart from the fact that it is straining language to describe Severus, who died a natural death, as cast down, it is impossible, in view of Eusebius' information about when the Homilies were first written down, to date the *Homilies on Psalms* as early as this. We may assume 247 as a probable date for this particular Homily, thirty years after the death of Caracalla, who was murdered in 217. But this does not necessarily mean that 247 is the date of the *publication* of these Homilies. We could put them late in 247 or early in 248.[4] To the same period we should perhaps attribute the recently discovered *Origen's Conversation with Heracleides and His Fellow Bishops on the Father, the Son, and the Soul*. Its editor, Scherer, links this *Conversation* with the activity of Origen in Arabia on his third visit there, mentioned in *H.E.* VI. 37. He very tentatively places it in the year 244 or 245; he thinks that the conversation recorded in it could not have been the actual synod referred to by Eusebius, but may have been an unofficial conversation connected with it (see pp. 54–6 of

---

[1] Op. cit. p. 226. Latko (*Origen's Concept of Penance*, pp. xxii–xxiii) puts these Homilies between 240 and 245, following Harnack and Bardenhewer. How he reconciles this with Eusebius' statement limiting the Homilies to after Origen's sixtieth year, I do not know· He places Origen's birth in 185. [2] *P.G.* XII, 1375

[3] Homily 1.2 (*P.G.* XII, 1323). The Migne editor's remark is *P.G.* XII, 1051–2.

[4] Only eight of these Homilies survive. See the Bibliography, p. 194.

Scherer's Introduction). The text refers to the doctrine of the Arabians, and implies that Origen had already discussed the matter with 'the other Heracleides and Celer who was before him', and that it was much agitated by 'certain persons among those present and among people in neighbouring parts' (p. 144 of the text). The question of the fate of the soul (which according to Eusebius formed the subject of debate during Origen's third visit to Arabia) is not the main one at this *Conversation*, though it is touched upon. It is reasonable therefore to link this *Conversation* with the third visit, and to date this visit about 245 or 246. We cannot be exact in our dating because all that we can learn from Eusebius is that he apparently regarded this visit as taking place in the reign of Philip.

There remain a number of works which we cannot date to a single year with any confidence, but which must be set within wider limits. We have already seen that the *Commentary on Revelation* must be placed after the *Commentary on Romans* (244), and the *Commentary on Daniel* before the *Commentary on Matthew* (246) but presumably after 231. Further we must assume that the *Commentary on Isaiah* mentioned by Eusebius (*H.E.* VI. 32) was written some time between 232 and 249, perhaps (as Eusebius mentions it along with the *Commentary on Ezekiel* and the *Commentary on the Song of Songs*) nearer 232 than 249. The *Letters to the Emperor Philip* and *to Severa* were written some time between 244 and 249, and that *to Pope Fabian* some time between 246 and 249. The *Commentary on Exodus* was composed after *Concerning Prayer* (234) but before the *Commentary on Ezekiel* (243; in view of the date of Maximin's persecution we might reduce the gap to 236–43). We must place the *Commentary on the Twelve Prophets* some time between 246 and 249 (*H.E.* VI. 36), and the *Homilies on Leviticus* (mentioned in the *Homilies on Jeremiah*) and those *on Ezekiel* in the same period, though we might extend the limit of these to 255, as they came after the *Homilies on Jeremiah*. The *Homilies on Joshua* we may place after the Decian persecution, to which reference seems to be made in one passage in them (IX).[1] As we have no particular knowledge about the date of the *Homilies on Lamentations*, we can only set these also between 246 and 255.

Of the *Homilies on Jeremiah* we can assume that they were written down in 246 or after, and, as Klostermann shows in his edition of these

[1] See Latko, pp. xxvi, xxvii.

Homilies,[1] that they know of the *Homilies on Leviticus*, but were written before the *Homilies on Ezekiel* and *on Joshua*. As we know nothing certain about the dates of any of these works, all that they can tell us is that the *Homilies on Jeremiah* were written at the earliest in 247 and at the latest in 249. This dating is confirmed by a passage in the Homilies (IV. 3) where Origen regrets the former days when persecution was raging and martyrdoms frequent and faith and zeal burning. Presumably they could not have been written after the Decian persecution.[2] Klostermann, indeed, speaks of these Homilies as written after '*seiner homiletischen Erklärungen zu den Psalmen*',[3] but the passages from the *Homilies on Jeremiah* which he quotes to support this assertion (VIII. 3; XVIII. 10) are references to two passages from what Migne calls *Selecta in Psalmos* and Lommatschz does not classify as Homilies. They are comments on verses of two late Psalms (134 and 140), and are therefore more likely to be quotations from fragments of Origen's *Commentary on Psalms*, which, as we have seen, had by 231 reached only to Psalm 25, and must have been finished some time after Origen's change of residence to Caesarea, say by 235. The same uncertainty renders us doubtful when we try to date the *Homily on 1 Samuel 28. 3–25*, which survives. In this Homily Origen uses the words: ὡς πρώην ἐλέγομεν ἐξηγούμενοι τὸν κα′ Ψαλμόν...μεμνήμεθα, εἴγε μεμνήμεθα τῶν ἱερῶν γραμμάτων· μέμνημαι γὰρ αὐτῶν εἰρημένων εἰς τὸν κα′ Ψαλμόν. Now this passage, though it is rather cryptic, obviously implies that to remember this comment on the Twenty-First Psalm (English version, the Twenty-Second) was a feat of memory. If we are to abide by our conclusions reached so far, to assume here a reference to the *Homilies on Psalms* would mean that Origen was (presumably about 249) alluding to a passage written about 247–8—no very great feat of memory. But if he were alluding to his *Commentary on Psalms* these expressions would be quite understandable, because we know that his *Commentary on Psalms 1–25* was written before 231; Origen would therefore in this place be alluding to a passage written at least fifteen years before, and probably more. We *could* then place this *Homily on 1 Samuel* between 246 and 249. We might indeed seriously

---

[1] Introduction, pp. ix, x.   [2] See Daniélou, pp. 53–4.

[3] Introduction, p. ix. The two passages from the *Homilies on Jeremiah* will be found in *P.G.* XIII, 339, 484; the reference to the exposition of Psalms in the first of these passages is to be found in the Latin translation only, which is curious.

consider transferring this Homily, as well as certain others, to a date at the very end of Origen's life. It may even have been delivered in Tyre. Porphyry's reference to his encounter with Origen when he was a young man does not suggest that at that period Origen was incapacitated from work. The point does not seem to have occurred to any other writers upon Origen,[1] but if we find difficulty in fitting all the Homilies between the years 246 and 249, I think that we might well assume that some of these were written between 250 and 255, either in Caesarea or in Tyre. Certainly it is not easy to fit all the Homilies into only three and a half years, though, in view of the amazing industry of Origen, nicknamed Adamantius, it is not impossible.

Origen's *Commentary on Luke* is fairly easily dated. It consisted of only five books, and for the passages in Luke found also in Matthew Origen was apparently content to reproduce what he had already said on them in his *Commentary on Matthew*.[2] We must therefore place the Commentary some time between 246 and 255. The dating of the *Homilies on Luke* is a more complicated business. There are specific references to a work on Luke in the *Commentary on John* and the *Commentary on Matthew*: viz. *Commentary on John* XXXII. 2, ἐν ταῖς εἰς τὸ κατὰ Λουκᾶν ὁμιλίαις συνεκρίναμεν ἀλλήλαις τὰς παραβολάς, καὶ ἐζητήσαμεν τί μὲν σημαίνει τὸ κατὰ τὰς θείας γραφὰς ἄριστον, τί δὲ παρίστησιν τὸ κατ᾽ αὐτὰς δεῖπνον. But no Homily on the relevant passage (Luke 14. 16–24) survives. In *Commentary on Matthew* XIII. 29, we read, τὰ δὲ περὶ τῶν ἑκατὸν προβάτων ἔχεις εἰς τὰς κατὰ Λουκᾶν ὁμιλίας, again a reference to a part of Luke (14. 5–7) on which we have no extant Homily; and in *Commentary on Matthew* XVI. 9 we find, ὅρα τοίνυν, εἰ δύνασαι, μεμνημένος τῶν ἡμῖν ὑπαγορευθέντων εἰς τὴν ἐν τῷ κατὰ Λουκᾶν εὐαγγελίῳ παραβολὴν τήν· ἄνθρωπός τις κατέβαινεν ἀπὸ Ἱερουσαλὴμ εἰς Ἱεριχὼ καὶ περιέπεσε λῃσταῖς, κ.τ.λ. The part of the Homily referred to here does survive in Homily XXXIV in Jerome's translation. Now if the word ὁμιλίαι in these passages means 'sermons taken down in shorthand and later published', then of course Eusebius' statement that Origen did not allow his sermons to be taken down in shorthand and published till after he was sixty is worthless. But we

---

[1] Except that Harnack (followed by Latko) dates the *Homilies on Joshua* 249–50, and Swete thinks that the Tetrapla was finished in Tyre. See above, p. 15, n. 3.

[2] See Rauer's Introduction to Origen's works on Luke, p. x.

cannot be sure that this is the meaning of the expression here. For instance, Pamphilus, in his *Apology for Origen*, distinguishes between the private and secret writings of Origen (by which he clearly means what we should call his commentaries), and the public ones where he might be contending for popular support,[1] but he does not, as far as we can judge through Rufinus' translation, use the words ἐξηγητικά and ὁμιλίαι to distinguish them. Rauer[2] expressly states that these Homilies are not sermons taken down in shorthand by others, but sermons composed deliberately by Origen himself, or perhaps material designed to serve for sermons later, and he quotes Zahn and Redepenning to support him. On the other hand he believes that these Homilies were eventually in some form preached, for they have the inscription '*dictae in diebus dominicis*'. Socrates (*H. Eccl.* v. 27) tells us that most of Origen's sermons were preached on weekdays and holy-days. Is it possible that we have here a means of distinguishing between those Homilies which were first taken down in shorthand after Origen's sixtieth year and other Homilies published earlier than that date? Jerome, indeed, suggests that the *Homilies on Luke* were a work of Origen's youth, but they cannot have been composed before Origen was thirty (see *H.E.* VI. 19). Rauer suggests that they must be placed either in Origen's first visit to Caesarea (215-16) or in his second one, when he came to reside there. He points out, too, that these are not Origen's earliest Homilies, for Homily XVII makes reference to an earlier: '*Memini, cum interpretarer illud quod ad Corinthios scribitur, "ecclesiae dei quae est Corinthi, cum omnibus qui invocant eum", dixisse me diversitatem esse ecclesiae et eorum qui invocant nomen domini.*' The work also refers (in Homily VI, where a fragment is extant in Greek) to the Hexapla, since it mentions τὴν πέμπτην ἔκδοσιν.[3] This evidence makes it essential for us to recognize the existence of some form of Homilies before the year 246, more ordered ones, probably, than those taken down in shorthand, and perhaps representing sermons, or material for sermons, preached on Sundays. The appearance of the *Homilies on Luke* as we have them does not suggest sermons taken

---

[1] See the *Apology* in Rufinus' translation, *P.G.* XVII, 557.

[2] Introduction, pp. xi-xii. But it is worth noting that ὁμιλία means 'sermon' or 'exhortation' as early as Ignatius (see his *Letter to Polycarp* v. 1: μᾶλλον δὲ περὶ τούτων ὁμιλίαν ποιοῦ). Xenophon and Aelian use it of a 'lecture'.

[3] For all these foregoing details, see Rauer, Introduction, pp. xiii, xiv, xv.

down in shorthand as they were delivered.[1] One of the dates suggested by Rauer is a quite impossible one. If they were composed in 215, and at Caesarea, of all places, why has Eusebius never heard of them? And how could Origen refer to τὴν πέμπτην ἔκδοσιν in 215?[2] It is not even at all certain that Origen had by 215 published any work of any description. They must, however, be placed before the end of the *Commentary on John*; we might say 233-4. In that case we must place the *Commentary on 1 Corinthians* about 232-3.[3]

The *Homilies on Judges* present us with a similar difficulty. In his Preface to the *Commentary on the Song of Songs* Origen speaks of '*in illis oratiunculis quas de libello Iudicum edidimus*', and mentions that there he had discoursed about the Song of Deborah.[4] In his *Homilies on Judges* he does treat of the Song of Deborah, and one would normally therefore incline to put these Homilies before 244. But in this *Commentary on the Song of Songs* Origen also refers to *Homilies on Exodus* and *on Numbers*, and to a work on Leviticus. Now it is extremely difficult to place the Homilies on all these books before 244. Latko, for instance, does not attempt to do so.[5] From the Latin words in the Commentary in question we can derive no safe conclusion about whether Origen was referring to Homilies or to works of a quite different nature. It is safer therefore to assume that we have not got here a reference to the *Homilies on Judges* known to us, and to place these somewhere between 246 and 255.[6]

The *Homilies on Numbers* afford us no clear evidence of date. Rufinus' Preface describes them as '*Adamantini senis in legem Moysi*

[1] Indeed the Greek fragments, where they are extant, do not suggest sermons at all.

[2] Presumably he may have referred to the Hexapla, or to parts of it, before it was actually published or completed, but not as early as this. Incidentally, how can we imagine him referring to anything as erudite as the Hexapla in a *sermon*? The status of these Homilies as sermons, in spite of the ascriptions found at the end of them in the Latin version, seems to me not certain.

[3] Fragments of this work survive and have been edited by C. Jenkins. See Bibliography.

[4] See *P.G.* XII, 947, and Latko, p. xxii, where he follows Harnack in placing the work after 235.

[5] Or to explain the apparent contradiction. The disadvantage of Latko's method of briefly summing up the evidence and the opinions of scholars on each book in dating it is that it leaves so many problems unsolved.

[6] They look very like sermons taken down in shorthand. Almost any sort of work by Origen on Judges would be likely to treat of the Song of Deborah.

dicta', which might be held to argue for a late date. In his twelfth Homily on Jeremiah Origen promises to discourse later about the priestly blessings in Numbers. These blessings are not mentioned in the *Homilies on Numbers* which we possess, but we possess only twenty-eight and there were originally thirty.[1] The work on the blessings may have appeared in the two Homilies lost to us, or it may have been a separate work, or part of one. We cannot be more precise than to place these Homilies between 246 and 255. Considerable fragments of Origen's *Commentary on the Epistle to the Ephesians* have been printed by J. A. F. Gregg in the *Journal of Theological Studies*,[2] and some indications in these suggest a date contemporary with the *Commentary on John*. Origen in these fragments refers very often to οἱ εἰσάγοντες τὰς φύσεις and he identifies Christ with σοφία, δύναμις, ζωή, and εἰρήνη.[3] Consistent with this is a fragment of the same work printed in Migne[4] where Origen carefully and specifically denies the view that our Lord '*per phantasiam manducabat*'. It looks very much as if he were deliberately counteracting the teaching of Clement of Alexandria here,[5] in which case we should place the work as near to Origen's Alexandrian period as possible. If we tentatively placed it in 233–4, this would be not inappropriate to his having recently completed a *Commentary on* 1 *Corinthians*. About the dates of the *Homilies on Exodus* and the *Homilies on Genesis* we know nothing certain, and must place them some time between 246 and 255.[6] A fragment of a *Commentary on the Epistle to Titus* survives, quoted by Pamphilus,[7] in which Origen mentions certain heretics who believe that Jesus Christ 'was a man foreknown and predestined, who did not exist substantially before his incarnation, but who, when he was born a man, had in him only the deity of the Father'. These heretics were evidently the followers of Berullus of Bostra, with whom we have seen Origen dealing in 243. We might then attribute this Commentary to that date,

---

[1] See *P.G.* XII, 583, 573 and XIII, 59, for this evidence.

[2] Vol. III (1902), pp. 233–44, 398–420, 554–76.

[3] See Sect. XI, p. 406 (on Eph. 2. 14).

[4] Quoted by Pamphilus in his *Apology for Origen*, *P.G.* XVII, 586.

[5] See *Stromateis* VI. ix (*P.G.* IX, 292), where Clement says that our Lord's body did not need nourishment from food, but he only ate in case his companions should acquire wrong ideas about him.

[6] Latko, following Harnack and Bardenhewer, puts them some time after 244.

[7] See *P.G.* XVII, 554–5; the fragment is on Titus 3. 10, 11.

and perhaps Origen's Commentaries on the rest of the Pastorals, which a few surviving fragments assure us were written.

There remain a number of works which we know Origen to have written, which have not survived, or have only survived in the tiniest fragments, and about whose dates we cannot be in any sense precise. There is a *Letter to Photius and Andreas, presbyters*,[1] and there are *Commentaries on Galatians, on Colossians, on Thessalonians, on Philemon*, and *on the Epistle to the Hebrews*; these presumably we must place between 231 and 249. Finally there are *Homilies on the Song of Songs, on Isaiah, on Acts*, and *on the Epistle to the Hebrews*, which we can only assign to the years 246–55. The question of the date of Origen's *Scholia*[2] falls outside this inquiry because I cannot find any evidence that they were published until after Origen's death. They consisted of collections of rough notes by Origen on various interpretations of passages in Scripture, and especially in the Psalms. S. Jerome called one collection of these, on the Psalms, ἐγχειρίδιον.[3] The various ἐκλογαί or anthologies of Origen's works published after his death often drew on these *Scholia*, and some Latin *Excerpta* from Origen were no more than rather polished translations of these *Scholia*. Jerome gives the name *Excerpta* to both *Scholia* and σημειώσεις. These latter were concise explanatory notes on definite points; they mostly appeared in the *Scholia*, but some were incorporated in Commentaries. The *Scholia* survived in Eusebius' library in Jerome's day.

We may therefore tentatively reconstruct the dates of the main events of Origen's life in a column opposite the main events of the secular history of his time, and in another table the dates of his works, as nearly as we can calculate them (see pp. 25–7). Works which still survive to any considerable extent are printed in capitals.

A very few personal references faintly confirming this scheme can be gleaned from Origen's works. In the *Commentary on Matthew* (xv. 3) he vigorously condemns the practice of self-castration. This would be, by our calculation, over thirty years after he had castrated himself, and it may be held to be his considered condemnation of the act he had

---

[1] See *P.G.* XVII, 28.

[2] See Cadiou, *Commentaires Inédits des Psaumes*, pp. 31, 32 (n. 1, 2), 41 (n. 3), 42.

[3] *Breviarium in Psalmos*, Prologue (*P.L.* XXVI, 821–3).

DATES OF MAIN EVENTS IN ORIGEN'S LIFE

Main Events of Secular History	*Main Events of Origen's Life*
—	186 Origen born at Alexandria.
193 Accession of Septimius Severus.	—
—	203 Martyrdom of his father in persecution.
	204 Head of Catechetical School.
211 Accession of Caracalla on death of Severus.	210–11 Self-castration. Conversion of Ambrosius.
	212 Visit to Rome.
	214 First visit to Arabia.
—	215 First visit to Palestine.
217 Murder of Caracalla; accession of Macrinus.	
218 Murder of Macrinus; accession of Elagabalus.	
222 Murder of Elagabalus; accession of Alexander.	—
232 Empress Mammaea and Alexander at Antioch.	231–2 Quits Alexandria. First visit to Athens.
—	232 Interview with Empress Mammaea at Antioch. Settles in Palestinian Caesarea.
235 Murder of Alexander; accession of Maximin.	235 Maximin's persecution. Origen in Cappadocian Caesarea.
237 Rise of the younger Gordian.	—
238 Murder of Maximin. Gordian sole Emperor.	238–43 In Palestinian Caesarea with Gregory.
	243 Second visit to Arabia (for Berullus of Bostra).
	243–4 Second visit to Athens. Encounter with Plotinus and Longinus.
—	—
244 Murder of Gordian; accession of Philip the Arab.	246 Third visit to Arabia
248 Festival of Millenium of Roman rule.	
249 Fall of Philip and accession of Decius.	249 Suffers in Decian persecution in Palestinian Caesarea.
251 Death of Decius; accession of Gallus.	—
253 Death of Gallus. Accession of Valerian. Gallienus associated with Valerian.	?253 Moves to Tyre. Meeting with Porphyry.
—	255 Dies at Tyre.

Main Events of Secular History	*Main Events of Origen's Life*
260 Fall of Valerian. Gallienus sole Emperor.	
	—
268 Murder of Gallienus; accession of Claudius.	

DATES OF ORIGEN'S WORKS

More Precisely Dated	Less Precisely Dated
	—
212 *Hexapla* begun by now.	
218 *On the Resurrection.*	
	220–30 *Comm. on Lamentations.* 'Little' Comm. on Song of Songs.
—	
222 *Stromateis.*	
223 *Concerning Demons.*	
224 *Comm. on Psalms* *Comm. on Genesis* } begun.	—
225 COMM. ON JOHN CONCERNING FIRST } begun. PRINCIPLES	
	231–46 *Comm. on Daniel.*
	231–49 *Letter to Photius and Andreas.* *Comms. on Galatians, Colossians, Thessalonians, Philemon,* and *Epistle to Hebrews.*
—	
232 Letter mentioned in *H.E.* VI. 19.	232–49 *Comm. on Isaiah.*
232–3 COMM. ON I CORINTHIANS	
233–4 CONCERNING PRAYER. COMM. ON EPHESIANS. HOMILIES ON LUKE.	233–40 COMM. ON REVELATION
235 EXHORTATION TO MARTYRDOM.	—
—	236–43 *Comm. on Exodus.*
	236–49 *Letter to Pope Fabian.*
242–3 *Commentary on Pastorals.*	
243 LETTER TO GREGORY. LETTER TO AFRICANUS. *Comm. on Ezekiel.* *Hexapla* probably finished by now.	—
244 COMM. ON THE SONG OF SONGS.	244–9 *Letter to Emperor Philip.* *Letter to Severa.*
—	
245 COMM. ON ROMANS.	

More Precisely Dated		Less Precisely Dated
246	COMM. ON MATTHEW. Homilies first taken down in shorthand. CONVERSATION WITH HERACLEIDES	
		246–9 *Comm. on Twelve Prophets.* HOMILIES ON LEVITICUS.
		246–55 *Homilies on Lamentations.* *Comm. on Luke.* *Homilies on Song of Songs.* *Homilies on Isaiah.* *Homilies on Acts.* *Homilies on the Epistle to Hebrews.* HOMILY ON 1 SAMUEL 28. HOMILIES ON JUDGES. HOMILIES ON EXODUS. HOMILIES ON GENESIS. HOMILIES ON NUMBERS.
247–8	HOMILIES ON PSALMS. HOMILIES ON JEREMIAH.	247–55 HOMILIES ON EZEKIEL.
248	AGAINST CELSUS.	
?253	*That the King Alone is Creator.*	249–55 HOMILIES ON JOSHUA.

committed as a young man. Again, we can find several uncomplimentary references to clergy, and especially to bishops, in which we can no doubt trace the influence of his unhappy experiences with Demetrius, and the trouble aroused by his own ordination. This attitude is particularly visible in the *Commentary on Matthew.* In XI. 15, he refers to teaching in the church which may become servile, or an excuse for greed or for pride, and in xv. 25 he carefully places ἀνεπιλήμπτους before ἐπισκόπους and ἀνεγκλήτους before πρεσβυτέρους in reckoning them as 'spiritual fathers and mothers'. In *Concerning Prayer* xxviii. 9, 10, he says that not even the bishops of his day can forgive idolatry or adultery or fornication.

The task of tracing a development in Origen's thought is a delicate and perilous one, in view of our uncertainty about the chronological order of his works. One sad example of the dangers of this task is provided by N. P. Williams, in his book *The Ideas of the Fall and of Original Sin.* Williams here propounds the theory that before 231, in his *Concerning First Principles,* Origen has no theory whatever of original sin, but that afterwards, when he encountered in Caesarea and elsewhere the practice of Infant Baptism, he began to see the necessity of formulating one.[1] Origen toyed, Williams believes, with the theory of 'quasi-material impurity' or 'bad mana' found in the Levitical law. For support for this Williams refers to passages from the *Homilies on Leviticus*, describing them as 'shortly after 231',[2] and from the *Homilies on Luke* ('some years later'). Later, however, Origen produced a more refined theory along the same lines, and for this development Williams appeals to the *Commentary on Romans*. Origen's fall-theory becomes at times one of *inquinamentum* (for this Williams quotes the *Commentary on the Song of Songs*),[3] but in the *Commentary on Romans* he took a more Pauline view, though even here he sometimes suggests his earliest view of all.[4] In *Against Celsus*, however, which Williams calls 'his last work', 'he appears, though it is impossible to be quite sure of his meaning, to revert to his earlier theory, that of an immense number of individual pre-natal falls'.[5] A consideration of chronology, however, quite upsets this carefully-devised scheme. The *Homilies on Leviticus* (246 at earliest) must have come after the *Homilies on Luke* (234 at latest), and possibly after the *Commentary on Romans* (245), and even after *Against Celsus*; they certainly did not appear 'shortly after 231'. The *Commentary on the Song of Songs* we put in 244, the *Commentary on Romans* in 245, and *Against Celsus* in 248. If Origen took one fall-theory in the first, another in the second, and the original one in the third, all in the space of four years, he must have had an inconstancy of intellect no one has hitherto suspected. The fact is that though it is true that Origen does mention Infant Baptism as an apostolical custom several times[6] in the *Commentary on Romans* (as Williams observes), it is unlikely in the extreme that this custom was only brought to his notice after 231. Before 231 he had, after all, visited already Rome (212), Arabia (214), and Palestine (215). Whatever views Origen held about original sin, it is clear that we cannot trace such a chronological development in them as Williams outlines, and the evidence for their having been influenced by the practice of Infant Baptism is utterly insufficient.

We can, however, if we work cautiously enough, trace a development in Origen's thought in certain matters, and Koch's view,[7] that there is

---

[1] See N. P. Williams, pp. 219–20. He here follows Bigg and Harnack, who both seem to be nodding.   [2] N. P. Williams, p. 224.

[3] Ibid. p. 227.   [4] Ibid. p. 228.   [5] Ibid. pp. 228–9.   [6] See below, p. 178.

[7] According to Molland, *The Conception of the Gospel*, p. 164.

no development to be found there, is a superficial one. Molland himself[1] thinks that Origen's eschatology had, by the time he wrote the *Commentary on Romans*, reached a conclusion concerning the possibility of human free-will's indefinitely defying God, determined by the conviction that 'love never faileth'. There are, moreover, several indications in the *Concerning First Principles* itself that it is an early work,[2] and Denis is thoroughly justified in saying[3] '*le περὶ Ἀρχῶν était peut-être une tentative prématurée*'. It has very little reference to the Marcionites, a class of heretics with whom Origen was to be much occupied later. In III. 3, 3, pagan poetry is described as inspired by evil spirits, but in *Against Celsus*, at the end of his life, Origen quotes pagan poetry pretty freely.[4] In *Concerning First Principles* there is an elaborate division of the sense of Scripture into ῥητόν, ψυχικόν, and πνευματικόν, and a careful systematization of allegory. Origen never consistently observed these rather subtle distinctions in his later works. For instance, in his *Homilies on Jeremiah* (247–8) he shows an obvious tendency to jump from ῥητόν to ψυχικόν and πνευματικόν without preserving much distinction between them. The earlier works, the *Commentaries on John* and *on Genesis* (in so far as they survive), and the *Concerning First Principles*, are full of typology and elaborate allegory designed to support Origen's particular doctrinal interests. But in the *Commentary on Matthew* he uses allegory much less and is surprisingly cautious about it when he does use it. For instance, in XII. 30, to a speculation of his motivated by his characteristically rationalistic view of eschatology he adds a note: 'But we say this without wanting to invalidate the literally interpreted Second Coming of the Son of God.' And in XVI. 9, before he allegorizes the story of the healing of the two

---

[1] Ibid.

[2] Even though Cadiou may describe it as 'not a work of his youth but of his maturity' (*La Jeunesse d'Origène*, p. 400).

[3] Denis, p. 390.

[4] This may be partly accounted for by the fact that Origen was writing *Against Celsus* specifically for pagans, but more, in my view, by the likelihood that when he was writing *Concerning First Principles* he was in conscious reaction against the author of an earlier *Concerning First Principles*—Clement of Alexandria. Clement commonly regards classical Greek literature as inspired, almost as much as the Bible is. In this softening attitude towards pagan culture observable later in Origen's life we have perhaps some slight support for the view which attributes the purely philosophical work, *That the King Alone is Creator*, to his last years.

blind men (Matthew 20. 29–34), he takes care to explain that he believes in the literal sense also. Cadiou sees a decrease in Origen's interest in Gnostic speculation concerning cosmology and the like as his life goes on, particularly in the later books of the *Commentary on John*: '*Un mouvement mystique finit par prédominer*.'[1] The *Exhortation to Martyrdom* almost entirely eschews allegory, naturally, because such speculations would be out of place in a book written to meet so serious a situation. *Against Celsus* is extremely sparing of its allegorization, both because it was designed for pagans who would not readily understand the allegorization of the Old Testament, and because one of the charges made by Celsus against the Christians was their unjustified use of allegory.

In the Homilies, as might be expected, Origen's style is simpler and his matter more directly edifying than in the Commentaries, and he is at greater pains to explain his points and to expand the context. In the Homilies he does indeed use allegory fairly freely, but not to support such doctrinal speculations as those of *Concerning First Principles* and the *Commentary on John* so much as to produce edifying moral and religious sentiments, and even then it is noticeable that he does not allegorize as freely as in his earlier works. There is, for instance, very little typology for the purpose of doctrinal discussion in the *Homilies on Leviticus* and much for spiritual edification. In his only surviving Homily on 1 Samuel he seems deliberately to eschew allegory, which makes it all the more surprising that Eustathius in decrying Origen's tendency to allegorize should apparently have chosen this work for his attack.

We shall see later on how we may perhaps detect in Origen a change of attitude towards the value of three works which we now place outside the Canon of Scripture, the *Shepherd* of Hermas, the *Acts of Paul* and the *Book of Enoch*, and also towards that book which formed the subject of his *Letter to Africanus*, the History of Susanna.

[1] *La Jeunesse d'Origène*, p. 339.

CHAPTER I

THE MEANING OF TRADITION

THE broadest sense that can be given to the word 'tradition' is, to put it in one sentence, What the Church knows of Christ. Christian tradition is therefore in this work taken to mean primarily that which is handed down from the very beginning of the Christian faith, the Christian teaching and gospel, the method by which it is handed over, and the sources from which it is derived. If we begin by asking ourselves what are the sources and depositaries of this knowledge, we shall at once find it necessary to reply, our Lord himself, and the evidence of apostles, disciples, and eyewitnesses of the Word. Any authoritative tradition must ultimately derive from these. But the question which is not so easily answered, and about which doubt and controversy have constantly arisen, is, How does the tradition derived from these sources reach Christians of succeeding generations, whether of the third century or the twentieth? How is this tradition handed down?

Tradition must at first have been entirely oral. All are agreed here. The earliest traditions must have been various fragments of our Lord's teaching, circulating in different communities in more or less independent units, and along with these must have circulated the stories of the Passion and Resurrection, in more than one form, and perhaps accounts of the early days of the Christian Church. It is possible, too, that very early credal formulae existed first in an oral form. Some, for instance, have seen such a formula in Romans 1. 1–4, and C. H. Dodd[1] has shown that something like a creed may be found behind the speeches in the early part of Acts.

But later on tradition was written down. Tradition was listed in order to aid Christian teachers to emphasize some important point, such as the Resurrection Appearances (1 Cor. 15. 3–8), or our Lord's actions at the Last Supper (1 Cor. 11. 23–5). Or Christian tradition was witnessed to and enshrined in early Christian documents such as letters written by, or attributed to, S. Peter and S. Paul. Or else tradition was deliberately written down as a conscious aid to teaching and preaching,

[1] *The Apostolic Preaching and its Developments*, pp. 29–73.

in order to distinguish fact from uncertainty and legend. Many had undertaken to draw up a narrative of Christian tradition, says S. Luke, but he was writing as an accurate author who was in a position to discriminate between genuine tradition and false, in order that Theophilus might know the certainty of the tradition (Luke 1. 1-4). This need accounts for the origin and the form of the four Gospels and of Acts.

Again, Christian institutions constitute one form of tradition. The institutions of Baptism and the Eucharist derive from a time as early as any oral tradition and earlier than any written.[1] The Christian ministry is also conceivably a source of such tradition. These possibilities must not be overlooked in our estimation of the sources of early Christian tradition.

Finally, it is possible that, though oral tradition must have been to a large extent written down during the first Christian century, inasmuch as all the written tradition which we now possess must at one time have been oral, yet some of this oral tradition may have survived. It may have been handed on from generation to generation in the Church, without being written down, and may either have been written down centuries after the Church's official writing down of tradition which we call the New Testament, or may never have been written down at all, and may still be preserved and available in the Church, oral but intact. Possible instances of such a tradition as this are the number, names, and authorship of the books of the New Testament, the practice of baptizing infants, and some primitive traditions forming the basis of dogmas later officially adopted in the Christian Church, or in parts of it, such as the doctrine of the Holy Trinity, the doctrine of the Prerogatives of Peter, and the doctrine of Purgatory. This possible source of Christian doctrine must also be explored as we approach the consideration of Christian tradition in general, and of Origen's doctrine of it in particular.

Among English theologians G. L. Prestige has in recent years dealt with this subject in a most interesting and useful way in the first chapter of his book *Fathers and Heretics*. He there says that in the Christian Fathers two meanings of the word 'tradition' are found most commonly. One denotes 'an accretion, enlargement, confirmation of the

---

[1] However instituted, Christian Baptism derives from a very early time and will answer the purposes of this argument. Personally, I think Baptism does derive from our Lord, though he did not 'institute' it exactly as he did the Eucharist.

faith'; this 'is to be expected and welcomed in the process of trans-mitting Christian truth...the whole of history adds material for testing the validity and illustrating the progress of Christian beliefs, and so enriches Christian tradition'.[1] In this material are included creeds,[2] and also, as well as fact itself,[3] the interpretation of fact—a feature which is to be found even in the New Testament. In short this form of tradition is almost a *philosophia perennis*: it is 'the accumulating wisdom of philosophically grounded Christianity'.[4] This tradition the Fathers called διδασκαλία.

The other sort of tradition they described as παράδοσις,[5] a 'handing over'. Christianity is a 'given', a revealed religion, given through inspired men. In the Old Testament it is divine truth which is given. But the New Covenant 'depended on personal relations with an historical figure who was both Man and Saviour, who revealed God and selected His own witnesses to testify to the fact and the significance of His work'.[6] From the side of Heaven this is described as redemption, from the side of man as faith in Christ. This is the 'faith once delivered to the saints'. Hence[7] this tradition is specially associated with the word 'apostolic', and later 'ecclesiastical'. The contents and substance of this tradition[8] are to be found in the Church's keeping, and 'for most practical purposes the tradition is enshrined in the Bible'.[9]

But what if heretics and catholics differed and yet both quoted Scriptural texts to support their arguments? By what standard is the Bible to be interpreted? Prestige answers this[10] by making three points which he says represent the Fathers' answer to this question. First, 'The original doctrine of tradition by the apostles to the Church continued to be the ultimate basis of Christian thought'. Second, a process of interpretation was necessary to extract the original tradi-tion from the Bible: 'Appeal was made, not to the Bible simply, but to the Bible rightly and rationally interpreted.' Third, 'There survives definite evidence that the meaning of the Bible was consciously sought in relation to its context in Christian institutions.' Instances of these institutions are spiritual order and discipline, sacraments, creeds, the episcopate. Hence it is[11] that Irenaeus appeals to 'the tradition of the

---

[1] *Fathers and Heretics*, p. 6. [2] Ibid. p. 7.
[3] Ibid. p. 10. [4] Ibid. p. 12. [5] Ibid. p. 13.
[6] Ibid. p. 22. [7] Ibid. p. 24. [8] Ibid. p. 26.
[9] Ibid. p. 27. [10] Ibid. p. 30. [11] Ibid. p. 33.

apostles', handed down through apostolic succession. This tradition is also derived from the Christian cultus. Basil can be quoted[1] as appealing to unwritten customs which he believed to have apostolic authority. Chrysostom confined such a tradition to practical matters, such as actions, not doctrines.[2] Summarizing, Prestige says: 'The voice of the Bible could be plainly heard only if its text were interpreted broadly and rationally, in accordance with the apostolic creed and the evidence of the historic practice of Christendom.'[3] This attitude rested on two presuppositions, the first that the Bible does provide all things necessary to salvation, the second that the Christian Church possesses sufficient inspiration to give a true interpretation of the records of the Christian faith.

Finally, Prestige asks himself whether in fact the Fathers were arguing in a circle. 'They interpreted the Bible by the tradition, and yet expounded the tradition out of the Bible.'[4] And he answers this question by saying that for the Fathers the tradition really came from only a small part of the Bible: 'The appeal was really from the Bible as a whole to the Gospel.'

J. F. Bethune-Baker, in his *Introduction to the Early History of Christian Doctrine*, says that in early times both oral and written tradition constitute 'the Tradition, the Canon or Rule of Faith', and adds in a footnote, 'The same terms, κανών, *regula (sc. fidei)*, παράδοσις, *traditio*, are applied to both'.[5] Later he tells us that 'the interpretations of the Church of post-apostolic times, whether contained in oral or in written tradition...henceforth constitute a separate source of doctrine.' In the same work[6] he discusses the Fathers' claim, originating in controversies with the Gnostics, that the Scriptures can only be understood in close connection with the tradition of the Church. 'Such a claim was quite in accordance with the primitive conception of tradition, not as an independent source of doctrine, but as essentially hermeneutic, forming with the written words one river of knowledge.'[7] Irenaeus, he says,[8] appeals to tradition as to something which, even if Scripture were not there, would serve us in good stead, as it is the tradition of teaching of the apostles, guaranteed by the consensus of the most ancient and apostolic churches about it. Bethune-Baker adds

[1] *Fathers and Heretics*, p. 40.   [2] Ibid. p. 42.
[3] Ibid. p. 43.   [4] Ibid. p. 44.   [5] Bethune-Baker, p. 42.
[6] Ibid. pp. 55–8.   [7] Ibid. p. 55.   [8] Ibid. p. 56.

in a footnote to the same page that 'though priority is claimed for the tradition, yet it is appealed to not as an independent source of doctrine but as a means of determining the true sense of the Scriptures'. Irenaeus 'to the pretended secret doctrine of the heretics opposes the public preaching of the faith of the apostolic churches'. Tertullian, in his *De Praescriptione Haereticorum*, asks: 'Whose are the Scriptures? By whom and through whose means and when and to whom was the discipline [i.e. the teaching or system] handed over which makes men Christians? Wherever you find the true Christian discipline and faith, there will be the truth of the Christian Scriptures and expositions and all traditions.'[1] 'It is', Bethune-Baker continues,[2] 'the Church which is the keeper and guardian of all these possessions, and therefore it is the Church and the Church only which can determine the truth.'

'In early times', says F. J. Badcock in his *History of the Creeds*,[3] 'the appeal in questions of doctrinal controversy was to the Scriptures and to the common faith of the Church, which had received a very incomplete embodiment in the slightly varying local creeds.' This conclusion seems to support Bethune-Baker's view of the matter.

A different and most interesting approach to the matter is taken in a series of essays on the general subject of Tradition and Scripture published in *The Eastern Churches Quarterly* in 1947.[4] The first is by L. Bouyer, on 'Holy Scripture and Tradition as seen by the Fathers'. He says[5] that to the Fathers the object of faith is not a series of propositions, but is fundamentally one. It is the grasping of this oneness which Irenaeus calls ὑπόθεσις (*Adv. Haer.* I. i. 15–20), and Origen μυστήριον. What Origen means by this is 'the impact of our Lord's personality, as God and as man, on the divine world and on the created one; it is closely akin to the "mysterion" of S. Paul, expressed so prominently in his later epistles, though perhaps not to be completely identified with it. It constitutes a key to the whole of Origen's conception of the allegorical understanding of Scripture and of all human history as well. He sees all things through that same medium converging and growing towards unity, so that his "mysterion" appears to be

---

[1] Ibid. pp. 57–8.   [2] Ibid. p. 58.   [3] p. 36.

[4] Vol. VII, Supplementary Issue. They represent a number of papers read at *The Eastern Churches Quarterly* Conference held at Blackfriars, Oxford, in October 1946, and at a discussion group of Dominican fathers and members of the Mirfield Community held in July 1946.

[5] *E.C.Q.* pp. 1–3.

an equivalent of the "anacephalaiosis" or recapitulation of Irenaeus, inasmuch as we see in it God reconciling all things, with Himself and between themselves. We may even say that the *gnosis* of which Origen makes so much is nothing else than seeing the development of that unity to its achievement in Christ through the Scriptures and through human and even cosmic history.' Athanasius calls this 'unified view-point' σκοπὸς ἐκκλησιαστικός (*Contra Arianos* iii. 58). And this 'unified view' Bouyer[1] virtually identifies with tradition, as distinct from Scripture. Clement of Alexandria speaks of 'the ecclesiastical canon', and that canon 'is nothing else than tradition itself, and that tradition is here [i.e. in Clement] seen as a key to the Scriptures and their profound unity brought to light at Christ's coming'.[2] Bouyer next quotes Rufinus' translation of Origen's *Concerning First Principles*, Book I, to show that in a list of points in the Christian faith which are beyond dispute the last on the list is the article that there is a spiritual sense hidden in Scripture, but that this sense is only known to those '*quibus gratia Spiritus Sancti in verbo sapientiae et scientiae condonatur*'.[3] This last item, says Bouyer, is not, as is usually held, one of Origen's private opinions, but 'the commonest view of tradition as such in all Christian antiquity'. This 'spiritual interpretation', he says,[4] 'was not created by Origen (though powerfully developed by him) but was inherited by him from S. Paul and our Lord', and 'it occupies a central place in all the Fathers' teaching of Christianity'.

Bouyer summarizes his conclusions under three heads:[5] First, in all the Fathers, the Incarnation and all that it implies are a key to the whole history of man and to the whole Bible. This is the meaning of Origen's μυστήριον and of Irenaeus' ἀνακεφαλαίωσις, and of Athanasius' σκοπὸς ἐκκλησιαστικός. Second, this interpretation, this revelation, is the legacy made by Christ through the Spirit to the apostles and by the apostles through the same Spirit to the Church. This is how the Church alone can truly interpret Scripture. Examples he finds in Tertullian, *De Praescrip.* XXXVII. i. 4; Irenaeus, *Adv. Haer.* i. 90–4; i. 207; ii. 10–15; ii. 56 (Harvey's ed.); Clement of Alexandria, *Stromateis* VI. xv. 135; Origen, *Homilies on Exodus*, Preface vii. 8 (Baehrens edition ii. 215), *Commentary on Song of Songs* I (Baehrens edition i. 9), *Concerning First*

---

[1] *E.C.Q.* p. 9.
[2] *E.C.Q.* p. 9.
[3] See *E.C.Q.* p. 10.
[4] *E.C.Q.* pp. 11–12.
[5] *E.C.Q.* pp. 12–13.

Principles IV. 2. 3. Thirdly, this tradition, says Bouyer,[1] gives the Church 'a large measure of freedom and even of independence.... Just because the Church keeps in its living κήρυγμα, always one with the tradition coming from the apostles and through them from our Lord, the gnosis which gives its true light to Scripture, in that same κήρυγμα she has an access to Christ and his teaching which, though always consonant with the Scriptures, does not depend upon them.... We have seen in [the Church's] living κήρυγμα the perpetual transmission of the κανών ἐκκλησιαστικός without which neither the letter nor the Spirit can be grasped.'

We are not therefore surprised to find Bouyer later[2] alluding to Basil's reference in his *De Spiritu Sancto*[3] to τὰ ἄγραφα τῶν ἐθῶν as essential to the κήρυγμα, and claiming that 'the *traditio non scripta* supplements Scripture, not as though it added anything foreign to it, but as preventing us from maiming its data through a minimizing or distorted interpretation'. This tradition, too, Bouyer seems to believe,[4] accounts for the Church's production of creeds and formulae of the faith.

Another essay in the same volume is by H. E. Symonds, on 'The Patristic Doctrine of the Relation of Scripture and Tradition'. He speaks of the handing on of the Christian faith, in Prestige's sense of παράδοσις, and then says:[5] 'This handing on is known as tradition, and through it, and through it alone, was the Christian faith spread until the formation of the collection of apostolic writings known as the Canon of the New Testament. Even then the New Testament did not become a substitute for this tradition. The Church in the person of her authorized teachers, the bishops, continued to hand on the same tradition, though constantly appealing to the Scriptures of both Old and New Testament to corroborate its truth.' For this appeal to apostolic tradition he quotes[6] Origen's *Concerning First Principles*, '*servetur vero ecclesiastica praedicatio per successionis ordinem ab apostolis tradita*', and later[7] he refers to the same passage to show that the discordant views of those who believe in Christ are to be brought to the test of the Church's tradition. He concludes:[8] 'It means that the

[1] *E.C.Q.* p. 13.   [2] *E.C.Q.* p. 14.
[3] *P.G.* XXXII, 188.   [4] *E.C.Q.* p. 15.
[5] *E.C.Q.* p. 59.   [6] *E.C.Q.* p. 61. *Concerning F.P.*, Origen's Preface, 2.
[7] *E.C.Q.* p. 66.   [8] *E.C.Q.* p. 70.

Church never claims to add new truths to the final revelation given by our Lord to His apostles, and has at the time of forming the canon of the New Testament (and in accepting that of the Old) decided that the truth handed down in the tradition is in fact embodied in the writings of the apostles and evangelists.'

The final essay in this series to which we must refer is that of R. Kehoe on 'The Scriptures as the Word of God'. 'The Scriptures', he says,[1] 'give the very word of God. What tradition gives us is the true sense of the Scriptures, the right understanding of them. It is not in the same sense a source of revelation. We are not presented with the anomaly of the Scriptural source providing us with the greater part of revelational truth, plus an appendix—of inferior verbal quality—containing a certain few truths which are there omitted. Formally speaking, Tradition means that instinctive mind of the Church, that inspired sense of hers, which enables her to handle the Word of God aright, to be the wise Mother of the Word and Bride of Christ.'

One more opinion on the general subject of the relation of Scripture to tradition is worth quoting, and this is from the French scholar, C. Mondésert. In his book, *Clément d'Alexandrie*,[2] he has a delightful simile for the relation of the two, which is almost Homeric in its quality: Scripture is the shepherd, tradition the flock. The flock may wander a little (it is a living flock), and the shepherd may even sometimes follow it. But it is the shepherd who fixes the limit of the flock's extravagances, and who guides it between morning and evening and from resting-place to resting-place.

How far this tradition, or indeed tradition in any of its senses, is related to a creed or creeds, seems to be very uncertain. Badcock[3] distinguishes carefully between 'the common doctrine and discipline of Christendom', called the Rule of Faith, and the Creed. This Rule of Faith 'whether stated by Origen or Irenaeus or Tertullian contained very much more than was ever found in the contemporary creed'. Later,[4] speaking of the *regula veritatis*, he quotes, 'Undoubtedly the baptismal formula...and the baptismal creeds of various churches, into which the formula naturally expanded, were never far from the thoughts of the writer who used the phrase; but the baptismal creed and

---

[1] *E.C.Q.* pp. 76–7.   [2] p. 256.
[3] Op. cit. p. 4.
[4] Badcock, p. 21; here he is quoting Mason in Swete's *Essays*, p. 51.

the *regula veritatis* are not convertible terms'. Badcock also[1] quotes Harnack as equating 'the Faith, the Rule of Faith, "Kerugma" (or "Proclamation"), "Truth", and "Rule of Truth"'; and he quotes some words of Ammundsen:[2] 'The Rule of Truth in Irenaeus *primarily* is not an institution, a formula, or a book; it is Christianity itself, the genuine apostolic Christianity. . . . The Truth—which is the rule—. . . comprehends the whole revelation. . . . Its main points are: the creation —the dispensation and prophecies in the Old Testament—Christ as the Second Adam, His supernatural birth, His words, His Death, His resurrection and ascension—the Holy Ghost—the Church—the Christian Ethics—the Eschatology.'

In his investigation of the origin of creeds, Badcock finds no direct connection between the Rule of Faith and the Creed. He derives, incidentally, all creeds from the Baptismal Creed.[3] But in fact by his account any given creed must also have been a summary of the Church's Rule of Faith, that is, of the Church's preaching at the time when the Creed originated.

A more recent authority, J. N. D. Kelly, in his *Early Christian Creeds* distinguishes carefully between Baptismal Formulae and Declaratory Creeds. These latter he thinks were used only in connection with the preparation before Baptism of Catechumens, and had no wide currency till the second and third centuries.[4] He too refuses to identify the Creed and the Rule of Faith. He says of Irenaeus and Tertullian: 'Though they frequently cite the rule of faith, it is plain that their citations are neither formulae themselves nor presuppose some underlying formula.'[5] It will be seen that inquiry into the Rule of Faith of both Clement and Origen tends to support this conclusion.

[1] Badcock, p. 22. The reference is to Harnack, *The Apostles' Creed*, pp. 54–8.
[2] In *J.T.S.* xiii, 578.
[3] Contrast O. Cullmann, who in *The Earliest Christian Confessions*, pp. 81 ff., derives creeds from five different sources: Baptism, Regular Worship, Exorcism, Persecution, and Polemic against Heretics.
[4] *Early Christian Creeds*, Ch. II, and Ch. III, pp. 95, 96, 98.
[5] Ibid. pp. 95–6. Kelly defines Tertullian's Rule of Faith as 'the body of teaching transmitted in the Church by Scripture and tradition' (p. 83), which is not an entirely clear account of it.

CHAPTER II

ORIGEN'S TRANSLATORS

THIS survey of contemporary opinions upon the subject of tradition in general is necessary if we are to consider Origen's doctrine of tradition fully and in its right setting. But before we begin to consider our main subject we must issue a warning, and take some time over emphasizing it. The Latin translators of Origen's works will have to be used very sparingly in evidence, because it is clear that both Rufinus and Jerome, the chief ancient translators of Origen's works, altered the sense of Origen's words when they thought fit; and we have definite evidence that Rufinus at least did so in cases where Origen's words referred to tradition.

In his Preface to his translation of Origen's *Concerning First Principles*, Rufinus expressly tells us that he omitted or altered, to suit the orthodox rule of faith, various passages in Origen's works on the grounds that they were later interpolations by heretical and malevolent persons.[1] He claims that he is in this practice only following the example of Jerome in his translations of Origen. And in his *Apologia in Hieronymum* he accuses Jerome of inserting bits into Origen's text in his translation of the *Homilies on Luke* as often as Rufinus did in his own translations, and he gives one example (though admittedly it is a very slight one). He adds the allegation that Jerome did the same in his translations of the *Homilies on Jeremiah*, *on Isaiah*, and *on Ezekiel*.[2] That, generally speaking, Rufinus' translation of Origen's Greek is loose and sometimes deliberately untrue to the original has been recognized by all commentators on Origen from the Migne editor onward, whose comments, '*Porro sollemne fuit Rufino pervertere omnia et ad libitum recoquere*', and '*Qui legit has homilias incertus sit utrum*

---

[1] *Concerning F.P.*, Rufinus' Preface, 2. Compare his equally candid admission in his Preface to his translation of Origen's *Commentary on Romans*. A. Ramsbotham, the editor of the Greek fragments of this work, says, 'with rare exceptions Rufinus is little or no help towards a reconstruction of a perfect text' (*J.T.S.* xiii, 1912, p. 210).

[2] *P.L.* xxi, 606. See Rauer, *G.C.S.*, Origen ix, pp. xvii–xviii.

legat Origenem an Rufinum', are very just.[1] Koetschau, indeed, goes so far as to say,[2] 'Rufinus' work represents a working over rather than a translation of the Greek original, and is in places so unreliable that it continually needs checking to be of any use'.

It is easy to see that Rufinus is, to say the least, very paraphrastic in his translation if we compare his Latin with any parts of Origen's translated works where a fragment has survived in Greek. To take concrete instances, a Greek fragment survives for *Concerning First Principles* I. 6. 5, whereby we can see that Rufinus has translated eleven lines of Greek into twenty-two lines of Latin, including among other superfluities a quotation of 1 Corinthians 11. 10, which is not in the Greek. Again, in Origen's *Homilies on Leviticus*[3] Rufinus makes Origen say that somebody might preach soundly and well on other doctrinal subjects, and yet ignore '*carnis resurrectionem*'. It is impossible to believe that this represents ἀνάστασιν σαρκός in the original Greek of Origen, and not ἀνάστασιν σώματος; it is highly likely that this is an example of Rufinus' changing Origen's sense. Compare, for a more certain and more flagrant example, a passage in Origen's *Commentary on Song of Songs*.[4] We can recover a fragment of the original Greek here from Procopius. It is a comment on the LXX version of a phrase in Song of Songs 2. 12, καιρὸς τῆς τομῆς ἔφθακεν; it runs οὗτος δέ ἐστιν ὁ τῆς αὐτοῦ παρουσίας, ἐν ᾧ δεῖ τὰ σωματικὰ τοῦ νόμου, καὶ τῆς ἐν τοῖς προφήταις ἱστορίας περιπεφυκότα τοῖς πνευματικοῖς περιτέμνεσθαι[5] καὶ μεῖναι τὰ κρείττονα. καιρὸς δὲ πάλιν καὶ τῆς τῶν ἁμαρτημάτων ἐκκοπῆς καὶ ἀφέσεως διὰ λουτροῦ παλιγγενεσίας. Rufinus does not like this belittling of the historical, so he translates, '*Sed et putationis tempus per fidem meae passionis et resurrectionis advenit. Amputantur enim et exsecantur ab hominibus peccata, cum in baptismo donatur remissio peccatorum.*' Again in his translation of Pamphilus' *Apology for Origen* we find a quotation from a passage in *Concerning First Principles* which deals with the Holy Spirit. The Greek original

---

[1] The first comment is from *P.G.* XIII, 62, on the Prologue to Rufinus' translation of Origen's *Commentary on the Song of Songs*. The second is from *P.G.* XII, 395, in a preface to Origen's works on Leviticus. Cf. Cadiou, *La Jeunesse d'Origène*, pp. 263–5.

[2] See Koetschau, *G.C.S.*, Origen v, Introduction, pp. cxxviii–cxxxv.

[3] v. x.　　　　　　　　　　　　　[4] *P.G.* XIII, 185.

[5] 'Those accretions of historical narrative upon the spiritual truths of the prophets.'

for this survives in the Emperor Justinian's *Letter to Mennas*. When we compare the two it becomes glaringly obvious that Rufinus has in his translation omitted Origen's explicit statement that the Holy Spirit is less than the Father and the Son and that the Son's power is greater than that of the Spirit, and has wrapped the whole in verbose paraphrase. It is possible (but not certain) that Rufinus is responsible for the apparent contradiction in Origen's *Homily I on Psalm 38*, where he seems to hold the opinion that the reference in Matthew 23. 35 to the Zechariah who was slain between the porch and the altar meant the prophet Zechariah.[1] In three other passages[2] Origen clearly expresses the opinion that this Zechariah was the father of John the Baptist.

It is not so easy to impugn Jerome's translations of Origen's works, apart from Rufinus' statements. Jerome translated the *Homilies on the Song of Songs*, the *Homilies on Ezekiel*, the *Homilies on Isaiah*, the *Homilies on Jeremiah*, the *Homilies on the Twelve Prophets*, and the *Homilies on Luke*; of these translations we only have parts of the second, fourth, and last. It has been suggested that he was also the translator of the *Commentary on Matthew* which we have,[3] but this view is not generally held now. The subject has been exhaustively treated by Klostermann and Benz.[4] They explicitly rule out Jerome as the translator[5] on grounds of style and diction, if on no others. And they rule out Rufinus, on the grounds that his translations of extracts quoted from this commentary in Pamphilus' *Apology for Origen* display a very different text from that which we find in the extant translation of the commentary. They mention Huet's conjecture that the translator lived in the time and belonged to the circle of Cassiodorus,[6] and suggest that if we are to accept this theory we may identify him with a man called Bellator who, we know from Cassiodorus, translated two Homilies of Origen on Ezra into Latin. But they do not

[1] Section I (*P.G.* XII, 1570).

[2] *Comm. on Matthew* (Pt. II, 25); fragment on Luke II. 51 (*P.G.* XVII, 356); *Comm. on Ephesians* xx (Gregg's edition of the fragments, p. 554). But *Comm. on Matthew* x. 18 appears to hold the other view.

[3] Migne's editor (*P.G.* XII, 395) quotes Gennadius to the effect that all Latin translations of Origen not by Rufinus are by Jerome.

[4] *Zur Überlieferung der Matthäusklärung des Origenes.*   [5] Ibid. p. 72.

[6] Cassiodorus lived 469/70–*c.* 560. He was a great statesman, a patron of monasticism and learning during 'the last flicker of Roman civilization under the Ostrogothic rule'. See the article 'Cassiodorus' in the *Dictionary of Christian Biography*.

think that the attribution of the translation to this man is at all certain. The Latin text of the translation, as we have it, may, they think,[1] represent a fuller form of the original than the Greek as we now have it does, and its omissions and additions as compared with the Greek may not be due merely to deviation on the part of the translator. The Greek may represent (as apparently Preuschen conjectured) an abbreviated form of the original. They incline to think that we must either assume a recension or redaction of the work after Origen's day or conclude, with Harnack and Zahn, that Origen himself produced two versions of the commentary in his lifetime. Whoever translated this commentary, however, cannot have been an impeccable translator, and was capable of altering the text in the interests of orthodoxy. In one passage (XVII. 9) Origen belittles 'the doctrine of the resurrection of the dead as it is believed in the Church', but the Latin translation significantly omits this sentence. Later on (Pt. II. 46) the survival of a Greek fragment enables us to see how much the translator has elaborated upon Origen's reference to the Church's rule of faith.

Where we are on sure ground with Jerome, for instance in his translation of the *Homilies on Luke*, we cannot help noticing that he is a much more accurate translator than Rufinus. Rauer, the editor of these Homilies,[2] says that though Jerome has certainly abbreviated in several places and made some additions, where he has translated he has done so accurately, almost word for word. He admits, however, that we cannot be sure that Jerome has not introduced doctrinal emendations into the text. In fact (though Rauer does not seem to have noticed this) in at least one place we can be fairly sure that he has. In Homily XIV[3] Origen is speaking of the possibilities of another baptism of the faithful after death: '*Ego puto quod et post resurrectionem ex mortuis indigeamus sacramento eluente nos atque purgante, nemo enim absque sordibus resurgere poterit, nec ullam posse animam reperiri quae universis statim vitiis careat. Unde in regeneratione baptismi assumitur sacramentum, ut quomodo Jesus secundum dispensationem carnis oblatione purgatus est, ita etiam nos spiritali regeneratione purgemur.*' And later in the same work, in Homily XXIV[4] he again suggests that the 'baptism with fire' is to take place after this life, and to involve all those who

---

[1] Op. cit. p. 86.
[2] See *G.C.S.*, Origen IX, Introduction, pp. xviii–xx.
[3] On Luke 2. 22.   [4] On Luke 3. 16.

need cleansing before they enter Paradise. But earlier in Homily XIV, Origen has said that to imagine that the spiritual body rises polluted and stained is a '*piaculum*'. The Migne editor suggests that in this last passage the text is corrupt, but it seems to me much more likely that it represents an attempt on the part of Jerome to modify the more daring flights of Origen's speculation.[1]

Several recent commentators upon Origen have also recognized that on the particular subject of Origen's doctrine of tradition Rufinus must be convicted of altering Origen's words. G. W. Butterworth, for instance, in his Introduction to his translation of *Concerning First Principles*[2] notes how Rufinus will convert a passage so as to make it express a desire to keep close to the faith of the Church and to test all things by the rule of piety, as well as his hesitation about reproducing Origen's statements which reject the literal interpretation of the Bible, and his fear of the lengths to which allegorical interpretation may go. Bardy[3] admits that in several passages where the phrase '*regula pietatis*' occurs in Latin translations of Origen there is no equivalent in the Greek, and recognizes the danger of basing arguments on the Latin text only, unsupported by the Greek, though it would suit his thesis well to do so. Von Balthasar even suggests[4] that Rufinus has in several places exaggerated Origen's esotericism, so that where Origen meant nothing more than *sapienti sat* Rufinus has interpreted it to mean *non mittendum canibus*. And Molland notes[5] that in Rufinus' translation of the *Commentary on Romans* one passage contains a reference to the Creed as a 'short word' which is irrelevant to the discussion and looks like an appendix inserted by Rufinus.

Several more instances, no less striking, can in fact be found. In one passage in *Concerning First Principles* (III. 1. 23) where Origen's Greek has ὥστε κατὰ τοῦτο, Rufinus translates '*ex quo magis convenit regulae pietatis*', though the Greek contains no reference whatever to the Church's rule of faith. Later still in the same work (IV. 3. 13, 14)

---

[1] *P.G.* XIII, 1836. Cf. Cadiou, *La Jeunesse d'Origène*, p. 266: '*On se gardera d'attribuer une autorité sans limite aux traductions de Jérôme.*' He adds that Jerome, whose spirit was so unlike Origen's, tends to warp Origen's thought.

[2] Page xxx.

[3] 'La Règle de Foi d'Origène', pp. 173, 180.

[4] 'Le Mystérion d'Origène', p. 516.

[5] *The Conception of the Gospel*, p. 127; the passage in the *Commentary on Romans* is VII. xix, on Romans 9. 28.

a Greek fragment enables us to observe that Rufinus omits a particularly daring speculation by Origen suggesting that Christ is crucified still in the heavenly places, and begins the next paragraph thus: '*Verum in his omnibus sufficiat nobis sensum nostrum regulae pietatis aptare et ita sentire....*' The Greek fragment stops before the next paragraph begins, but we strongly suspect that this is another example of an insertion by Rufinus of a reference to the Church's rule of faith. So in the *Commentary on Romans* I. xviii, a long parenthesis introduced by the words '*quamvis iuxta ecclesiae fidem consequenter explanari videantur*', and not at all relevant to the subject of Origen's discussion, suggests the hand of Rufinus. Most remarkable of all, perhaps, is the instance noted by J. E. L. Oulton in an article on 'Rufinus' Translation of the Church History of Eusebius' in the *Journal of Theological Studies*.[1] In his summary of Origen's *Letter to Africanus* about the History of Susanna, Rufinus described Origen as saying 'that that alone should be deemed true in the divine scriptures which the Seventy interpreters had translated, since it had been confirmed by apostolic authority'. In fact what Origen wrote was πρὸς ταῦτα δὲ σκόπει εἰ μὴ καλὸν μεμνῆσθαι τό· οὐ μὴ μεταθήσεις ὅρια αἰώνια ἃ ἔστησαν οἱ πρότεροί σου. And this tendency on the part of Rufinus to alter Origen's references to what Rufinus had learnt to call the Canon is confirmed by some passages in his translation of Origen's *Commentary on the Song of Songs*. Throughout this commentary Origen quotes freely from the Book of Wisdom; for instance, in Book II of the Commentary (on Song of Songs I. 8) he quotes Wisdom 7. 17, 18 along with Psalms, Matthew, and Luke, without making any distinction between them, and later in the work (Book III, on Song of Songs 2. 19), he calls the author of Wisdom '*ille scriptor divinae sapientiae*', and refers to his words, quoted in the text, as '*his Scripturae sermonibus*'. Yet in his Preface to this Commentary,[2] we find the statement that the Church of God has accepted no songs of Solomon's as worth reading except the Song of Songs, and that no works of Solomon are in the Jewish canon except Proverbs, Ecclesiastes, and the Song of Songs (the Latin for 'are in the Canon' is '*habeatur in canone*'). The statement goes on to say that writers in the New Testament often do quote books known neither to the Jews nor to the Christian Church, and that no doubt the Holy Spirit had his reasons for that. Then: '*Illud tamen palam est, multa vel ab apostolis vel ab evangelistis exempla esse prolata, et Novo Testamento inserta, quae in his scripturis quas canonicas habemus numquam legimus, in apocryphis tamen inveniuntur, et evidenter ex ipsis ostenduntur assumpta. Sed ne sic quidem locus apocryphis dandus est; non enim transeundi sunt termini quos statuerunt patres nostri.*' It is just possible that this may be a fair representation of what Origen wrote here, if we assume that he is referring only to *songs* written by Solomon, and that he does not consider the Book of Wisdom a song.[1] But it cannot be an exact translation, as it is impossible to believe (as we shall see later) that Origen used the words κανών and κανονικός in this sense, and anyway the fragments of Greek printed by Migne from Procopius' quotations of Origen's works on the Song of Songs show that Rufinus was extremely free in his translation and expanded and elaborated generously. It is much more likely that Rufinus is here expounding, under cover of Origen's words, his own theory about the Canon. The reference in this passage to Proverbs 22. 28 may be original, or may betray Rufinus' memory of the passage from Origen's *Letter to Africanus* quoted above.

When therefore we find such scholars as Bouyer or Prat making statements about Origen's belief in the Church's control of her tradition and supporting them by references to Rufinus' translation of *Concerning First Principles* or of other works, we must point out how inconclusive such arguments are, and insist that to support their views these scholars must rely on the original Greek of Origen himself and not on the Latin of his translators.[2] There are many tempting passages in Rufinus' translations for those who hold views similar to these scholars',[3] but no good purpose is served by using them. This does not

[1] This is the explanation of Merk in an article in *Biblica*, in which he criticizes Harnack for concluding that Origen was contradicting himself in this matter. Merk does not seem to realize that Rufinus' translation cannot always be taken *au pied de la lettre*, and this solution does not seem to have presented itself to Harnack either. This is another small but significant demonstration of how important it is for those who write about Origen to take seriously the problem of his translators. See Merk's article, 'Origenes und der Kanon des alten Testaments', in *Biblica* for 1925, Vol. VI, pp. 200–5.

[2] See Prat, *Origène, le Théologien et l'Exégète*, pp. 8–13, and especially p. 17, where he claims that Origen's definition of the faith is essentially that of the 'sens scolastique' as well: '*C'est la prédication ecclésiastique, c'est-à-dire le magistère vivant et infaillible de l'Église qui règle et délimite l'objet de la foi.*'

[3] E.g. *Con. First P.*, Origen's Preface, 2: '*servetur vero ecclesiastica praedicatio per successionis ordinem ab apostolis tradita et usque ad praesens in ecclesia permanens, illa sola credenda est veritas quae nullo ab ecclesiastica et apostolica traditione*

mean of course that we can entirely ignore the Latin translations of Origen as sources for our inquiry. It does mean that we must take his words extant in Greek as our primary authorities, and realize that any reference to tradition, in particular in a translation by Rufinus or by Jerome, may very well have been touched up or even interpolated by the translator.[1]

discordat'; *Comm. on Romans* v. i (on Rom. 7. 9): '*nos autem apostoli sensum secundum pietatem ecclesiastici dogmatis advertamus.*' Both these, I am fairly sure, are examples of Rufinisms. Symonds quotes the first (*E.C.Q.* p. 61). Compare too *Con. First P.* I. 5. 4: '*ut in rebus tam difficilibus quid magis veritati sit proximum, vel quid secundum pietatis regulam opinandum sit, consequamur*', where Origen has a few sentences before appealed to Scripture and logic, but not the rule of faith.

[1] A particularly bad offender in this matter is E. F. Latko in his book, *Origen's Concept of Penance.* He does not attempt to take seriously the possibility of Origen's translators having altered his words. Indeed, he scarcely seems to realize the existence of such a possibility, and he quotes the translators' Latin far more freely than the original Greek. A superficial reader might even conclude from his book that Origen had written most of his works in Latin! The result is to render many of his conclusions almost valueless. See my review of the book in *Theology*, October 1949.

CHAPTER III

THE BIBLE AS THE SOURCE OF THE CHURCH'S TRADITION IN CLEMENT AND ORIGEN

As we explore Origen's doctrine of tradition we shall for almost all our points examine first the evidence of Clement of Alexandria upon the subject, because Clement was, quite clearly, the main source from whom Origen drew, at least in his doctrine of tradition, and all scholars are agreed that they both belong to the same school of thought. This does not, of course, imply that Origen borrowed slavishly or wholesale from Clement (though he invariably borrowed without acknowledgement) or that he did not differ from him in many points. But a knowledge of Clement's doctrine of tradition is an essential preliminary for the understanding of Origen's.

Let us then see, as our first subject of examination, how far these two theologians regarded the Bible as the source of the Church's tradition. Prestige alludes[1] to passages where Clement professes to draw all his arguments from Scripture, but in fact this should be amended to 'from Scripture rightly interpreted'. There are indeed many of these passages, the clearest being *Stromateis* VII. xvi,[2] a discussion of how to refute the heretics. The keynote all through the chapter is, 'Explain the Scriptures by the Scriptures'. Clement says that we have the Lord given to us in the Scriptures as τὴν ἀρχὴν τῆς διδασκαλίας, and that since, if you ask for a standard of judgement (κριτήριον) of ἡ ἀρχή, it ceases to be ἡ ἀρχή, the Scriptures must be the standard of judgement of the Scriptures. And heretics err in taking the wrong sense of the Scriptures, not comparing them together, and not admitting all of them. 'For those people desire notoriety who deliberately misrepresent by alien speculations the doctrines naturally derived from the inspired words handed down by the blessed apostles and teachers, resisting the divine tradition [θείᾳ παραδόσει, i.e. the interpretation of the Scriptures] for the sake of supporting their sect. In truth, what argument of Marcion,

---

[1] Prestige, p. 29.   [2] *P.G.* IX, 529–33, 544.

for instance, or of Prodicus, or of similar people who do not walk the right road, would stand among such men [i.e. the apostles and teachers], I mean, if we are to follow the Church's interpretation [τὴν ἐκκλησιαστικὴν γνῶσιν]? For they could not so excel in wisdom the men who went before them as to find out something additional to what was truly said by them; but they should have been content had they been able to learn what had previously been handed down. Therefore it is only the Gnostic man who has grown old in the Scriptures themselves and preserves the apostolic and ecclesiastical true interpretation of belief [τὴν ἀποστολικὴν καὶ ἐκκλησιαστικὴν ὀρθοτομίαν τῶν δογμάτων] who lives most rightly by the standard of the Gospel.... For, I think, the life of the Gnostic is nothing else than actions and words which are consistent with the tradition of the Lord.' In other words, the Scriptures are the source of doctrine, even for the intellectual *élite* of the Christian fold, but the Scriptures as interpreted by the Church. This is a consistent attitude, and one not unlike Origen's, though not entirely identical with his. Unfortunately (as we shall see) it is not consistently maintained by Clement. This passage alone, however, is enough to modify considerably the statement of Mondesert[1] that Clement never raises the question of the authority of the Bible. He does so specifically here, though he does not spend much time on the question.

The most cogent argument for the view that Origen believed that Scripture was the sole source of doctrine for himself or for any other Christian is that (unlike Clement) he never quotes any other source as his authority for doctrine, and usually assumes without question that in any discussion the deciding factor is the evidence of the Bible. There are, however, several passages where this conclusion is clearly implied, and we must now consider some of these.

In *Against Celsus* II. xiii he is speaking of the enemies of Christianity, and he says, 'Surely they will not assert that those who knew Jesus and heard him handed down the teaching of the Gospels without committing it to writing, and left the disciples without written memoirs of Jesus'. The clear implication here is that the tradition about Jesus is contained in the written documents of the Scriptures. A little later on in the same book (II. lxxi), he says, speaking of Christ, 'He, when he discoursed about God, declared the facts about God to his true

---

[1] *Clément d'Alexandrie*, p. 121.

disciples; and because we find the traces of this teaching in the written books, we possess the foundations of our own theology'. In the *Commentary on Matthew* (Pt. II. 18), commenting on Matthew 23. 16–22, where our Lord refers to swearing by the Temple, Origen produces an allegorical explanation. The Temple is Scripture, the gold is '*sensum Scripturae*'; 'every interpretation which was outside Scripture (however wonderful it may seem to some people) is not holy'. No one should therefore bring his own private interpretations of Scripture, 'unless he shall have shown them to be holy, from that which is contained in the divine Scriptures as in some Temple of God'. Origen's standard of interpretation here seems to be the whole of Scripture and nothing else. Later in the same work (Pt. II. 47), he claims that the Church alone does not add to or subtract from the word and the meaning of Scripture. And in one passage in *Concerning First Principles* (III. 6. 6), he derives 'the faith of the Church' from Scripture. He has just refuted a theory of some Greek philosophers about the body; '*Non fides ecclesiae recipit*', he says, and for two reasons: first, it cannot be found in Holy Scripture, and second, the circumstances themselves ('*ipsa rerum consequentia*') forbid us to accept it.

This double appeal to the Scriptures and to logic or common sense, and to nothing else, is highly characteristic of Origen. We find it occurring over and over again. In his *Against Celsus* (III. xv), he says that the Christians expound to those under instruction what Christ was, 'both from the prophecies about him (and they are many), and from those things which have been carefully handed down to those who can hearken with an understanding mind to the Gospels and to the words of the apostles'. In the very next section of the work (III. xvi), he speaks of teaching concerning God's judgement to be found partly in the Scriptures and partly from common sense (ἀπὸ τοῦ εἰκότος λόγου). Later on in the same work (IV. viii, ix), he says that 'there are certain secret and inexplicable systems and logical trains of argument about the dispensation of different destinies to different souls', and for these and similar doctrines 'the educated man will need to calculate the principles of the doctrine by various sorts of explanations, both from the inspired writings and from the logical development of the principles themselves (τὰς ἐν τοῖς λόγοις ἀκολουθίας)'.[1] Similarly in *Concerning First Principles* we find three passages to the same effect:

[1] See below, p. 81, for another quotation of this passage.

the teaching of the Church, says Origen, is based upon 'either the evidence to be found in the sacred Scriptures, or that to be discovered by the investigation of the logical consequences of the Scriptures and adherence to accuracy'.[1] Later again (I. 5. 4), he has been arguing for the freedom of the human will, and he lets us see the source from which he draws his doctrine: 'But that we may not appear to make statements on such important and difficult subjects by following the principles of logical deduction only, and to compel our hearers to agree with us merely by our own speculations, let us see if we can take any statements from the Holy Scriptures, by whose authority these views may be more firmly commended to our belief.' And later still (II. 5. 3) he professes to refute an heretical opinion 'from the authority of the Scriptures', but he also adds some arguments taken 'from the logic of reason itself'. Prestige notices this double appeal to Scripture and reason as generally characteristic of all the early Fathers.[2]

It will be observed how very much more Origen stresses the sole sufficiency of the Bible to supply the Church's doctrine than does Clement. Harnack has remarked[3] that Origen is distinguished from Clement of Alexandria by his 'unbedingten Biblicismus'. It is not merely that far more of Origen's works have survived than have of Clement's; we have here a genuine difference of emphasis between them. Origen, as we shall see, does not neglect or deny the Church's function of interpreting the Bible. He can appeal to the Church's teaching against heretical doctrines as readily as Clement. For instance, in his *Homilies on Numbers* (IX. i), he can explain that the Church's faith appears truer and clearer by its very comparison with heretical perversions, and add, 'For if, to take an example, I were to take the sayings of Marcion or of Basilides or of any other heretic you like, and I were to refute them by the words of truth and the evidences of the divine Scripture, would not their wickedness seem clearer by the very comparison?' Here Origen is saying very much what Clement said in the passage from the Seventh Book of the *Stromateis* quoted at the

---

[1] *Con. First P.*, Origen's Preface, 10. 'Adherence to accuracy' is my translation of Rufinus' '*recti tenore*'. Cadiou (*La Jeunesse d'Origène*, p. 268) paraphrases this phrase as '*dogmes secondaires définis par la recherche que dirige la règle de foi*'. This is a quite illegitimate translation, as I show quite clearly below, p. 116, n. 3.

[2] Prestige, p. 30.

[3] Quoted by Koetschau in his Introduction to his edition of *Con. First P.*, p. xiii.

beginning of this chapter, but his emphasis is (if we may so express it) not on the fact that the Bible is the *Church's* book (that is Clement's emphasis), but on the fact that it is the *Bible* that is the Church's book.[1]

[1] For the terms which Origen uses to describe the Bible—θεῖα βιβλία, γραφή (γραφαί), γράμματα, παλαιὰ διαθήκη, εὐαγγελικαὶ παραβολαί, νεώτεραι γραφαί, κ.τ.λ.—see Koetschau's Introduction to his edition of *Against Celsus*, Section III, and also Molland's *The Conception of the Gospel*.

CHAPTER IV

CLEMENT'S DOCTRINE OF THE RULE OF FAITH AND OF SECRET TRADITION

WHEN we have established that both Origen and Clement profess to draw their doctrine from the Bible, we have not nearly exhausted what they have to tell us on the subject of tradition. They both say much about the rule of faith of the Church on the one hand, and about a secret tradition of doctrine on the other, and to these two subjects we must now turn our attention. We shall first examine the evidence in Clement of Alexandria, because Origen owes more to him, perhaps, in his treatment of these subjects than he does on any other point, and because in Clement the two are combined as they are not in Origen.

Clement does not consistently display that distinction between the uses of παράδοσις and διδασκαλία which Prestige attributes to all the Fathers.[1] He uses διδασκαλία of the teaching of the Logos in doctrine and theology (as contrasted with education and preparation) in a wide but special sense. It cannot be identified absolutely with 'the accumulating wisdom of philosophically grounded Christianity',[2] but Clement does state that it is only to be found in the Church.[3] It certainly is in no sense contrasted with παράδοσις. In *Stromateis* I. i,[4] for instance, he says that the teachers under whom he studied preserved τὴν ἀληθῆ τῆς μακαρίας διδασκαλίας παράδοσιν, meaning the secret teaching not divulged to all, as distinguished from the Scriptures.

Clement certainly believes that he has access to a secret tradition of doctrine, which he usually calls γνῶσις, but sometimes παράδοσις.[5] In the passage in *Stromateis* I just mentioned he gives a list of various teachers from whom he has derived this tradition—an Ionian, somebody from Coele Syria, another from Egypt, others from the East (including an Assyrian, and a 'Hebrew' from Palestine), and, 'last in time but

---

[1] Prestige, pp. 12, 13; but see the instance quoted on p. 39.
[2] Prestige, p. 12.   [3] *Paidagogos* III. 12 (*P.G.* VIII, 681).
[4] *P.G.* VIII, 697–704.
[5] *Strom.* v. x (*P.G.* IX, 96) γνωστικὴ παράδοσις; VI. xvi (*P.G.* IX, 377) ἀληθὴς γνῶσις.

greatest in worth', a Sicilian in Egypt (apparently Pantaenus), who προφητικοῦ καὶ ἀποστολικοῦ λειμῶνος τὰ ἄνθη δρεπόμενος ἀκήρατόν τι γνώσεως χρῆμα ταῖς τῶν ἀκροωμένων ἐγέννησε ψυχαῖς. These teachers, as we have seen, preserved τὴν ἀληθῆ τῆς μακαρίας διδασκαλίας παράδοσιν, deriving it from 'Peter and James, John and Paul, the holy apostles'. This tradition is only for the select few, the intellectual Christians who can understand it. In fact, the Lord (for the tradition of course derives from him) 'did not reveal to many what was not the concern of many, but of the few whom he knew it did concern, those who are capable of receiving it and being moulded by it'; and Clement adds, τὰ δὲ ἀπόρρητα, καθάπερ ὁ θεός, λόγῳ πιστεύεται, οὐ γράμματι.

That this conception of a secret tradition, available only to the intellectual *élite*, is influenced by Philo is very likely. Philo played a great part in moulding Clement's thought, even more than he did in influencing Origen's, and we can trace the beginnings of this doctrine in Philo without difficulty. Philo draws a distinction between two types of learners in *De Sacrificiis Abelis et Caini* (ii. (7)). There are those who μαθήσει καὶ διδασκαλίᾳ προκόψαντες ἐτελειώθησαν, and the nobler class ἀνθρώπων μὲν ὑφηγήσεις ἀπολελοιπότες, μαθηταὶ δὲ εὐφυεῖς θεοῦ γεγονότες. Again, even more clearly, he says in *De Abrahamo* (xxix): ἡ μὲν οὖν ἐν φανερῷ καὶ πρὸς τοὺς πολλοὺς ἀπόδοσις ἥδ' ἐστιν· ἡ δ' ἐν ἀποκρύφῳ καὶ πρὸς ὀλίγους, ὅσοι τρόπους ψυχῆς ἐρευνῶσιν, ἀλλ' οὐ σωμάτων μορφάς, αὐτίκα λεχθήσεται. Similarly, in the same work (xxxvi), the story of Abraham's sacrifice of Isaac in Genesis 22 is allegorized to mean οἱ τὰ νοητὰ πρὸ τῶν αἰσθητῶν ἀποδεχόμενοι καὶ ὁρᾶν δυνάμενοι. Again, Philo has probably influenced Clement in his use of the language of the Greek mystery-religions. In *Stromateis* I. xxiii[1] Clement says that he derived some information about Moses, which is very like some form of Midrash, from people whom he calls οἱ μύσται; so in *Stromateis* II. xx[2] he says that certain parts of animals are either allowed or forbidden for sacrifice in the Jewish law for reasons which ἴσασιν οἱ μύσται, meaning apparently the people who receive the secret tradition. And in *Stromateis* VI. iv,[3] he uses explicitly mystery-religion language of the giving of the ἀληθὴς παράδοσις to the Christian initiate. Mondésert[4] notes how visible is the influence of the mystery-religions on Clement's doctrine of γνῶσις

[1] *P.G.* VIII, 899.   [2] *P.G.* VIII, 1049.
[3] *P.G.* IX, 435.   [4] Op. cit. pp. 59–61.

in his use of such words as 'initiation', 'hierophant', 'revelation', 'mystical vision' (ἐποπτεία), etc. This practice derives in part at least from Philo, who speaks of himself as an initiated hierophant leading others into the mysteries of Moses (*De Cherubim* xiii and xiv). He also speaks of himself in more than one place as achieving by his superior knowledge something not unlike a state of mystical contemplation of the idea of God. For instance, he gives an opinion which, he says, comes from his soul εἰωθυίας τὰ πολλὰ θεοληπτεῖσθαι καὶ περὶ ὧν οὐκ οἶδε μαντεύεσθαι (*De Cherubim* ix. 27). Clement's conception of his secret tradition often seems to be one of a similar divine intuition. This special knowledge, says Lebreton,[1] is not just speculation, but '*une connaissance religieuse plus haute, due à une révélation privilégiée; c'est une intuition, qui initie celui qui en jouit à des mystères interdits à la foule; elle transforme sa vie morale et religieuse, elle le tire de la condition servile commune à tous les hommes, elle en fait un ami de Dieu, égal ou même supérieur aux anges*'. Similarly Mondésert tells us[2] that Clement's secret knowledge is mystical rather than rational; its aim is 'a knowledge which is as much a moral and spiritual condition of the whole soul, will, and intellect, as the pure apprehension of existence by the reason'.

As we have already seen,[3] one of the words which Clement uses for this secret tradition is ἀπόρρητος. It is a significant word, because we find Origen using it for the same purpose, in an almost technical sense. Clement may have learnt the special use of the word from Plato, because in one place (*Strom*. III. iii)[4] he quotes a phrase from the *Phaedo*, ὁ μὲν οὖν ἐν ἀπορρήτοις λεγόμενος περὶ αὐτῶν λόγος (the λόγος being a theory that in the body men are in prison). But a much more obvious influence upon him in his use of ἀπόρρητος is once more Philo. Philo uses ἀπόρρητος once to mean 'indecent' (*De Josepho* XII), twice to describe 'things which should have been kept quiet', in a bad sense (*De Fuga et Inventione* xxxiv; *De Specialibus Legibus* II. xiv), five times to mean 'secret' generally,[5] once to describe the secrets of

---

[1] 'Le Désaccord de la Foi Populaire et de la Théologie Savante dans l'Église Chrétienne du IIIe Siècle', *Revue d'Histoire Ecclésiastique*, tom. 19, p. 493.

[2] Mondésert, pp. 47–8.

[3] See the quotation of the passage from *Strom*. I. i on pp. 53, 54.

[4] *P.G.* VIII, 1121.

[5] *De Plantatione* xlii; *De Mutatione Nominum* xxxvi and xliii; *In Flaccum* xiii (iii)—of secret instructions brought by a junior officer to his commander; *Hypothetica*, Part I, para. 359.

philosophy (*De Somniis* I. xxxix), once to mean 'something which young ears should not hear', but in a good sense ('esoteric' rather than 'shocking': *De Sacrificiis Abelis et Caini* xxxix (131)), and twice to mean 'unspeakable', as Paul uses ἄρρητα in 2 Corinthians 12. 3.[1] Clement uses the word once to mean 'the private parts of the body' (*Paidagogos* II. vi),[2] once to mean 'unspeakable' in a bad sense (*nefandus*: ibid. III. iii),[3] and once to mean 'mysterious' generally (*Strom.* v. i);[4] but much more often he uses it to refer to his secret tradition. S. Paul, he says, might have been referring to ἀνδρικῶν καὶ ἐντελεστέρων μαθημάτων διδαχὰς ἄλλας ἀπορρήτους in 1 Corinthians 14. 20 (*Paidagogos* I. vi);[5] τὰ ἀπόρρητα are entrusted by God to oral, not written transmission (*Strom.* I. i), and they are merely set out but not adequately interpreted by him in the *Stromateis*;[6] the higher angels sinfully repeated them to women (*Strom.* v. i);[7] there is a risk in publicly displaying τὸν ἀπόρρητον λόγον before those who will not appreciate it (ibid. I. ii);[8] we must look in Scripture for τὸ τῆς γνώμης ἀπόρρητον of our Lord (*Quis Dives* v).[9]

This secret tradition Clement contrasts with the παράδοσις πάνδημος. He calls it in one place τὰς ἀποκρύφους τῆς ἀληθοῦς γνώσεως παραδόσεις (*Strom.* I. xii).[10] In *Stromateis* IV. xvi,[11] he contrasts ἡ γνῶσις with τὴν κοινὴν διδασκαλίαν τῆς πίστεως, and in *Stromateis* v. iv,[12] γνωστικῆς τελειότητος with τὴν κοινὴν πίστιν. In *Stromateis* v. x,[13] he says that 'the mysteries which were hidden until the apostles' time and were handed down by them as they received them from the Lord, and were hidden under the Old Covenant and revealed to the saints, were one thing'; but the ordinary revelation to the faithful was another matter. This distinction between the Christian Gnostic's privileged access to the secret tradition and the ordinary believer's simple ration of faith is sometimes carried to almost shocking lengths. He says, for instance, in

---

[1] *De Legum Allegoria*, Book II, 57 (οὐ γὰρ πᾶσιν ἐπιτρεπτέον τὰ θεοῦ καθορᾶν ἀπόρρητα), and Book III, 27 (God thought Abraham's soul worthy τῶν ἀπορρήτων μυστηρίων).

[2] *P.G.* VIII, 453.   [3] *P.G.* VIII, 585.

[4] *P.G.* IX, 17—Christ is ἀπόρρητον τῆς μεγάλης προνοίας ἅγιον γνώρισμα.

[5] *P.G.* VIII, 289.

[6] *P.G.* VIII, 704–8—a passage already referred to twice, pp. 53, 54.

[7] *P.G.* IX, 24.   [8] *P.G.* VIII, 709.   [9] *P.G.* IX, 609.

[10] *P.G.* VIII, 753.   [11] *P.G.* VIII, 1305.   [12] *P.G.* IX, 45.

[13] *P.G.* IX, 93.

one passage (*Strom.* IV. xviii)[1] that though love is the fulfilling of the law (Romans 13. 10), the law can be thus fulfilled ἤτοι διὰ πίστεως ἢ καὶ γνωστικῶς. And later in the same passage,[2] he says that the Gnostic is rewarded by 'things which eye hath not seen nor ear heard, neither hath it entered into the heart of man' (1 Corinthians 2. 9), whereas the simple believer (τῷ δὲ ἁπλῶς πεπιστευκότι) is rewarded by the sufficient but calculable 'hundredfold'.

The secret tradition is, moreover, a completion of the ordinary faith. S. Paul, he says (*Strom.* VI. xviii),[3] preached the 'gnosis' at Corinth, and this 'is a perfecting of faith, and goes beyond the ordinary instruction, following the abundance of the Lord's teaching and the Church's rule of faith'.[4] Caspari[5] quotes this passage and interprets it to mean that the κανὼν ἐκκλησιαστικός is the norm both of the κοινὴ πίστις and of the γνῶσις. But, as we shall see, this view is impossible, because the γνῶσις *is* the κανὼν ἐκκλησιαστικός. 'Gnosis' is indeed sometimes contrasted with 'pistis' as something different. '"Gnosis" is handed down through tradition (ἐκ παραδόσεως) by the grace of God and is committed as a trust to those who show themselves worthy of the teaching (διδασκαλία). For it is said, "To him that hath shall be added"; to faith knowledge, to knowledge love, to love the inheritance' (*Strom.* VII. x).[6]

Clement specifically describes this tradition as unwritten (see *Strom.* I. i, the passage already referred to three times). In *Strom.* VI. vii[7] we find the phrase γνῶσις... ἡ κατὰ διαδοχὰς εἰς ὀλίγους ἐκ τῶν ἀποστόλων ἀγράφως παραδοθεῖσα. Later in the same book (xv),[8] he says: αὐτίκα διδάξαντος τοῦ Σωτῆρος τοὺς ἀποστόλους ἡ τῆς ἐγγράφου ἄγραφος ἤδη καὶ εἰς ἡμᾶς διαδίδοται παράδοσις, καρδίαις καιναῖς κατὰ τὴν ἀνακαίνωσιν τοῦ βιβλίου τῇ δυνάμει τοῦ θεοῦ ἐγγεγραμμένη. This clearly refers to an unwritten tradition of interpreting the Scriptures delivered by our Lord to his apostles and by them to succeeding generations, independent of the Bible and available to Clement in his own day. It is possible that Clement borrowed something from Philo

---

[1] *P.G.* VIII, 1321.　　　[2] *P.G.* VIII, 1322.　　　[3] *P.G.* IX, 397.

[4] γνῶσιν τελείωσιν οὖσαν τῆς πίστεως, ἐπέκεινα περισσεύειν τῆς κατηχήσεως κατὰ τὸ μεγαλεῖον τῆς τοῦ Κυρίου διδασκαλίας καὶ τὸν ἐκκλησιαστικὸν κανόνα.

[5] 'Hat die alexandrinische Kirche zur Zeit des Clemens ein Taufbekenntniss besessen, oder nicht?', p. 371.

[6] *P.G.* IX, 477.　　　[7] *P.G.* IX, 284.　　　[8] *P.G.* IX, 356.

even in this respect, for Philo in one passage (*De Specialibus Legibus* IV. xxviii)[1] indulges in praise of the ἄγραφος παράδοσις of custom, and the virtue of obeying it. Indeed, in most of his references to this tradition, Clement seems to have conceived of it as nothing else than an interpretation of the Scriptures.[2] In one place (*Strom.* VI. vii),[3] he says that the γνωστικὴ παράδοσις can be learnt from the prophets, and consists of the same doctrine as Christ in his earthly ministry taught to the apostles. That this secret doctrine existed long before the Incarnation we have learnt already from the passage about the fallen angels' betraying τὰ ἀπόρρητα to women.[4] So in *Strom.* VI. viii[5] Clement claims that James, Peter, John, and Paul, and the rest of the apostles, were Gnostics, 'for prophecy as it was given by the Lord [i.e. in the Old Testament] is full of "gnosis", and as it was explained again by the Lord to the apostles'. He sometimes describes this 'gnosis' as consisting of a general conspectus or harmonization of all Scripture. For instance, *Strom.* III. x[6] runs: νόμος δὲ ὁμοῦ καὶ προφῆται σὺν καὶ τῷ εὐαγγελίῳ ἐν ὀνόματι Χριστοῦ εἰς μίαν συνάγονται γνῶσιν. In VI. xi[7] we read: συμφωνίαν τὴν ἐκκλησιαστικήν, νόμου καὶ προφητῶν ὁμοῦ, καὶ ἀποστόλων σὺν καὶ τῷ εὐαγγελίῳ. And in VI. xv:[8] παραθήκη γὰρ ἀποδιδομένη θεῷ ἡ κατὰ τὴν τοῦ Κυρίου διδασκαλίαν διὰ τῶν ἀποστόλων αὐτοῦ, τῆς θεοσεβοῦς παραδόσεως σύνεσις καὶ συνάσκησις.

Later (ibid. VII. xv)[9] he equates this 'gnosis' with the Church's interpretation of Scripture, and with the rule of faith of the Church: ἀποδείξεως δ' οὔσης ἀνάγκη συγκαταβαίνειν εἰς τὰς 3ητήσεις, καὶ δι' αὐτῶν τῶν γραφῶν ἐκμανθάνειν ἀποδεικτικῶς ὅπως μὲν ἀπεσφάλησαν αἱ αἱρέσεις, ὅπως δὲ ἐν μόνῃ τῇ ἀληθείᾳ καὶ τῇ ἀρχαίᾳ ἐκκλησίᾳ ἥ τε ἀκριβεστάτη γνῶσις καὶ τῷ ὄντι ἀρίστη αἵρεσις. In VII. xvi[10] he associates closely the 'gnosis' handed down through the Scriptures and the

---

[1] The Loeb editor, F. H. Colson, at this point (Appendix on this passage, Vol. VIII, p. 435) notes that Philo in his turn is recalling a passage of Aristotle (*Rhetoric* I. 14. 7) on the subject of unwritten laws. But it seems to me more likely that Clement's view of unwritten tradition is indebted to Philo rather than to Aristotle. In *De Legatione ad Gaium* 16, Philo makes special mention of τῶν ἀγράφων ἐθῶν as part of the Jewish religion.

[2] See pp. 48, 49, above. [3] *P.G.* IX, 284.
[4] See p. 56 above. [5] *P.G.* IX, 289. [6] *P.G.* VIII, 1172.
[7] *P.G.* IX, 309. [8] *P.G.* IX, 348–9. [9] *P.G.* IX, 528.
[10] *P.G.* IX, 545.

κανὼν τῆς ἐκκλησίας. Allegorization of the Scriptures in his own 'gnostic' manner he claims to be part of the rule of faith of the Church. To Clement, says Bigg,[1] the true Christian Gnostic must be an allegorist. But no writers about Clement's thought, not even Bigg, have properly grasped the fact that Clement *identifies* his secret tradition with the Church's rule of faith, that there is no evidence at all that he kept them separate in his thought. Indeed, we cannot fully decide how far we are to take Clement seriously, or how he resembles and differs from Origen, until we have appreciated the significance of this identification.

An analysis of Clement's use of the word κανών and its antecedents in Philo (for here once more Philo's influence upon Clement becomes visible) will make this identification clear. In Philo the word κανών means either a rule or a standard. Twice he uses it for the rules of allegorizing Scripture,[2] once for rules of conduct,[3] once for rules of living in a community,[4] and once for the guiding lines of right education.[5] He also uses the word to describe standards of truth,[6] evidence as determining a case,[7] and the standard of judgement which governs God's law;[8] and he speaks of legislators who are not 'landmarks and canons of justice',[9] of Moses as a κανών and law for rulers,[10] of Abraham as a κανών to all proselytes,[11] and of the Essenes' three canons of good—love of God, love of virtue, and love of man.[12]

Clement uses κανών once in its original sense of a ruler for writing or drawing (*Strom.* VI. iv),[13] and speaks four times of a κανών of chastity kept by the Gnostic.[14] Twice he uses the word to describe the Old Testament;[15] and twice he uses εὐαγγελικὸς κανών to mean the rule of

---

[1] See Bigg, *Christian Platonists of Alexandria*, p. 125.

[2] *De Somniis* I. xiii; *De Specialibus Legibus* I. lii.

[3] *Quis Rerum Divinarum Heres* xxxv.   [4] *De Decalogo* III.

[5] *De Specialibus Legibus* IV. xxi.   [6] *De Josepho* xxiv.

[7] *De Decalogo* xxvii.   [8] *De Specialibus Legibus* III. xxv.

[9] Ibid. III. xxx.   [10] *De Virtutibus* xi.   [11] Ibid. xxxix.

[12] *Quod Omnis Probus Liber Sit* xii. If *De Aeternitate Mundi* is by Philo, we have another example in cap. xxi: Ἰσότητος κανόσι καὶ δικαιοσύνης ὁρίοις. Indeed, Philo seems to like the association of κανών and δίκαιος.

[13] *P.G.* IX, 253.

[14] *Strom.* III. xi, xii (*P.G.* VIII, 1172, 1180), κανὼν ἐγκρατείας; III. xviii (*P.G.* VIII, 1208, 1212), τὸν ὑγιῆ κανόνα τῆς εὐσεβείας (twice).

[15] *Strom.* I. i (*P.G.* VIII, 704–8), κατὰ τὸν εὐκλεῆ καὶ σεμνὸν τῆς παραδόσεως κανόνα; IV. i (*P.G.* VIII, 1216), ἡ γ' οὖν κατὰ τὸν τῆς ἀληθείας κανόνα γνωστικῆς παραδόσεως φυσιολογία. Caspari ('Hat die alexandrinische Kirche',

life set out in the Gospel.[1] On three occasions κανών refers to the Gnostic's standard both of faith and of behaviour, in contrast, explicit or implicit, with that of the ordinary believer: *Stromateis* VII. iii,[2] where he says that gentleness, benevolence, and highmindedness are the κανόνες of the Gnostic; IV. xvi,[3] where he contrasts κοινὴν πίστιν with γνωστικοῦ κανόνα; and V. i,[4] where τὸν κανόνα τὸν γνωστικόν means the Gnostic's articles of faith or practice. In *Stromateis* VII. vii[5] we find an intermediate stage between the κανών of the Gnostic and the κανών of the Church, in the phrase τὸν τῷ ὄντι κατὰ τὸν ἐκκλησιαστικὸν κανόνα γνωστικόν. In I. xix[6] he speaks of heretics' being referred to in Proverbs 9. 16, 17, and describes them as ἄρτῳ καὶ ὕδατι κατὰ τὴν προσφορὰν μὴ κατὰ τὸν κανόνα τῆς ἐκκλησίας χρωμένων. Here the practice of the Church is undeniably his meaning. In VII. xvi,[7] he speaks of heretics' interpreting Scripture wrongly: οὐ γὰρ χρή ποτε, καθάπερ οἱ τὰς αἱρέσεις μετιόντες ποιοῦσι, μοιχεύειν τὴν ἀλήθειαν, οὐδὲ μὴν κλέπτειν τὸν κανόνα τῆς ἐκκλησίας, ταῖς ἰδίαις ἐπιθυμίαις καὶ φιλοδοξίαις χαριζομένους. Here the κανών has become the Church's interpretation of Scripture. But it is noticeable that in this chapter (which has already been referred to, p. 48) he associates closely this κανών of the Church with the 'gnosis' handed down through the Scriptures, and earlier in the same chapter[8] he has said that the heretics will always err 'unless they receive the rule of truth (τὸν κανόνα τῆς ἀληθείας) from the truth itself, and hold it fast'. The 'truth itself' can in the context only mean the Scriptures, but Clement goes on to say that a man of God and a man of faith has ceased to be one who is ὁ ἀναλακτίσας τὴν ἐκκλησιαστικὴν παράδοσιν. But the man who returns from this sort of deceit and hearkens to the Scriptures becomes a man of God again. Later[9] he accuses the heretics of not having learnt τὰ τῆς γνώσεως τῆς ἐκκλησιαστικῆς μυστήρια. Again, we are told (*Strom.* VI. xviii)[10] that S. Paul at Athens preached a doctrine beyond that of ordinary faith 'according to the greatness of the Lord's teaching and the Church's rule'. In *Stromateis* IV. xv[11] Clement modifies his version

---

p. 369, n. 3) takes κανόνα in this passage to refer to the article of creation in the Church's rule of faith, but, in view of *Strom.* I. i and VII. xvi, this is unlikely. For further treatment of this passage, see below, p. 64.

[1] *Strom.* III. ix; IV. iv (*P.G.* VIII, 1168, 1229).   [2] *P.G.* IX, 417.
[3] *P.G.* VIII, 1308.   [4] *P.G.* IX, I.   [5] *P.G.* IX, 457.
[6] *P.G.* VIII, 813.   [7] *P.G.* IX, 545.   [8] *P.G.* IX, 529–33.
[9] *P.G.* IX, 536.   [10] *P.G.* IX, 397.   [11] *P.G.* VIII, 1305.

of 1 Corinthians 10. 31 (which is 'whatever therefore ye do, do to the glory of God') by the clause ὅσα ὑπὸ τὸν κανόνα τῆς πίστεως ἐπιτέτραπται ποιεῖν. The most explicit statement of the meaning of the Church's κανών occurs in *Stromateis* VI. xv,[1] where he says that we are to hand on the right interpretation of Scripture κατὰ τὸν τῆς ἀληθείας κανόνα. Our Lord spoke all things in parables, and the Law and the prophets are not easy parables to interpret. But understanding minds can interpret them who carefully expound the Scriptures κατὰ τὸν ἐκκλησιαστικὸν κανόνα. Then he adds: κανὼν δὲ ἐκκλησιαστικὸς ἡ συνῳδία καὶ ἡ συμφωνία νόμου τε καὶ προφητῶν τῇ κατὰ τὴν τοῦ Κυρίου παρουσίαν παραδιδομένῃ διαθήκῃ.

Caspari, in an article already referred to,[2] discusses the content and significance of this κακὼν ἐκκλησιαστικός in Clement. He defines it as 'the essence of the mutually consistent teaching of the Scriptures of the Old and New Testament',[3] and says that 'It is the rule for the interpretation of Scripture and for the true Gnosis and the true Gnostic'.[4] He even thinks, as we shall see a little later, that this κανών may be identified with a formal confession of faith and was given in pre-baptismal catechetical instruction.[5] But this is altogether too vague and confused an interpretation of the meaning of κανὼν ἐκκλησιαστικός in Clement. It cannot possibly be maintained, in view of the evidence which has been presented in the last few pages, that Clement preserved any clear distinction between the secret tradition and the Church's rule of faith. Once it is granted that the Gnostic's κανών and the Church's κανών are the same κανών (and I do not see how this conclusion can be avoided), then it becomes positively demonstrable that the Church's κανών *is* the secret tradition, and not simply a rule or guide for it. Both the 'gnosis' and the 'canon' are described as a harmony of the Scriptures. We cannot imagine two separate traditions, each of them consisting of a harmony of Scripture, as existing in Clement's thought. We are driven to the conclusion that in Clement's theological system the 'gnosis' is the 'canon', the 'canon' is the 'gnosis'.

The word κανών, then, for Clement retains its two fundamental meanings which it has in Philo, that of 'rule' and that of 'standard'. In

---

[1] *P.G.* IX, 348–9.   [2] See p. 59, n. 15, above.

[3] '*Der Inbegriff der übereinstimmenden Lehre der Schriften des alten und neuen Bundes*' ('Hat die alexandrinische Kirche', p. 368).

[4] Ibid. p. 369, n. 3.   [5] Ibid. p. 371.

so far as he uses it of the life of the Gnostic it tends to have the meaning of 'rule', or even 'discipline', but when he uses it to mean a κανών of faith or a doctrinal κανών, it has rather the meaning of 'standard'. He believed in the existence of a standard of faith maintained by the Church, or rather, it would be more accurate to say, a standard way of interpreting her tradition (the Bible) employed by the Church. And there is no evidence whatever that Clement made any distinction between this ecclesiastical κανών and the secret tradition of the Gnostic called 'gnosis', but sometimes called κανών, which he quite certainly believed to have survived to his day independently of the Bible through a succession of teachers deriving originally from our Lord and his apostles. Had Clement's work κανών ἐκκλησιαστικὸς ἢ πρὸς τοὺς 'Ιουδαΐзοντας, which Eusebius (*H.E.* VI. 13) tells us he wrote, survived, we might know more about his conception of the κανών, but this much at least is certain.

This tradition is taught by the Church side by side with Scripture, the difference being that Scripture is a confirmation of what is taught. In the *Eclogae ex Propheticis Scripturis* xxvii,[1] Clement has some interesting remarks on why οἱ πρεσβύτεροι [i.e. the first Christians after the apostles][2] οὐκ ἔγραφον: 'They did not want to give time from their responsibility for teaching the tradition (τὴν διδασκαλικὴν τῆς παραδόσεως φροντίδα) to the responsibility of writing, or to occupy, in writing, their opportunities for meditating upon what they were to speak. And perhaps because they were convinced that to carry through successfully the task of compiling books and to teach were not suitable to the same temperament, they left the task to those who were by nature fitted for it.' Then he goes on to point out how useful a written tradition is as 'a written confirmation of the teaching' (ἔγγραφος διδασκαλίας βεβαίωσις). Then: 'The message with which the elders were entrusted, speaking through the Scripture, uses the writer as an agent for the handing on of that which is read.' Here Clement virtually identifies written and unwritten tradition, as far as their content is concerned. A comment of Mondésert is relevant

---

[1] *P.G.* IX, 712. It is not certain whether these are genuine fragments of Clement. The emphasis they lay upon the importance of the written tradition and of the unwritten διδασκαλία, however, is very characteristic of the doctrine of tradition in Clement's undisputed works.

[2] And specifically the bearers of the secret tradition.

here.[1] He speaks of Clement's view of revelation as '*une donnée révélée, qui lui est transmise par la tradition de son église et par son livre sacré, la Bible, les deux étant pour lui inséparables*'. A similar passage, in *Stromateis* VII. xvii,[2] is devoted to showing that the tradition of the Church is older than that of the heretics. The text of this passage is corrupt in places, but it is clear that Clement's method is to show that the apostles of Christ, from whom the Church derives, long antedate the heresiarchs. He ends by saying: μία γὰρ ἡ πάντων γέγονε τῶν ἀποστόλων ὥσπερ διδασκαλία, οὕτως δὲ καὶ ἡ παράδοσις, where by these two terms (which in this instance do approximate closely to Prestige's connotation) he means, as is clear from the preceding chapter, the Scriptures, or the prior tradition which was written down in the Scriptures ('paradosis') on the one hand, and on the other the Church's witness to them and interpretation of them ('didascalia').

It is not easy to determine what exactly were the contents, as distinct from the function, of this secret tradition, as Clement conceives them. Molland even denies that Clement gives us an account of the contents of this 'gnosis';[3] and Caspari believes that we do not find a list of the articles of the κανὼν ἐκκλησιαστικός.[4] It certainly is true that Clement is unwilling to parade this tradition openly, especially before sophists and pagan philosophical writers.[5] 'There is considerable risk', he says, 'in publicly displaying the secret doctrine (τὸν ἀπόρρητον λόγον) of that which really is philosophy before those who are ready to contradict everything unsparingly, not fairly, but hurling at us every unsuitable name and epithet.'[6] But it is not in fact the case that we can never find mention in Clement of the articles of this tradition. In point of fact we can.

It seems to consist, we must admit, of suspiciously Alexandrine speculations, and certainly a thoroughgoing licence for allegorization is part of it.[7] His First Book of the *Stromateis*, which is full of allegorizing speculations, he calls ὁ κατὰ τὴν ἀληθῆ φιλοσοφίαν γνωστικῶν

---

[1] Mondésert, p. 210.   [2] *P.G.* IX, 552.
[3] *The Conception of the Gospel*, p. 83.
[4] 'Hat die alexandrinische Kirche', p. 375.
[5] See *Strom.* I. iii (*P.G.* VIII, 711–14).   [6] *Strom.* I. ii (*P.G.* VIII, 709).
[7] See *Strom.* v. xiv (*P.G.* IX, 129) for the association of allegorizing with ἡ γνωστικὴ ἀλήθεια; also v. viii (*P.G.* IX, 84), where the sin of Joseph's brothers is said to have consisted in their failure to resort to the allegorization of the Law.

ὑπομνημάτων Στρωματεὺς περαιούσθω.[1] At the end of his Fifth Book he says: ὧδε μὲν οὖν καὶ ὁ πέμπτος ἡμῖν τῶν κατὰ τὴν ἀληθῆ φιλοσοφίαν γνωστικῶν ὑπομνημάτων Στρωματεὺς περαιούσθω.[2] In a later Book he claims that the 'gnosis' handed on to the select few by the apostles assists θεωρία (spiritual vision, or mystico-intellectual contemplation).[3] But the clearest account of the contents of this tradition is given in *Stromateis* IV. i.[4] This is an account of the subjects with which he intends to deal in the book. The articles of ordinary tradition in this list comprise the aid Greek philosophy received from non-Greek thought, a general argument against both Jews and Greeks, a discourse on the natural philosophy of the Greeks, and a discussion of prophecy, of how the Scriptures are guaranteed by the authority of God Almighty, and of how all heresies can be refuted from them. Then we find a description of 'Gnostic' teaching, and this is quite clearly defined as advanced and spoken of in the deliberate language of the mystery religions (τὰ μικρὰ πρὸ τῶν μεγάλων μυηθέντες μυστηρίων). This passage runs: 'The natural philosophy, or rather illumination, which is according to the canon of truth of the Gnostic tradition, begins with the account of the creation of the world, and advances thence to the subject of theology. Consequently we shall reasonably take the beginning of our tradition from the creation spoken of by the prophets, and to some extent also compare the heretics' views, trying as well as we can to refute them.'[5]

It is perhaps going too far to call this a list, though it is noteworthy that twice in this passage Clement refers to these subjects as a παράδοσις. He is really giving us a sketch of the lines which his speculations are going to take. Clement does not in fact deal with all these subjects in the Fourth, or indeed with all of them in any, Book of the *Stromateis*. But we should observe that he apparently here proposes in his treatment both of ordinary and of 'Gnostic' teaching to attempt very much what Origen accomplished in his *Concerning First Principles*, that is, to give a systematic theology for the intellectual *élite*, dealing with the creation

---

[1] *Strom.* I. xxix (*P.G.* VIII, 929).   [2] *Strom.* v. xiv (*P.G.* IX, 204).
[3] *Strom.* VI. vii (*P.G.* IX, 284).   [4] *P.G.* VIII, 1216.

[5] ἡ γοῦν κατὰ τὸν τῆς ἀληθείας κανόνα γνωστικῆς παραδόσεως φυσιολογία, μᾶλλον δὲ ἐποπτεία, ἐκ τοῦ περὶ κοσμογονίας ἤρτηται λόγου, ἐνθένδε ἀναβαίνουσα ἐπὶ τὸ θεολογικὸν εἶδος. ὅθεν εἰκότως τὴν ἀρχὴν τῆς παραδόσεως ἀπὸ τῆς προφητευθείσης ποιησόμεθα γενέσεως, ἐν μέρει καὶ τὰ τῶν ἑτεροδόξων παρατιθέμενοι, καὶ ὡς οἷόν τε ἡμῖν διαλύεσθαι πειρώμενοι.

and cosmogony generally, and embodying all his favourite speculations and trying to base them on Scripture.

Can we find mention of a Creed in Clement? Harnack committed himself to the opinion[1] that Clement does not identify the Church's teaching with a confession, baptismal or otherwise. There is only one passage where Clement seems to refer to a confession, he thinks, a sentence from *Stromateis* VII. xv,[2] and this passage is not enough for the deduction that Clement identified the Church's teaching with a Creed. Caspari, in an article already referred to several times, dissents strongly from this opinion. The passage may be solitary, he contends, but it is very significant. It runs thus: οὕτως καὶ ἡμεῖς κατὰ μηδένα τρόπον τὸν ἐκκλησιαστικὸν παραβαίνειν προσήκει κανόνα καὶ μάλιστα τὴν περὶ τῶν μεγίστων ὁμολογίαν ἡμεῖς μὲν φυλάττομεν, οἱ δὲ παραβαίνουσι. In this passage, says Caspari,[3] the phrase τὴν περὶ τῶν μεγίστων ὁμολογίαν is in contrast to the less important ἐκκλησιαστικὸν κανόνα. By τὰ μέγιστα he means the important, essential, not merely incidental or subordinate, things. Clement does not describe what these are in this passage, but he does in other passages.[4] For instance in *Paidagogos* I. vi[5] he speaks of one Father, one Logos, one Holy Spirit, and one Church, as articles of faith. In *Stromateis* V. xiv[6] he speaks of ἡ ἁγία τριάς, Spirit, Son, and Father. In *Paidagogos* III. xii,[7] he mentions Father, Son as Paidagogos and Didascalos, and Holy Spirit; in *Stromateis* VII. xvii,[8] one true Church which is genuinely ancient, one God, and one Lord; in *Protrepticos* x,[9] the Man and God, who has suffered, who is worshipped as the living God, who was dead; and in *Stromateis* VII. ii,[10] him who for our sake took passible flesh. Caspari concludes that we can therefore assume that τὰ μέγιστα meant for Clement of Alexandria, roughly speaking, 'a Trinitarian baptismal confession, in a more or less anti-Gnostic form'.[11]

---

[1] *Lehrbuch der Dogmengeschichte*, Bd. I, pp. 267–71.   [2] *P.G.* IX, 525.
[3] 'Hat die alexandrinische Kirche', p. 357.   [4] Ibid. p. 357, n. 3.
[5] *P.G.* VIII, 301. So Caspari; but I cannot find any reference to the Church here.
[6] *P.G.* IX, 156.   [7] *P.G.* VIII, 680–1.   [8] *P.G.* IX, 552.
[9] *P.G.* VIII, 224.   [10] *P.G.* IX, 409.
[11] 'Hat die alexandrinische Kirche', p. 359. Caspari then plunges into a conjecture that in the Alexandrian Church there were two forms of baptismal confession: one, a very short confession of Father, Son, and Holy Spirit, used interrogatively at the actual baptism itself, and known as ἡ ὁμολογία; and the

So far, Caspari's case is a convincing one, and we may well conclude that Clement did know of a confession of faith which he called a ὁμολογία. But Caspari goes on to claim[1] that ἡ ὁμολογία was closely connected in Clement's thought with ὁ κανὼν ἐκκλησιαστικός because at his baptism the Christian repeated what he had learnt during catechetical instruction, and during that instruction he had also learnt the κανὼν ἐκκλησιαστικός. 'The promise which he undertook in his repetition of the baptismal confession, the covenant which he made in it with God, was valid also for the ecclesiastical canon and could therefore be extended to this as well.'[2] Here, I think, Caspari goes too far. The very fact that the ecclesiastical canon is so closely associated with that 'gnosis' which is contrasted with the common faith, indeed is perhaps itself contrasted with the common faith by Clement,[3] suggests that it is most unlikely that it should have been taught as a regular thing to the catechumen. All Clement's references to it suggest rather that the ecclesiastical canon is something which the instructed Christian may learn of, if he is intellectual enough, but not that the ordinary Christian should learn it before baptism. No doubt he would have agreed that the ὁμολογία made by ordinary Christians was a summary—the iron ration of a Christian, so to speak—of the important matters among those with which the ecclesiastical canon dealt. But we are not justified by the words of the passage in *Stromateis* VII. xv, or of any other, in going further than this.

What, then, are we to think of the secret tradition of Clement of Alexandria? Various censures upon it have been passed by various writers. Eusebius apparently believed in its authenticity, for he tells us (*H.E.* VI. 13)[4] that Clement committed to writing in his work περὶ τοῦ πάσχα the παραδόσεις which he had chanced to hear παρὰ τῶν ἀρχαίων πρεσβυτέρων. Lebreton notes this claim of Clement to

---

other a longer form used in the instruction of catechumens before baptism, and known as ἡ πίστις. See n. 1 to p. 359, which extends to p. 360 as well. But much more evidence would have to be produced in support of this theory before we were convinced.

[1] 'Hat die alexandrinische Kirche', pp. 372–3.

[2] '*Das Versprechen, das er bei der Ablegung des Taufbekenntnisses leistete, der Vertrag, den er in ihr mit Gott schloss, galt auch dem kirchlichen Kanon und konnte daher auch auf diesen übergeführt werden.*'

[3] See the quotation from *Strom.* VI. xviii on p. 57 above.

[4] See Lawlor and Oulton, p. 199.

a secret tradition,[1] but criticizes it no further than to say, '*ce christianisme est fortement imprégné d'un hellénisme hautain, aristocratique, très peu évangélique*'. Molland, after a rather inadequate treatment of Clement's 'gnosis', calls it 'ecclesiastical Christianity mystically coloured'.[2] Of Clement's phrases ὁ κανὼν τῆς πίστεως and διδασκαλίας παράδοσις Tollinton says, 'we are never sure of the exact implication of these terms', and he believes that their content may be 'as often moral as doctrinal'.[3] Later he deals with Clement's secret tradition at greater length,[4] but he does not realize two important facts about that tradition —the source from which Clement derived the conception of such a secret store of doctrine, and the fact that he unmistakably identifies it with the rule of faith of the Church. Mondésert indeed explicitly says that '*la tradition ecclésiastique*' in Clement must be distinguished completely from '*la tradition secrète, ou gnostique*'.[5] But this is (as, we trust, has been made clear), in view of the evidence that Clement identified the two, an entirely untenable opinion.

Otherwise, Mondésert does more justice than his predecessors to Clement's own description of the tradition.[6] He makes no secret of his entire disbelief in the authenticity of this secret tradition. He notes that Fénelon under the influence of Bossuet denied any authority to Clement's conception of a secret tradition,[7] and he claims that Clement never in any passage explicitly says that he himself has personally received this oral tradition,[8] though he believes that it exists. Indeed, Mondésert roundly asserts that this theory of a secret tradition is absolutely contradictory to the Christian conception of tradition, which he defines as '*cette continuité vivante du magistère et de l'Église entière, gardant le sens de la vérité écrite et consignée dans les livres sacrés*'.[9]

There can be no doubt that Mondésert's judgement upon this point is a wise one. Quite apart from the justice of his remark that such a conception of a secret tradition vitiates dangerously the significance and value of the public and official tradition (however we define it),

[1] Lebreton, 'Le Désaccord de la Foi', tom. 19, pp. 497, 501.
[2] Molland, p. 83. [3] *Clement of Alexandria*, Vol. II, p. 117.
[4] Ibid. Vol. II, pp. 205–8.
[5] Mondésert, p. 119; but on p. 110 (n. 2) he makes some rather reluctant concessions to the view that Clement associates this general 'gnosis' with his secret tradition.
[6] See Mondésert, pp. 51, 111, 117, as well as the passages cited below.
[7] Mondésert, p. 56. [8] Ibid. p. 57. [9] Ibid. p. 58.

two tell-tale facts compel us to discard Clement's claim to be in possession of a secret, unwritten tradition of doctrine independent of the Bible, on the grounds that it is entirely untrustworthy. The first is that when we examine the contents of this tradition we find it to consist of theological speculations which have a suspiciously Alexandrian ring about them, and which we cannot possibly imagine to have emanated from our Lord and his apostles. The second is that we can with very fair probability determine whence Clement derived both the idea that such a tradition might exist and the conviction that it did exist. The first of these sources is Philo. We have seen how Clement has borrowed both vocabulary and ideas on this subject from him. The other is the *Epistle of Barnabas*. Writers on Clement have noticed that he seems to ve bor rowed his phrase ἡ γνῶσις from this work,[1] but no one has apparently gathered all the evidence, as it can be gathered, to show how likely it is that Clement derived his whole theory of secret tradition from the *Epistle of Barnabas*. Clement quotes the Epistle several times, and appears to regard it as tradition as authentic as that of any New Testament epistle.[2] In *Stromateis* v. x[3] he describes the *Epistle of Barnabas* as σαφέστερον γνωστικῆς παραδόσεως ἴχνος παρατιθέμενος. In a fragment of the *Hypotyposeis* (Book VII) quoted by Eusebius,[4] he says: 'The Lord gave the secret knowledge (παρέδωκε τὴν γνῶσιν) to James the Just, to John, and to Peter, after the Resurrection. They handed it on to the other apostles, and the other apostles to the Seventy, *of whom Barnabas was one.*' It is noteworthy too that documents of the second and third centuries spuriously written in the names of the apostles describe Barnabas as having been sent eventually by S. Peter to be the apostle of Northern Italy. The *Clementine Recognitions* say that Barnabas came first of all the apostles to Rome and converted Clement of Rome.[5] The conclusion is almost irresistible that

---

[1] E.g. Bigg (*Christian Platonists*, p. 125), who quotes especially *Ep. Barnabas* VI. 9; IX. 8 (τίς οὖν ἡ δοθεῖσα αὐτῷ γνῶσις;); x. 10. I would add XIX. 1, where the author calls 'the way of light' ἡ δοθεῖσα αὐτῷ γνῶσις. So also Mondésert, p. 110. More will be said later about Clement's use of this work. It is perhaps worth noting here that Clement follows the *Epistle of Barnabas* in using the word σημεῖον, without a definite article or further explanation, to mean the Cross. See *Ep. Barnabas* XII. 5.

[2] For further information on this point, see below, pp. 129, 130.

[3] *P.G.* IX, 96.   [4] *P.G.* IX, 749.

[5] *Clementine Recognitions* i. 7. See Badcock, *History of the Creeds*, p. 176.

Clement of Alexandria was influenced enough by his reading of the *Epistle of Barnabas*, and by the existence of quite a large body of legend about the Barnabas of the New Testament, to exalt the Epistle's 'gnosis'—that is its system of allegorizing the Old Testament and especially the Law-books—into a theory that Barnabas received a special secret tradition through the apostles from Christ.[1] The main content of this tradition Clement apparently believed to be the allegorization of the Old Testament so as to yield support for all sorts of speculations appealing to his own mind and to the mind of his teachers. And he persuaded himself that this supposed secret teaching of Barnabas had been maintained independently of the New Testament up to his own day.[2]

It is necessary to emphasize that this teaching was treated by Clement as secret and as a tradition, for it has been held by some writers that there is no evidence that he regarded it as anything more than the result of individual scholars' being given special inspiration by God, or that he imagined it to have been handed down in a continuous tradition from the apostles' time, or that he ever intended that it should be *withheld* from anybody and not merely that those who were not fit for it should not expect it. Mondésert, for instance, says of Clement: '*Il se réfère à une doctrine secrète, il croit la posséder, mais rien dans toute son œuvre ne permet de penser qu'il la détient, et qu'il la cache dans un langage dont il faudrait avoir la clef.*'[3] It should be clear enough, from what has already been said, that the evidence that Clement believed himself to possess a continuous tradition, not merely a divine inspiration enabling him to reproduce wonderful truths which others had independently discovered, is very strong. The fact that he constantly refers to his secret teaching as παράδοσις is significant; it is indeed difficult to

---

[1] Incidentally, Clement calls Barnabas ὁ ἀπόστολος Βαρνάβας in *Strom.* II. vii (*P.G.* VIII. 965, 969), and in *Strom.* II. xx (*P.G.* VIII, 1060) ὁ ἀποστολικὸς Βαρνάβας, and says that he was one of the Seventy and a fellow-worker with Paul. But then elsewhere (see *Strom.* IV. xvii–xix) he calls Clement of Rome an ἀπόστολος.

[2] It may be that he was influenced in forming this theory by his belief, stated in *Strom.* V. x (*P.G.* IX, 96), that ἦν γάρ τινα ἀγράφως παραδιδόμενα τοῖς Ἑβραίοις. As he goes on to quote Hebrews 5. 12–14 and 6. 1, it is very likely that he here means tradition given by Christ to the Jews and surviving unwritten indefinitely.

[3] Mondésert, p. 61.

imagine how this word could be used without implying continuous tradition. More telling, however, is his statement in *Stromateis* I[1] that he derived this παράδοσις from certain teachers. Even though this παράδοσις were in fact no more than an intuition or inspiration, not separable into distinct articles of teaching, still an intuition derived from teachers who went before *is* a continuous tradition, particularly if Clement imagines (as he clearly does) that these teachers derived this special teaching ultimately from the apostles. Again, the manner in which Clement connects this teaching with Barnabas cannot be ignored. If Clement imagined that his 'gnosis' were only the result of God's providential guidance given to certain select souls from time to time, he would not trouble to give his 'gnosis' the pedigree traced through Barnabas, as he does. There is finally the close association or identification of this 'gnosis' and the Church's 'canon'; quite apart from other passages not easy to explain away,[2] there can be no doubt whatever that Clement describes both 'gnosis' and 'canon' as a conspectus or harmony of Scripture. We cannot imagine that the 'canon' of the Church did not represent a continuous tradition handed down from one generation to another; we have therefore no right to assume that Clement did not believe the same about the 'gnosis'.

The evidence about the secrecy of this tradition is as strong. When Mondésert, in the quotation given above, states that nothing in Clement's works allows us to assume that he withholds the secret tradition, he is making an unjustified generalization. Several passages have already been quoted which suggest quite a different view,[3] and the analogy from the mystery religions which Clement, following Philo, so often draws, would suggest this anyhow. But there is one more passage, not yet quoted, which, we venture to think, puts the matter beyond doubt. It occurs in *Stromateis* VII. ix,[4] where Clement is speaking of the 'Gnostic' man. He says that he will sometimes hide certain things from the less instructed καθάπερ ἰατρὸς πρὸς νοσοῦντας ἐπὶ σωτηρίᾳ τῶν καμνόντων ψεύσεται. He is here in fact merely reproducing an idea which he found very fully developed in Philo. In

---

[1] See the passages quoted on pp. 53–4 above.

[2] *Strom.* VI. xviii; VII. xvi. See pp. 57, 58–9 above.

[3] E.g. one from *Strom.* I. i quoted on p. 53; and the phrase τὰς ἀποκρύφους τῆς ἀληθοῦς γνώσεως παραδόσεις (*Strom.* I. xii) quoted on p. 56.

[4] *P.G.* IX, 475–6.

his *Quod Deus Immutabilis Sit* (xiii) Philo is discussing the fact that God is in the Pentateuch sometimes said to have parts and passions like a man, and he explains this difficulty as follows: 'Thus too in dealing with dangerous sicknesses of the body, the most approved physicians do not allow themselves to tell the truth to their patients, since they know that this will but increase their disheartenment and bring no recovery from the malady, whereas under the encouragement which the opposite course of treatment gives they will bear more contentedly their present trouble, and at the same time the disease will be relieved. For what sensible physician would say to his patient, "Sir, you will be subjected to the knife, the cautery, or amputation", even if it will be necessary that he should submit to such an operation? No one.... Whereas if, through the physician's deceit, he expects the opposite, he will gladly endure everything with patience, however painful the methods of saving him may be.'[1] Now if Clement can reproduce this principle from Philo, by whom it was already well accepted, there can be no further doubt that the thought of deliberately withholding advanced doctrine from the simpler and less educated Christians would have caused him no trouble at all. We must in fact accept the evidence that this policy is just what he recommends.

It is not of course contended here that Clement really did possess a genuine continuous tradition of secret teaching. On this point Mondésert is quite accurate. Clement's secret teaching did, as far as we can reconstruct it, consist of speculations, intuitions, and inspired (or not so inspired) theologizing, which had no connection with any oral teaching given by our Lord or his Apostles; and (as we have pointed out) it was intimately connected with his own devotional life. But we believe that, however often Clement may speak of it as if it were no more than this, to deny that in other places he claims that it represents a continuous tradition of teaching deriving from our Lord through his apostles, through Barnabas, through Clement's teachers and their predecessors, up to Clement himself, and that this tradition is a secret one in as far as it is withheld from certain people who would not understand it, is to deny facts supported by quite plain evidence.

It is clear, then, that Clement has confused in his theory of secret tradition at least three separate things: First, his own private

---

[1] The Migne editor quotes a similar passage from *De Cherubim* and one from Plato's *Republic*, Bk. III.

speculations, which are often of a Gnostic cast; second, a tradition of doctrinal speculation inherited from eminent teachers before him, not least among whom were (as we can see from Clement's own writings) Philo, and (as he tells us himself) Pantaenus,[1] a tradition which he attributed quite mistakenly to Barnabas, whom he imagined to have derived it through the Twelve from our Lord; third, what Prestige calls διδασκαλία, the Church's interpretation of her tradition in teaching and preaching. It is not surprising that this confusion should have arisen, because doubtless all its constituents were more fluid, and their limits less sharply defined, than they were in later ages. That this confusion had arisen, however, we must recognize if we are to understand the doctrine of tradition of Clement of Alexandria, and if we are to profit by it in our exploration of Origen's doctrine, both by the many points of agreement which Origen has with Clement, and by the few but noteworthy instances in which he disagrees with him.

[1] See p. 54 above.

CHAPTER V

ORIGEN'S DOCTRINE OF
SECRET TRADITION

WHEN we come to examine Origen's doctrine of secret tradition, the first fact to be observed is that Origen uses the words παράδοσις and διδασκαλία in no such special sense as Prestige attaches to them, to mean the Church's tradition and the Church's expansion of her tradition in teaching respectively. In all the works and fragments of Origen that survive in Greek the word παράδοσις occurs forty-six times; thirty instances of it signify Rabbinic or Jewish tradition, and seven mean traditions independent of the Bible connected with the Christian faith; one instance may refer to the Bible, and eight occurrences have meanings quite irrelevant to our inquiry. Origen never uses the phrase 'apostolic' or 'ecclesiastical' παράδοσις. His instances of tradition outside the Bible are small and comparatively unimportant pieces of information.[1] Twice, indeed, Origen quotes a saying of our Lord not found in the New Testament; but he does not call any of these a παράδοσις. Some of these traditions, whether called παραδόσεις or not, are probably intelligent guesses,[2] and some perhaps derived from popular legend or gossip.[3] The occasion where παράδοσις probably means the Bible is in a comment on Psalm 1. 5,[4] where his phrase τὴν τῶν ἀρχαίων παράδοσιν apparently means the Scriptural doctrine of the resurrection of the body. But this instance is not, of course, sufficient to prove, against the testimony of the others, that Origen uses the word παράδοσις to express the sense of tradition which, in Prestige's account, attaches to it in the Fathers generally. In fact, as has been shown, Origen quite demonstrably does not so use it. If further proof is needed, it is supplied by a passage in *Against Celsus*[5] which runs: 'For [the enemies of Christianity] surely will not assert that those who knew Jesus and heard him handed down the teaching of the Gospels without committing it to writing' (χωρὶς γραφῆς τὴν

---

[1] See below, pp. 145–6.   [2] Compare *Hom. on Genesis* XIV. iii.
[3] Cf. *Against Celsus* I. li; II. lxii, lxviii; *Hom. on Jeremiah* XX. 8.
[4] *P.G.* XII, 1092 ff.   [5] II. xiii.

τῶν εὐαγγελίων παραδεδωκέναι διδασκαλίαν). According to Prestige's theory, this should have read δεδιδαχέναι παράδοσιν. This does not, of course, imply that Origen does not derive the sort of tradition to which Prestige gives the name παράδοσις from the Bible. As we have seen, there is every reason for thinking that Origen does derive this primary tradition from the Bible, though he does not call it παράδοσις,[1] and that he is here entirely at one with the other Fathers quoted by Prestige.

An investigation of the word διδασκαλία in Origen is no more rewarding than that of the word παράδοσις, and serves to bring us to the same conclusion, namely, that in the narrowly philological field Origen does not very obviously bear out Prestige's conclusions about the meaning which the Fathers attached to the word. Διδασκαλία occurs 260 times in Origen: sixty-three instances are quite irrelevant to our study; 114 instances refer to the teaching of our Lord, and fifteen to that of evangelists, apostles, or disciples; in two cases it means the teaching of the Bible generally, in seven that of the Law or of the Old Testament, and in forty-seven that of Christianity or of God, so generally as to be of no use in our inquiry. In four instances it signifies the teaching of Christianity in particular relation to those outside the Church, and in eight explicitly the teaching of the Church.[2]

But that Origen believed in a tradition of secret doctrine in many ways similar to Clement's is undeniable. His secret tradition, however, is not independent of the Bible, but derived from it by the intellectual élite of the Church. In *Concerning First Principles* I,[3] Origen tells us that the apostles preached about some things to all men, clearly and as of necessity to salvation, but leaving the reason of them to be sought by those who were given special gifts of knowledge and grace by the Spirit. About other things they stated, 'that they are, but how and why they are they do not state', in order to give succeeding generations an opportunity of exercising their ingenuity and wisdom. And then he goes on to give a list of things which Christ and his apostles preached as necessary.[4] In *Against Celsus*, when he defends Christianity against

---

[1] He does, however, frequently use the word παραδιδόναι in connection with this primary tradition, as in the instance quoted above. Cf. *Against C.* III. xvii; *Comm. on Matthew* XIII. 1; etc.

[2] One of these instances is from a fragment on Psalm 78. 30, 31, derived from a Catena (*P.G.* XVII, 141), where there is a possible reference to teaching leading up to Baptism.

[3] Origen's Preface, 3.   [4] See below, p. 116.

Celsus' charge that Christians kept their belief secret, Origen denies the charge as far as the general outlines of the faith are concerned. But he adds,[1] 'but that there should be certain doctrines as it were taught in addition to the superficial teaching (τὰ ἐξωτερικά), which do not reach the majority of people (μὴ εἰς τοὺς πολλοὺς φθάνοντα), is not peculiar to the Christian system alone, but also belongs to that of the philosophers'. These doctrines appear, for instance, in S. Paul's writings, but deliberately hidden. In his *Commentary on Romans*[2] he says: 'I think he has this intention, with which the Scriptural prophecies agree, to prevent the pronouncements of divine inspiration being openly displayed before men who are uncultured and have made little progress in faith or study, and, as I might say, being spread out to be trodden under their feet; but rather that...the secret of S. Paul's king should reach only a few, and those secretly.' So, later in the same work,[3] he says, discussing Romans 11. 25–7: 'We should, however, always remember that the apostle wanted the passage before us[4] to be considered a mystery, whereby doubtless those who are faithful and qualified are to conceal among themselves the meanings of this sort of thing in the silence of God like a mystery, and not expose it indiscriminately to those who are unqualified and less accomplished. For, says Scripture, it is good to hide the mystery of the king.'[5]

Sometimes he implies that these 'mysteries' were imparted to chosen disciples by the apostles. In his *Homilies on Joshua*,[6] he says as much, discussing the incidence of names in Joshua: 'Consequently, to prevent your becoming contemptuous when you read this book, and imagining it to be a worthless piece of writing, because it is crammed with many words denoting names, we say that you must on the contrary realize that unspeakable mysteries are implied in these names, mysteries which are greater than either human speech can pronounce, or mortal ear

---

[1] *Against Celsus* I. vii. Kelly (*Early Christian Creeds*, p. 170) misunderstands this passage. Origen is not here referring to sacraments, but, as the context makes clear, to his own esoteric doctrine. Kelly in the same place refers to *Hom. in Leviticus* IX. x, and makes exactly the same mistake; as the words show, Origen is here referring to doctrine which the simpler-minded cannot understand ('*non ergo immoremur in his quae scientibus nota sunt et ignorantibus patere non possunt*'), not to sacraments which the catechumens should not see.

[2] VI. viii.   [3] VIII. xii.

[4] Rom. 11. 25, 'I would not have you ignorant of this mystery'.

[5] Tobit 12. 7.   [6] XXIII. iv.

listen to. These mysteries, in my opinion, can be worthily explained, not only not by me, who am least, but not even by those who are much better than I. Indeed, I am not sure if they are expounded fully and entirely by the holy apostles themselves. I did not say that they are not fully understood, but that they are not fully expounded. For it is certain that they were known and fully grasped by him who was "caught up to the third heaven", who, needless to say, when in heaven saw heavenly sights, saw Jerusalem, the true city of God, saw there too the Mount Sion, whatever it is, saw also Hebron, saw too all those territories which the book tells us were divided by lot. And he not only saw them but understood in his spirit their principles, because he admits that he heard words and traditions.' Paul, Origen goes on to say, could not disclose these to ordinary men. 'But perhaps he used to tell them to those who do not walk according to man. He used to tell them to Timothy, he used to tell them to Luke and to the other disciples whom he knew to be fit to receive unspeakable mysteries.' Again, in *Against Celsus*[1] Origen adduces instances to show that people in the Bible were given revelations which they could not, or might not, write down. He quotes Ezekiel 2. 9, 10, and 3. 1, 2, and 2 Corinthians 12. 4. Jesus, he says, spoke some things privately to his disciples, and some things he spoke which have not been written. Some things were οὐ γραπτέα, others οὐ ῥητά.[2] Similarly, he believes that the Ephesians had been put in possession of ἀπορρήτων λόγων by S. Paul's teaching.[3]

There also are a number of passages where Origen begins to speculate on some subject, and then breaks off on the grounds that he will not dare to commit such speculation to paper, either because the subject is too solemn, or because he does not want to arouse opposition. In his *Commentary on Matthew*,[4] he indulges cautiously in the speculation that certain men become angels before the general resurrection, but admits that this line of thought would be repulsive to most people and says that he would rather not entrust to paper further speculation about it. Later in the same work,[5] the Latin translation reads, '*haec prolixius*

---

[1] vi. vi.

[2] For one other example of Origen's belief in an unwritten tradition, see below, p. 179. This is the only other example I know of, and it of course does not refer to *doctrine*. There is no proof that Origen shared Clement's belief in an unwritten tradition of doctrine.

[3] *Comm. on Ephesians* VIII, p. 242, on Eph. 1. 13.

[4] XVII. 30.   [5] Pt. II, 16.

*et manifestius tradere per atramentum et calamum et chartam visum mihi
est non esse cautum; utinam et haec ipsa quae dicimus non videamur temere
et periculose dixisse'*. He had been discussing hell. Later still[1] he
refuses to commit his speculations about the foundation of the world
to paper, lest it might be exposed to the eyes of 'men of bad character
and slanderers and favourers of doctrinal innovation'. We have found
much the same reluctance in Clement of Alexandria.[2] So in his
Commentary on Romans[3] Origen can say of the speculation that good
souls out of their bodies labour with the angels for our good and bad
ones similarly assist the fallen angels to harm us, 'Let this too be
thought of as among the secrets of God and as mysteries not to be
entrusted to paper'. In his *Homilies on Genesis*[4] he refuses to discuss
the question of predestination raised by the birth of Esau and Jacob
described in Genesis 25, on the grounds that he will be unfairly
attacked over it. He sometimes attributes the same cautious motives to
S. Paul: '*plura tamen et multo plura scierit quam scripserit*', but he
thought it over-daring to commit everything to writing.[5] Similarly, on
the question of Pharaoh's heart being hardened by God—very much
a *locus vexatus* to Origen and his contemporaries—Origen refuses to
divulge what is his real opinion,[6] but adduces the example of S. Paul,
who (according to Origen) on this very point refused to answer and
would not commit the secret to writing.[7]

This method of Reserve (as Bigg calls it) sometimes brings Origen
(as it frequently brought Clement) to an almost Gnostic view of the
Christian faith. S. Paul rejoices that the treasures of God's wisdom
hidden in Christ should now be revealed even to the simplest Christian
believer, but not so Origen. The man who has found the treasure of
hidden meaning in the Scriptures, he says,[8] hides it, οὐκ ἀκίνδυνον
εἶναι νομίζων τὰ τῶν γραφῶν ἀπόρρητα νοήματα ἢ τοὺς ἐν Χριστῷ
θησαυροὺς σοφίας καὶ γνώσεως ἐκφαίνειν τοῖς τυχοῦσι. Here we encounter
that significant word ἀπόρρητος, which we have found to be something
of a key-word with Clement.[9] And just as Clement can shock us by his

---

[1] Pt. II, 71.

[2] *Strom.* I. ii. See pp. 56, 63.   [3] II. iv.   [4] XII. iv.

[5] *Commentary on Romans* x. xi.

[6] It is in fact, as is clear from other passages, that Pharaoh was given a second
chance by God in the next life.

[7] *Hom. on Exodus* IV. ii.   [8] *Comm. on Matthew* x. 6.

[9] See above, pp. 54, 55, 56.

dichotomy between God's gracious dealing with the *élite* and his rather less than gracious dealing with the simple,[1] so can Origen. 'We who profess to say truly, "Even if we have known Christ once according to the flesh, now we no longer know him", know that it is the primary work of the Word to save the more understanding people (συνετωτέρους); for they are more appropriate to him than the more unintelligent.'[2] So in his *Homilies on Ezekiel* he can say: 'These are "little ones", and cannot profitably learn that they are loved by the Father, in case they should be spoiled, and should despise God's goodness.'[3] Lebreton cites an instance where Origen says that there are two sorts of Christians, '*aliqui pro caritate adhaerentes Deo, alii pro metu et timore futuri iudicii*'.[4]

Though Origen frequently describes this tradition of doctrine as secret or hidden, this does not mean that his readers, especially the more intellectual ones, may not learn it. Indeed, ἀπόρρητος does not imply 'unspeakable' (i.e. incommunicable) to Origen, any more than it does to Clement.[5] We can with confidence make out quite a long list of the main contents of this secret tradition. In *Against Celsus*[6] Origen seems to equate the 'teaching given privately by Jesus to his true disciples' with the σύμβολον and the admission to the sacraments of Baptism and Holy Communion imparted to the fully qualified catechumen. This is the only passage where he appears to do this. Its significance will be discussed later on.[7] In one place in *Concerning First Principles*[8] he gives a list of the first intentions of the Holy Spirit in introducing allegory into the Bible. He wanted, says Origen, to impart knowledge concerning τῶν ἀπορρήτων μυστηρίων τῶν κατὰ τοὺς ἀνθρώπους πραγμάτων, that is to say, concerning the salvation of souls and how they need God's help, and about God and his only-begotten Son, and

---

[1] See instances on pp. 56, 57, above.

[2] *Comm. on Matthew* XI. 17.   [3] I. iii.

[4] *Hom. on Genesis* VII. iv. See Lebreton, 'Les Degrés de la Connaissance', p. 274. He also refers to *Hom. on Joshua* VII. iv.

[5] Cf. fragments of a *Comm. on Proverbs* (*P.G.* XIII, 25) where (on Prov. 1. 6) he defines a 'riddle' as διέξοδόν τινα περὶ ὡς γεγονότων μὴ γεγονότων, μήτε γενέσθαι δυναμένων, σημαινόντων δ' ἐν ἀποκρυφῇ ἀπόρρητόν τι, and then instances Joash's parable in Judges 9. 8, where ἀπόρρητον can mean nothing more than secret. Cf. too a fragment of the *Comm. on Ephesians* v, p. 240 (on Eph. 1. 9), where Origen glosses μυστηρίων as τῶν θείων καὶ ἀπορρήτων καὶ μὴ ἐπιτηδείων φθάνειν εἰς πολλούς.

[6] III. lx.   [7] See below, p. 121.   [8] IV. 2. 7.

several points of Christology. Consequently knowledge about angels, fallen and unfallen, must be included in 'the principles of the divine teaching' (τοὺς λόγους τῆς θείας διδασκαλίας), and also that about the differences of souls, the origin and nature of the world, and the origin and extent of evil. Prestige[1] is anxious to identify this list with the secondary form of tradition, to which he gives the name of διδασκαλία, and to make it equivalent to the Creed of Origen's day. But the identification with a Creed, it will be seen very clearly from the paraphrase of the passage given above, is impossible. There is no evidence that such things as doctrine about fallen and unfallen angels, the differences of souls, and the origin and extent of evil, formed articles of a Creed of any period, far less Origen's. Besides, the use of the phrase τῶν ἀπορρήτων μυστηρίων is against this view. This is clearly a list—the fullest we possess—of the articles of Origen's secret teaching. The use of the word ἀπόρρητος is noteworthy, and also that the tradition seems to have had a great deal to do with speculation.

These two features reappear in other articles of the secret tradition as we can recover them from Origen's works. In *Against Celsus*[2] Origen remarks that the story of the Tower of Babel has a deep mystical significance, which need not be expounded in this context, 'so that the doctrine of souls' being bound into bodies by no process of reincarnation may not be cast before any chance audience, nor that which is holy given to the dogs, nor pearls cast before swine. For that would be irreverent, involving a divulging of the secret (ἀπορρήτων) oracles of the wisdom of God.' His cryptic reference to 'souls' being bound into bodies by no process of reincarnation' means Origen's own speculation about the pre-existence of souls (which involves their ultimate incarnation, but not, as in Pythagoras' theory, *reincarnation* later). Similarly in the *Commentary on Matthew* he gives it as his opinion that the pre-existence of the soul is hinted at in the class of workers who stand all day idle till the eleventh hour, but he only suggests this diffidently, in default of an alternative explanation. He calls this τὸν περὶ ψυχῆς ἀπόρρητον λόγον.[3] In his *Commentary on John*[4] he throws out the suggestion that the Jews before our Lord's day had a knowledge of such ἀπόρρητα as this doctrine of the transmigration of souls. He does not reject the doctrine, but he does not adopt it either. He only says that it needs exploration.

---

[1] Prestige, p. 120. [2] v. xxix. [3] xv. 34. [4] vi. 12, 13, 14.

That Origen believed that the Jews possessed some knowledge of this secret tradition is clear. This need not surprise us, for we have seen that Clement of Alexandria believed that fallen angels had repeated τὰ ἀπόρρητα to women,¹ and that prophecy in the Old Testament is 'full of "gnosis"'. In the *Commentary on Matthew*² Origen says that the chief priests and elders of the people who interrogated Jesus about his authority (Matt. 21. 23) must have known λόγοι βαθεῖς καὶ ἀπόρρητοι on the subject of various types of authority. He describes them as εἴτε ἐκ παραδόσεων ἐπιβάλλοντες εἴτε καὶ ἐξ ἀποκρύφων (οὐκ οἶδα εὐλόγως ἢ καὶ ἀλόγως) κινούμενοι.³ Similarly, in *Against Celsus* he can say that a philosophical training is necessary in order to understand the deep doctrines of his esoteric tradition, because they 'were treated philosophically by the prophets of God and the apostles of Jesus'.⁴

To our list of esoteric doctrines an examination of the Fifth Book of the *Commentary on Romans*⁵ enables us to add two more. In the passage under discussion, Paul, says Origen, was only hinting at deeper mysteries which he could not fully disclose. 'Even so through the obedience of the one shall the many be made righteous' (5. 19), is what Paul wrote; he did not write 'shall all be made righteous', Origen suggests, 'because he wanted to leave the simpler and slacker an incentive for striving for salvation'. Yet *'perfectioribus divinae bonitatis secreta non claudat'*. In other words, Paul was hinting at that universal salvation which was one of the features of Origen's theological system. And later in the same passage, speaking of the 'trespass' which involved the whole human race, he says: *'Licet ubi, quando et quomodo ab unoquoque similitudo ista praevaricationis admissa sit tutum non crediderit apertius proloqui. Sed qui eruditus est ex lege Domini scit intellegere obscurum sermonem dictaque sapientium et aenigmata.'* Origen is probably here referring cryptically to his own doctrine of a pre-mundane Fall. In *Against Celsus*⁶ he is discussing the doctrine of our Lord's

---

¹ See above, p. 56.   ² XVII. 2.

³ He has been speaking of ἐξουσιῶν and ταγμάτων connected with the heavenly mysteries, so presumably ἐπιβάλλοντες here must mean 'with their attention attracted more strongly on the subject of authorities', etc. The Latin translation has *'cognoscentes'*, but this is the only meaning I can give it which bears any resemblance to the meanings of ἐπιβάλλω given in Liddell and Scott's *Lexicon*.

⁴ III. lviii.   ⁵ ii; he is discussing Rom. 5. 12–21.   ⁶ I. xxxi.

atonement for sin, and he uses these expressions about it: ὁρῶντες δὲ ταῦτα οἱ τοῦ Ἰησοῦ μαθηταὶ καὶ ἄλλα τούτων πλείονα, ἃ εἰκὸς αὐτοὺς ἐν ἀπορρήτῳ ἀπὸ τοῦ Ἰησοῦ μεμαθηκέναι...κ.τ.λ. We notice the use of the word ἀπόρρητος again, and the word εἰκός is, as we shall see later, significant. In the same work[1] he mentions a class of Christians who 'are acquainted with principles which are far from contemptible, but on the contrary deep, and, as any Greek would say, esoteric and for the highly initiated'. And among these principles is the question of who deserves to be called God and who does not.

Another article of the esoteric tradition is the reasons for the precise time at which the Incarnation took place. The reasons for this, says Origen,[2] are a deep mystery which the ordinary Christian cannot understand, but which can be derived by the 'intellectual' method from such passages as Deuteronomy 32. 8, 9: 'for there are certain secret and inexplicable systems and logical trains of argument about the dispensation of different destinies to different souls'. Similarly for the duration of Christ's reign and the End and Judgement to follow, 'the educated man will need to calculate the principles of the doctrine by various sorts of explanations, both from the inspired writings and from the logical development of the principles themselves'.[3] But for the uneducated the doctrine of αὐτὸς ἔφα, or some such explanation, will have to suffice. In his work *Concerning Prayer*[4] Origen adds another article to this list. John the Baptist, he suggests, knew certain doctrines about prayer ἅπερ εἰκὸς ὅτι οὐ πᾶσι τοῖς βαπτιζομένοις ἀλλὰ τοῖς πρὸς τὸ βαπτίζεσθαι μαθητευομένοις ἐν ἀπορρήτῳ παρεδίδου. We are perhaps here approaching the conception of this secret tradition, as a form of mystical contemplation, which we have found occasionally in Clement.[5] In his *Exhortation to Martyrdom* Origen speaks of how those who attain to the point of martyrdom understand what he calls ἄρρητα no longer 'in a mirror' or 'darkly', but γυμνῇ σοφίᾳ φωνῶν καὶ λέξεων καὶ συμβόλων καὶ τύπων.[6] But he warns us that these things can only be learnt when you have left the body behind. And in his *Homilies on Jeremiah*[7] he has this sentence: ἐν ᾧ γὰρ οἰκοδομεῖται τὰ περὶ τοῦ θεοῦ

---

[1] III. xxxvii.   [2] *Against C.* IV. viii.

[3] τὰς ἐν τοῖς λόγοις ἀκολουθίας. See p. 50 for a previous quotation of this passage.

[4] II. 5; note the ἀπόρρητος and the εἰκός again.

[5] See above, p. 55.   [6] *Exhort. Mart.* xiii.   [7] Fragment lviii.

μυστήρια καὶ ἄρρητα δόγματα, ἐν τούτῳ ναός ἐστι τοῦ θεοῦ καὶ τὰ ἅγια τῶν ἁγίων καὶ ὅλης οὗτος τῆς 'Ιουδαίας μητρόπολις. Though in these two passages the word he uses is ἄρρητα (no doubt after 2 Corinthians 12. 4), and not ἀπόρρητα, there can be little doubt that Origen imagined that some form of mystical contemplation of divine truth was part of his esoteric doctrine, just as Clement did. Another article of this secret tradition is Origen's interpretation of the resurrection of the body. This interpretation in *Against Celsus*[1] he reserves for the better-informed Christians, calling it ἀπόρρητόν τι καὶ μυστικόν.

Among these esoteric doctrines of Origen Lebreton would count the doctrine of the Holy Trinity,[2] but he also notes how many of these doctrines seem to represent simply Origen's private speculations. There is, however, one more on this list to be dealt with, and that a particularly important one, which has already been referred to, in the quotation of Bouyer made at the beginning of our discussion.[3] That one is the allegorical interpretation of Scripture. This certainly formed part of Origen's esoteric tradition, quite apart from the fact that it was only by the use of allegorization that he was able to extract from the words of Scripture most of the other doctrines in this tradition. In his *Commentary on Matthew*,[4] we read that among the doctrines for the *élite* was the interpretation of the parables of our Lord which have no interpretation given in the Bible. And he notes that only a suitably clean heart can achieve the interpretation of such things, another indication that there is something of spiritual as well as of intellectual enlightenment in his conception of this tradition. Again, in his *Against Celsus*,[5] discussing the text, 'I have yet many things to say unto you, but ye cannot bear them now' (John 16. 12), Origen says that among these 'many things' was the explanation of 'what is the true law and what are the heavenly things for whose pattern and shadow the divine service among the Jews was carried out, and what were the good things to come of which the law about eating and drinking and new moons and sabbaths possessed a shadow'. It was, Origen believes, after his Passion and Resurrection that Jesus revealed these things, and he indicates thereby his belief that this abrogation and allegorization of the law was part of the esoteric teaching of Jesus.

---

[1] v. xix.   [2] 'Les Degrés de la Connaissance', p. 280.   [3] See above, p. 36.
[4] XIV. 12. See below, pp. 123–4, for an interesting parallel to this in Irenaeus.
[5] II. ii.

Now it will have become obvious from the examples of Origen's secret tradition given hitherto that he expects the Christian intellectuals of his own day to derive this esoteric doctrine, not from any tradition of teaching handed down by gifted teachers independently of Scripture (as does Clement), but from Scripture itself. That is in fact what Origen himself does in handling his advanced or esoteric theology. And when he speaks of Paul's or of anybody else's referring in a veiled or deliberately obscure way to a secret doctrine, he does not mean usually that the secret doctrine is not to be found in their writings, but that it is to be found only by the enlightened, those, in short, who are acquainted with all Origen's favourite speculations, and especially with his method of allegorizing the Bible. If further proof is needed that it is from the Bible, and the Bible only, that Origen imagines that secret doctrine to be derived in his own day, it can be supplied. In the *Commentary on Romans*,[1] we find these words: '*Et nos ergo si aliquid de secretis Dei et reconditis desideramus agnoscere, si desideriorum et non contentionum viri sumus, occultius in divinis litteris inserta Dei iudicia fideliter et humiliter requiramus.*' And later in the same work[2] (on the subject of 'esteeming days', mentioned in Romans 14. 5, 6), we find: '*Si quis ergo sit qui ita divinis litteris operam impendat ac studium, ut omnem diem et omnem sensum Scripturae divinae discutiat et diiudicet, ita ut non eum transeat de lege iota unum vel unus apex, hic omnem diem videbitur iudicare. Qui autem non est tantus ingenio, alternos, id est paucos ex multis, capiat sensus, qui si non ad plenitudinem scientiae sufficiant, at certe ad summam fidei satis sint.*' Both the ordinary and the esoteric doctrine, this passage implies, are to be derived from Scripture. The same meaning seems to be intended by a later passage still in this Commentary,[3] which discusses 'the mystery which hath been kept in silence through times eternal' (Rom. 16. 25). The revelation of this mystery, says Origen, was intended only for the elect few capable of understanding it. The prophets knew of it and it was manifested through them: '*sed hominibus, id est vulgo, non manifestaverint nec patefecerint, sed silentio texerint secundum praeceptum aeterni Dei usquequo tempus adesset ut caro Verbum fieret et habitaret in nobis.*' From the Scriptures of the Old Testament also, then, can be extracted this esoteric doctrine for the Christian intelligentsia. A final and, in my view, clinching proof that Origen does not imagine that his secret

---

[1] VII. xvii.   [2] IX. xxxvii.   [3] X. xliii.

tradition derives from our Lord independently of the Bible is provided by a passage in the fragments of his *Commentary on 1 Corinthians*.[1] On the phrase 'not to go beyond the things that are written' (1 Cor. 4. 6) Origen comments: 'The followers of sects profess to have traditions and say "These are in addition to the things that are written, because our Saviour delivered them in a secret communication (ἐν ἀπορρήτῳ) to the apostles, and the apostles to so-and-so and so-and-so"; and thus by this sort of mythical talk they deceive the minds of the guileless.' At the beginning of this fragment Origen has hinted that you can only go beyond what is written when you understand what is written. It is perfectly obvious that he means that you can by allegory extract from what is written certain esoteric doctrines, and that he knows of no tradition independent of the Bible and derived from our Lord.

In this, therefore, Origen differs strikingly from Clement in his doctrine of esoteric tradition. He does not give a direct and continuous ancestry independent of the Bible to his secret tradition, as Clement does. He does not profess to derive it from anywhere else than the Bible. The very fact that in referring to this secret tradition he uses on several occasions the word 'perhaps' betrays this.[2] Neither does he use the word γνῶσις for this secret tradition, as Clement does. Lebreton suggests that this is because the word had by Origen's day an heretical flavour.[3] In Origen, as Cadiou notes,[4] γνῶσις does not mean '*la communication instantanée du divin*', but 'religious knowledge', almost 'religious education'.[5] Origen can even on occasion use the phrase πᾶσι τοῖς ἀπόρρητα ἐπαγγελλομένοις τοῖς ἑτεροδόξοις,[6] as if he himself had never professed to teach esoteric doctrine! And in one of his *Homilies on the Psalms*,[7] we find a fine vindication of the superiority of the simple, uneducated believer who has 'the one thing needful', to even the very well-educated pagan. Origen is not always a Gnostic.

[1] *J.T.S.* ix, p. 357, xix.

[2] See the references above to εἰκός as it occurs in *Against C.* I. xxi; *Con. Prayer* II. 5. See too the 'perhaps' in the passage from *Hom. on Joshua* XXIII. iv quoted on pp. 75, 76.   [3] 'Le Désaccord de la Foi', tom. 20, p. 15.

[4] *La Jeunesse d'Origène*, p. 96.

[5] And in this respect at least Bouyer is inaccurate when he uses the phrase 'the *gnosis* of which Origen makes so much'. See the quotation from Bouyer on p. 36 above.

[6] Fragments from *Comm. on Psalms* (P.G. XII, 1413), on Ps. 41. 6. Cf. *Hom. on Ezekiel* II. v, '*audi haereticos, quomodo traditiones apostolorum habere se dicant*'.

[7] *Homily* III on *Ps. 37. 1* (P.G. XII, 1340–1).

Yet Origen undoubtedly does profess to have a body of esoteric doctrine, and certainly does believe in the practice of Reserve, or withholding the more advanced articles of Christian doctrine from the simple believer. It is perhaps unnecessary to argue this point any more strongly than has already been done; the quotations from the *Commentary on Romans* VI. viii and VIII. xii[1] should alone make it unmistakably clear that Origen did intend these secret doctrines to be *deliberately withheld* from those who were incapable of understanding them. Indeed, we have seen instances where he withholds them himself;[2] and we shall presently see that he uses the significant phrase τὰ σιωπώμενα δόγματα in a fragment on the Song of Songs.[3] But it is perhaps worth observing that Origen echoes Clement's and Philo's conviction that in certain circumstances it may be legitimate to lie to people for their ultimate good, but instead of doing what Clement did[4] and attributing this licence to the 'Gnostic', Origen, more faithfully reproducing Philo, allows it to God himself. Discussing in his *Homilies on Jeremiah*[5] the old crux raised by the text Jer. 20. 7, 'Thou has deceived me, O Lord, and I was deceived', he argues that God may legitimately deceive: 'If the doctor said to the patient, "You must submit to amputation, to cauterization, you must endure even more painful treatment than this", the patient would not submit himself to the treatment. So sometimes the doctor makes some other pretext, and hides the instrument in question, the steel which cuts, under the sponge, and again hides in honey, if I may so express it, the true nature of the bitter medicine and the unpleasant draught, with the intention, not of hurting, but of healing, his patient.' The debt to Philo and Clement is clear, though Origen in this place in fact claims the thought as his own. The idea reappears in *Against Celsus* (IV. xix), where Origen says that God may have in the Bible related things which were not true in order to improve men: 'Certainly some stories told in a manner which is false rather than in one which is true influence certain types of character, just as similar devices of surgeons are used on sick people.' If Origen can hold such a doctrine as this, it becomes frivolous to imagine that he never intended his secret teaching to be withheld from certain people in the Church.

Defences for these peculiarities, or at least explanations of them, have

---

[1] See above, p. 75.
[2] See above, pp. 76, 77.
[3] See below, p. 96.
[4] See above, pp. 70, 71.
[5] xx. 3.

been made by modern scholars. Bigg has observed how the Alexandrians' difference from their contemporaries in their theological opinions drove them to this resort. 'On many points', he says,[1] '—the explanation of those much-contested words, Priest, Altar, Sacrifice, the Body and Blood of Christ, the Power of the Keys, Eternal Life, Eternal Death—they were at variance with the spirit of the age. Hence they were driven to what is known as Reserve. The belief of the enlightened Christian becomes a mystery that may not be revealed to the simpler brother, for whom the letter is enough.' Later[2] Bigg explains this practice of Reserve as 'the Alexandrine *disciplina arcani*', and adds that 'the Allegorism of Clement and Origen is a plea for the utmost freedom of thought, on condition that it keeps within the teaching of Christ and is couched in a learned language'.

Lebreton notes that this secret doctrine is not merely speculation.[3] It is '*une connaissance religieuse plus haute, due à une révélation privilégiée; c'est une intuition, qui initie celui qui en jouit à des mystères interdits à la foule; elle transforme sa vie morale et religieuse, elle le tire de la condition servile commune à tous les hommes, elle en fait un ami de Dieu, égal ou même supérieur aux anges*'. And later he says, of both Clement and Origen: '*Au-dessus de la foi vulgaire, accessible à tous les chrétiens, ils ont imaginé une connaissance religieuse qui viendrait d'une tradition secrète, qui aurait le caractère d'une intuition immédiate et qui transformerait toute la vie, pour toujours. Cette conception aventureuse ne se rencontrera plus dans l'Église catholique après Origène.*'[4] Earlier Lebreton had put this practice of Reserve in its setting in the history of the development of Christian doctrine:[5] '*On reconnaît ici la théorie de la tradition secrète: très répandue chez les Gnostiques, elle n'est accueillie que tardivement dans la grande Église, et seulement chez les Alexandrins: on la trouve d'abord chez les maîtres gnostiques de Clément, puis chez Clément lui-même, chez Origène. Dans la suite elle s'efface, non cependant sans marquer encore de son empreinte quelqu'uns des disciples d'Origène, par exemple saint Basile.*' And in an earlier work[6] he delivers a final condemnation of the whole theory, calling it '*la théorie la plus éloignée de l'enseignement catholique et la plus choquante*'.

---

[1] *Christian Platonists*, pp. 85-7. [2] Ibid. pp. 178-84.
[3] 'Le Désaccord de la Foi', tom. 19, p. 493.
[4] Ibid. tom. 20, p. 5. [5] Ibid. tom. 19, p. 504.
[6] 'Les Degrés de la Connaissance', p. 274.

But, illuminating as these comments upon the theory of secret tradition among the Alexandrines are, Lebreton does not seem to realize that Origen never claims (as Clement does claim) to possess a secret tradition which he knows to have been derived independently of Scripture from our Lord and his apostles.[1] Cadiou is more accurate in this particular. He states plainly in a note, quoting Harnack, that Origen recognized no official secret tradition, least of all a written one.[2] The only conclusion that will fit all the facts in this matter is that Origen believed that the intellectual Christians of his day were intended to derive from their study of the Bible a number of secret doctrines beyond the understanding of the average believer (and in fact identical with the speculations of Origen himself and his school of thought), and that he assumed that Christ and his apostles had taught such doctrines privately to their more intelligent disciples, as Origen was teaching them to his; but that there is no evidence that any continuity of delivery in the Church existed between such alleged secret teaching by Christ and his apostles on the one hand and Origen's secret teaching on the other, or even that Origen believed such continuity to exist.

Lebreton suggests that as well as having Clement of Alexandria as his source for such a theory of secret teaching, Origen had the speculations of some Rabbinic schools of thought, and also of the Gnostics.[3] It is conceivable that these last two influences may have played some remote and indirect part in forming this theory in Origen's mind,[4] but (as we shall see) this is not the particular way in which those Rabbinic circles with which Origen undoubtedly was in touch were likely to influence him, and though his association with Gnostics gave him a good idea of some of their doctrines, it can hardly have led him to borrow that feature of their teaching which was, according to Irenaeus,[5] one of the principal doctrines which distinguished their teaching from the faith of the Church. The clearest, most direct, and most obvious

---

[1] See ibid. pp. 287–92.

[2] *La Jeunesse d'Origène*, p. 80. Harnack's phrase is '*förmliche Geheimtradition*'.

[3] 'Les Degrés de la Connaissance', p. 293.

[4] The contact between Origen and contemporary Jewish thought is discussed in Chapter VIII below.

[5] Cf. Irenaeus, *Adv. Haereses* III. ii. 1, 2 (chapter-divisions according to the Ante-Nicene Christian Library); the Gnostics claimed that 'the apostles gave their teaching with reserve, and replies according to the opinions of their questioners'. See J. N. Sanders, *The Fourth Gospel in the Early Church*, p. 70.

influence upon Origen in his theory of esoteric tradition is Clement of Alexandria, and it is only because nobody before has made a thorough examination of the teaching of both these Fathers upon this point that the dependence of Origen upon Clement has never been properly emphasized. It is, we may truly say, the point where their theological systems (in so far as Clement can be said to have a theological system) most clearly coincide. This doctrine of Reserve which we find in Origen, and this tendency to allot to the uneducated simple believers a kind of faith which is not fully faith but has in it an ingredient of fear which is wholly absent from the faith of the Christian intellectual, are, as we have seen, a direct borrowing from Clement. Origen does not make the cleavage between simple believer and intellectual as wide as Clement does, but he still believes in the existence of the cleavage. Again, we have noted the use made by both writers of the same word ἀπόρρητος, in an almost technical sense, to describe their secret tradition. We have observed that both writers evidently conceived of this secret tradition as being known to select souls and handed down by them even in Old Testament times. And we have seen that both can on occasion infuse into the tradition a note which is one almost of mysticism; this note is more obvious in Clement than in Origen, partly, I think, because Clement is borrowing much more directly from Philo here than is Origen, but it is not absent from Origen. Finally, we have detected a similarity between the contents of this secret tradition in both authors, where they allow us to have a glimpse of its contents.[1] We have even been able to discover a likeness between the list of speculations assigned by Clement to his secret tradition in the Introduction to the Fourth Book of the *Stromateis*, and the contents of Origen's *Concerning First Principles*.[2]

On the other hand, we must note several important points in which Origen differs from Clement in his treatment of secret tradition. We have already emphasized sufficiently the interesting fact that Origen does not claim to know of any line of teachers deriving in continuous succession from the apostles who taught this secret tradition, whereas Clement does. He does not bring the *Epistle of Barnabas* into prominence, as Clement does; indeed, he only very rarely quotes from the

[1] For further comparison of the contents of this tradition in Origen and Clement, see below, p. 122.
[2] See above, pp. 64, 65.

Epistle at all,[1] and does not associate Barnabas with the delivery of his esoteric tradition. Neither does he use the language of the mystery-religions concerning this tradition, as we have seen Clement doing,[2] again mainly, I suspect, because Origen is less directly influenced by Philo than is Clement. Further, Origen gives a fuller account of the contents of this tradition than Clement does; and this is not only because more of Origen's work has come down to us than of Clement's, but because Origen is noticeably less secretive about the tradition than is Clement. Origen's motive for secrecy is the fear that his daring speculations may upset the simple and exasperate the orthodox. Though this motive is discernible in Clement also, he has the added incentive for secrecy in that he regards his secret tradition more as the initiate of a mystery-cult regards the secrets with which he has been solemnly entrusted. Finally, whereas Clement confuses or identifies his secret tradition with the rule of faith of the Church, Origen tends to keep the two quite separate in his mind, as we shall see. This does not mean that some of the contents of his rule of faith may not be identical with some of the contents of his esoteric tradition (in fact they are), but the two still perform two quite separate functions in his mind, so much so that we shall be able to give examples where he contrasts the two.

This comparison between Origen and Clement of Alexandria in their doctrine of secret tradition inevitably raises the question of the relation of these two Christian Fathers to each other. This question cannot be finally dealt with until we have finished our whole survey of Origen's doctrine of tradition. But we may at the moment note that while Origen obviously owes a great deal to Clement, he holds himself perfectly at liberty to depart from him in several important particulars. The mystifying point in the relation of the two men is that Origen never once in any of his works which have come down to us in any form mentions Clement of Alexandria. He mentions several people to whom he is far less indebted—Philo, Melito of Sardis, Ignatius of Antioch, Clement of Rome, for instance—but never Clement of Alexandria. Eusebius tells us[3] that Origen was one of Clement's pupils in the Catechetical School at Alexandria; most scholars accept this as true, and Origen's undoubted indebtedness to Clement would seem to confirm

---

[1] But he certainly believes that it is 'canonical', in so far as we can attach that word to Origen's doctrine of tradition.

[2] See above, pp. 54, 55.   [3] *H.E.* VI. 6.

it. But chronological considerations forbid us to allow that he can have sat under Clement for more than a short time.[1] Clement mentions in *Stromateis* III. iii (*P.G.* VIII. 1116) a περὶ ἀρχῶν λόγος which he intends writing; and in *Quis Dives* xxvi (*P.G.* IX. 632), he uses the phrase ὅπερ ἐν τῇ περὶ ἀρχῶν καὶ θεολογίας ἐξηγήσει μυστήριον τοῦ σωτῆρος ὑπάρχει μαθεῖν. Koetschau is confident (and it is hard to disagree with him) that this means that Clement certainly did write, not merely plan, such a work. He conjectures that in it Clement dealt with the Greek and non-Greek philosophers, comparing them with a summary of Christian theology, that he intended (and here Koetschau follows Zahn) to outline a true physiology, grounded on Biblical cosmogony, to crown his theology, that he did not carry out this idea in fact, and that it was to complete this plan that Origen wrote his own περὶ Ἀρχῶν.[2] But it seems to me much more likely that Clement did carry out this plan in the lost περὶ Ἀρχῶν, and that Origen composed *his* περὶ Ἀρχῶν as a sort of counterblast, as an orthodox corrective of the near-Gnostic περὶ Ἀρχῶν of that suspect and unmentionable man, Clement of Alexandria. If Clement, Origen's predecessor in Alexandria, really *did* write a περὶ Ἀρχῶν, Origen's failure to mention him is most marked and can be explained on almost no other hypothesis than this one.[3] Perhaps I should say no more at this point than that the suggestion that Origen avoided mentioning Clement because, by the time Origen was writing, Clement's name was associated with heresy seems to me an attractive one.[4]

[1] Cf. Lawlor and Oulton, p. 194: 'The form of the sentence seems to imply that Origen was only for a short time a pupil of Clement.'

[2] Introduction to *G.C.S.*, Origen v, p. xiv.

[3] Koetschau points out (Introduction, p. xv, n. 1) that Clement had also intended writing a περὶ Ἀναστάσεως, an intention which Origen in fact accomplished.

[4] This suggestion has already been adumbrated by Lebreton's observation about Origen's avoidance of the word γνῶσις for his esoteric tradition, quoted on p. 84 above.

CHAPTER VI

ORIGEN'S DOCTRINE OF THE RULE
OF FAITH

WE have said that Origen keeps his doctrine of secret tradition separate from his doctrine of the Church's rule of faith. This has yet to be established by evidence. For the rule of faith of the Church and for the general belief of Christians (to Origen the two are identical), one of the commonest words that he uses is κανών.[1] In his *Commentary on John*[2] he speaks of 'the rule of faith (κανόνα) prevalent among the majority of the Church', and contrasts it with the belief of the Christian intellectual. One fragment of the *Commentary on 1 Corinthians*[3] has survived where the word stands for the whole gospel or content of the Christian faith (as it does in Irenaeus and Tertullian). Paraphrasing the words of 1 Cor. 14. 36, 'was it from you that the word of God went forth? or came it unto you alone?', Origen says: ἆρ' οὖν ἡ ἀλήθεια καὶ ὁ κανὼν ὁ ἐκκλησιαστικὸς εἰς ὑμᾶς μόνους τοὺς Κορινθίους κατήντησεν; In his *Homilies on Jeremiah*[4] he identifies the κανών with 'the Church's principles' (λόγος) and 'the intention of sound teaching' (τὴν πρόθεσιν τῆς ὑγιοῦς διδασκαλίας). In the *Commentary on Matthew*[5] we find a dark reference to people who ignorantly attack '*viros verbo et vita provectos et ecclesiarum canonem non relinquentes, propter prounditatem autem dogmatum suspectos*'. We cannot be sure that

---

[1] Origen can, of course, use κανών in a quite secular sense, as Philo and Clement do; e.g. in *Comm. on Ephesians* xxxvi (p. 575, on Eph. 6. 21, 22) he speaks of τὸν κανόνα τοῦ βίου, parallel with τὴν τάξιν τῶν πράξεων, of Tychicus' standard of life. Cf. *Comm. on 1 Corinthians: J.T.S.* ix, p. 500, XXXIII.

[2] XIII. 16.   [3] *J.T.S.* x, p. 42, LXXIV.

[4] v. 14. The passage in Greek (in which he is commenting on Jeremiah 4. 4, 'Circumcise yourself to the Lord') runs thus: εἰσὶν δὲ καὶ ἄλλοι λόγοι παρὰ τὸν λόγον τῆς ἀληθείας, παρὰ τὸν λόγον τὸν τῆς ἐκκλησίας. περιτέμνονται τὰ ἤθη καὶ τὴν καρδίαν ὥς τε εἰπεῖν σωφρονίζουσιν οἱ φιλοσοφοῦντες, σωφρονίζουσιν οἱ ἀπὸ τῶν αἱρέσεων, καὶ γίνεται αὐτοῖς περιτομή. ἀλλὰ περιτομὴ μέν, οὐ τῷ θεῷ δέ· περιτομὴ γὰρ λόγῳ ψευδεῖ παρ' ἐκείνοις γίνεται. ὅταν δὲ κατὰ τὸν ἐκκλησιαστικὸν κανόνα, κατὰ τὴν πρόθεσιν τῆς ὑγιοῦς διδασκαλίας, κοινωνικὸς ᾖς, οὐ περιτέτμησαι μόνον, ἀλλὰ περιτέτμησαι τῷ θεῷ.

[5] Part II, 28, where, of course, only a Latin translation survives.

'*canonem*' here represents an original κανόνα, but it seems very probable. Later in the same work,[1] we find the word used in a sense which approaches that of the later 'Canon' of Scripture, and yet one which is obviously not identical with it. Commenting on Matthew 24. 26,[2] he says that when heretics try to prove their heresy by reference to authentic Scriptures,[3] they are saying, 'Behold, he is in the inner chambers'. A Greek fragment enables us to recover the original of the next sentence. It runs: ὁ μὲν ἔξω τῆς πίστεως καὶ τοῦ τῆς ἐκκλησίας κανόνος καὶ τῆς γραφῆς λέγει· ἰδοὺ ἐν τῇ ἐρήμῳ.[4] This sentence might conceivably be translated, 'He who is outside the faith and the rule of the Church and of Scripture...', but the Latin translation is against it, and it is much more natural to translate, 'He who is outside the Church and the rule of faith and Scripture...', and conclude that Origen does regard the κανών of the Church as separate from Scripture, even though closely linked with it. There is a very interesting passage in *Concerning First Principles*[5] which mentions this κανών. Origen has been describing various classes of people who hold errors about Scripture. The fault of them all, he says, is understanding Scripture literally, not spiritually. These errors will be corrected if students of the Bible will follow Origen's exposition, and 'hold fast to the rule of Jesus Christ's heavenly Church according to the succession of the apostles (ἐχομένοις τοῦ κανόνος τῆς Ἰησοῦ Χριστοῦ κατὰ διαδοχὴν τῶν ἀποστόλων οὐρανίου ἐκκλησίας)'. There is one passage in Clement of Alexandria which is remarkably like this one. It occurs in the Sixth Book of the *Stromateis*,[6] where Clement is speaking of 'gnosis' in interpreting the prophets and as taught by Christ to the apostles. He describes it as ἡ κατὰ διαδοχὰς εἰς ὀλίγους ἐκ τῶν ἀποστόλων ἀγράφως παραδοθεῖσα. The wording is similar enough for us to conjecture that Origen had this passage in mind when he wrote the passage in *Concern-*

---

[1] Part II, 46.

[2] On the words, 'Behold, he is in the wilderness'.

[3] The word in the Latin translation is '*canonicas*', but this cannot represent an original κανονικάς.

[4] Incidentally the Latin translation of this runs: '*sed nos illis credere non debemus, nec exire a prima et ecclesiastica traditione nec aliter credere nisi quemadmodum per successionem ecclesiae Dei tradiderunt nobis*', which shows how much the translation embroiders on the original.

[5] IV. 2. 2.

[6] Cap. x (*P.G.* IX, 284). The passage has already been quoted on p. 57.

ing First Principles quoted above. Now Molland[1] discusses this very passage in *Concerning First Principles* and approves the view of Kattenbusch that ὁ ἐκκλησιαστικὸς κανών in Origen means 'the canon of Scripture as recognized by the authority of the Church', and that in this passage Origen is in fact referring to what we now know as the Canon. This view is one which cannot stand examination. In the first place, in this passage in Origen the most natural sense of κανὼν τῆς ἐκκλησίας (indeed almost the only possible one) is 'the Church's custom of allegorizing the Scriptures', and the parallel passage in Clement makes this interpretation certain. In the second place, I have shown that κανών, or even κανὼν τῆς ἐκκλησίας, as used in other passages by Origen, cannot be exactly identified with the Canon of Scripture any more than it can in Clement. Thirdly, I shall show later in this work[2] that neither Clement nor Origen has a conception entirely equivalent to an official list of inspired Scripture guaranteed by the Church as authentic. No doubt Kattenbusch and Molland have been misled, as too many other commentators on Origen have, by the use of the words '*canonizatus*' and '*canonicus*' on the part of the Latin translators of Origen, all of whom lived at least one hundred years after his day. Finally, it has been shown in a careful study of the word κανών by H. Oppel[3] that the word does not occur meaning 'the list of documents acknowledged by the Church as documents of the divine revelation' until we reach Athanasius.

What then did Origen mean by the word κανών or κανὼν ἐκκλησιαστικός? Caspari gives in a footnote an account of this word which is remarkable rather for its inaccuracy than its cogency.[4] He says that Origen uses the phrase only three times, a statement which anybody who has read this work thus far will be able at once to correct; and the three instances which he gives are: in the *Commentary on the Epistle to Titus*[5] (where Rufinus has '*ecclesiastica regula*', a translation of whose accuracy we cannot be at all sure), in the *Commentary on John* XIII. 16 (where Caspari omits to notice the vitally important fact that Origen

---

[1] Molland, p. 92. He refers to Kattenbusch's *Das apostolische Symbol*, vol. II, p. 137.

[2] See below, Ch. VIII.

[3] 'KANⲰN', pp. 70, 71, where he derives his information from Zahn's *Grundriss der Geschichte des Neutestamentlichen Kanons*.

[4] 'Hat die alexandrinische Kirche', pp. 371–2 (n. 7 to p. 371).

[5] *P.G.* XVII. 554–5, quoted in Pamphilus' *Apology for Origen*.

says that you can *transcend* the Church's 'canon'), and in *Concerning First Principles* IV. I. 9 (the passage quoted just above, where, as we shall see, it is very difficult to agree with Origen's contention that allegorizing is part of the rule of faith of the Church). Caspari goes on to assert that Origen uses more often the phrase κανών τῆς εὐσεβείας, a quite incorrect statement which he supports by quoting several passages where Rufinus has '*regula pietatis*', and which are all suspect; one of them, indeed, *Concerning First Principles* IV. I. 26, is almost certainly an addition of the translator. We can, however, agree with Caspari when he says that for Origen κανών ἐκκλησιαστικός meant the same as τὸ κήρυγμα ἐκκλησιαστικόν.

In an article in the *Recherches de Science Religieuse*,[1] entitled 'La Règle de Foi d'Origène', G. Bardy discusses the question of κανών ἐκκλησιαστικός in Origen. He is very well aware of the danger of relying upon translations of Origen by Rufinus for evidence upon this point, even where the phrase '*regula pietatis*' occurs.[2] He quotes three of the passages already mentioned in this discussion: *Commentary on John* XIII. 16,[3] *Concerning First Principles* IV. 2. 2,[4] and *Commentary on Matthew*, Pt. II, 46.[5] The first two passages, he admits, imply that '*les Écritures elles-mêmes constituent la règle inviolable qui dirige le croyant*',[6] while the third suggests nothing more than that '*hors de l'Écriture, il ne saurait pas être question de règle de foi*'.[7] He is anxious to establish a distinction in Origen's thought between his use of the words κανών ἐκκλησιαστικός and his use of such phrases as κήρυγμα ἐκκλησιαστικόν (corresponding to the Latin '*fides ecclesiastica*').[8] He thinks that Origen did not use the term κανών to mean '*une règle de foi, un symbole imposé aux fidèles au nom de l'Église*', but that he meant by it little more than the Church's interpretation of Scripture.[9] The 'symbol' or κήρυγμα in Origen would, he thinks, be some more or less definite list of dogmas distinct from the κανών.[10]

Cadiou has an interesting note on this point. '*Le canon ecclésiastique*', he says, '*ne se réduit pas à une formule. Au sens le plus large, il est*

---

[1] Tom. IX, 1919, pp. 162–96.   [2] Ibid. pp. 173, 180.
[3] See above, p. 93.   [4] See above, p. 92.   [5] See above, p. 92, n. 4.
[6] 'La Règle de Foi d'Origène', pp. 175–7.
[7] Ibid. p. 178.   [8] Ibid. pp. 181–2.   [9] Ibid. p. 180.
[10] The question of the relation of the rule of faith in Origen to the Creed is dealt with below, and for the moment we are only considering what light Bardy can throw on Origen's use of the word κανών.

la croyance de la masse des fidèles, la règle de la vraie religion, opposée à l'impiété des hérétiques.' But it can also mean in a general and wide-embracing sense the Church's interpretation of Scripture. And he points out in a footnote that κανών in Origen should be distinguished from σύμβολον. He notes that in the *Concerning First Principles* the authority of the Bible is regularly invoked to confirm the teaching and the theology of the argument, and later he says: *'Les textes de la Bible ne seront donc pas seulement appelés à confirmer la doctrine, ils lui donneront son fondement.'*[1]

The evidence which we have already considered makes it very probable that both Bardy and Cadiou are right in insisting that in his use of κανών and κανών ἐκκλησιαστικός Origen did not refer to any list of articles of belief or creed, and that, whatever his κανών was, it was very closely linked with the Scriptures, though not identical with them. On the other hand, the use of κανών as 'the belief generally held by the faithful in the Church' is one which would fit all the cases of it which we have examined, as long as we understand that Origen regarded this κανών primarily as the Church's interpretation of Scripture. The κανών was apparently to Origen simply the way the Church always had interpreted Scripture, as far as he knew. Here he reproduces one of the most important meanings that Clement attaches to the word;[2] but he does not specifically identify the κανών with his secret tradition, as Clement does.

With this provisional definition in mind, we can go on to explore further Origen's doctrine of the rule of faith. The first point we must note is that it is impossible to distinguish, as Bardy does, Origen's conception of the Church's κανών from his conception of the Church's κήρυγμα, or articles of belief. The fact is that Origen uses several other words and phrases to express virtually the same idea as the κανών, and among them is κήρυγμα. But before we reach the word κήρυγμα itself, it will be useful to examine some of the others. We have already seen one instance where Origen seems to identify ὁ κανών with ὁ ἐκκλησιαστικὸς λόγος and ἡ πρόθεσις τῆς ὑγιοῦς διδασκαλίας.[3] The expression ἐκκλησιαστικὸς λόγος is one which Origen uses several times. In his

---

[1] *La Jeunesse d'Origène*, pp. 269, 272, 286; cf. also p. 332: *'Il faisait appel à son autorité pour appuyer les dogmes, ou pour confirmer les conjectures.'*

[2] See above, p. 60.

[3] *Hom. on Jeremiah* v. xiv. See above, p. 91.

Commentary on Matthew[1] he describes as ξένοι τοῦ ἐκκλησιαστικοῦ λόγου those who teach a doctrine of the migration of souls of humans to and from the souls of animals.[2] On the other hand, Origen's solution to the problem of how John the Baptist could be Elijah οὐδὲ λυπεῖ τὸν ἐκκλησιαστικὸν λόγον.[3] Further on in the same work,[4] he says that to disbelieve the words of Scripture as not representing what Jesus really said would be to act contrary to ὁ ἐκκλησιαστικὸς λόγος. In the *Commentaries on Psalms*[5] we have a reference to 'the mind of the Church' (γνώμη ἐκκλησιαστική). 'The mind of the Church', he says, 'contemplates the truth and is therefore called Sion; we must grasp its doctrines with our mind. Understand her teaching intelligently and examine each article separately.' Again, in his *Commentary on Matthew* he speaks of people ἐπαγγελλομένων κατήχησιν ἐκκλησιαστικὴν καὶ διδασκαλίαν, and he clearly means well-instructed Christians.[6] In his *Commentaries on Psalms*[7] he can also write of someone agreeing φρονεῖν τὰ ἐκκλησιαστικά all the days of his life, and later of someone τὰ ὑποβεβηκότα δόγματα ('the foundation-doctrines') τῆς ἐκκλησίας ὁρῶν, and he instances the doctrine of the Trinity as one of these. So, in fragments *on Proverbs and the Song of Songs*,[8] he uses the phrase ἕκαστον δόγμα τῆς καθολικῆς καὶ ἀποστολικῆς ἐκκλησίας, and can contrast τὰ σιωπώμενα δόγματα with τὰ πεπιστευμένα δόγματα. He also refers to 'the intention of the Church' (βούλημα).[9] In *Against Celsus* he mentions certain heretics who deny the Scriptural doctrine of the resurrection of the body. Here he says, τηροῦμεν καὶ τὸ βούλημα

---

[1] XI. 17.

[2] It is worth noting that in refuting this doctrine Origen begins, ἡμεῖς δέ, μηδαμῶς τοῦτο εὑρίσκοντες ἐν τῇ θείᾳ γραφῇ, φαμέν, κ.τ.λ.

[3] *Comm. on Matt.* XIII. 2.

[4] XVII. 35. Cf. fragments on *Exodus (P.G.* XII, 287) for another use of this phrase; and *Comm. on* 1 *Corinthians: J.T.S.* ix, p. 507, XXXVII.

[5] On Psalm 48. 12 (*P.G.* XII, 1441). The Greek runs: τῆς γνώμης τῆς ἐκκλησιαστικῆς σκοπευτικῆς οὔσης τῆς ἀληθείας καὶ διὰ τοῦτο Σιὼν καλουμένης, περιληπτέον αὐτῆς ἐν διανοίᾳ τὰ δόγματα. ἐπιστημονικῶς τοίνυν κατανοήσαντες τὴν ταύτης διδασκαλίαν διαιρετικῶς ἕκαστον ἐξετάζετε.

[6] XV. 7.

[7] On Psalm 27. 5 (*P.G.* XII, 1280). This should perhaps be classed as a reference to a Creed. See below, pp. 118–121.

[8] *P.G.* XVII, 225 (on Prov. 24. 6) and 272 (on Song of Songs 4. 3, 4).

[9] Cf. the ἡ πρόθεσις τῆς ὑγιοῦς διδασκαλίας of the *Hom. on Jeremiah* v. 14, quoted above, p. 91.

τῆς ἐκκλησίας τοῦ Χριστοῦ καὶ τὸ μέγεθος τῆς ἐπαγγελίας τοῦ θεοῦ, adding that he does so, 'establishing its possibility not merely in profession but by logic'.[1]

With these instances before us, it is hard to imagine that there is any substance in Bardy's distinction between the κανών of the Church and the κήρυγμα of the Church.[2] All these expressions seem to mean much the same thing as κανών does, that is, in its broadest sense, the Church's interpretation of the Bible. This includes the allegorization of Scripture; it includes the Church's teaching upon important or disputed points, in contrast to that of the heretics; and it includes specific doctrines of the Church, which presumably might be in the process of being included in official creeds in Origen's day. The composition of the κήρυγμα, when we come to examine it, we find to be altogether too loose and comprehensive to be equated with a Creed, which is essentially a summary, though it is not impossible that the Creed of Origen's day was a summary of the κήρυγμα. In *Concerning First Principles* a fragment of the Greek survives in one passage where this κήρυγμα is mentioned.[3] We are told here ἐν τῷ κηρύγματι καὶ τὸ εἶναί τινας ἀγγέλους καὶ δυνάμεις...παραδέδοται, but that the creation of angels, and other details, are not in the κήρυγμα. And later in the same section he says that such truths as these must be worked into a system 'either by the evidence to be found in the sacred Scriptures, or by that to be discovered by the investigation of the logical consequences of the Scriptures and adherence to accuracy'.[4] Later on in the same work,[5] he has a sentence which begins: ἐπεὶ δὲ ἐν τῷ κηρύγματι τῷ ἐκκλησιαστικῷ περιέχεται ὁ περὶ κρίσεως δικαίας λόγος. What then is this κήρυγμα? It certainly seems to be something capable of division into a list of articles of what the Church preaches, as the name implies, but it can hardly be a baptismal creed, both for the reason given above, and because Origen does not call it a Creed (i.e. σύμβολον), but a κήρυγμα. Further, it is unprecedented to find in a Creed of any period the mention of angels alone, in no connection with our Lord's Ascension or Second Coming.[6] On the other hand, if this is, not a Creed, but an account of

---

[1] v. xxii.

[2] The most perhaps that we might concede to this view is that κανών means 'rule as standard generally', whereas κήρυγμα means 'rule as thing preached'.

[3] Origen's Preface, 10.

[4] For this translation, see below, p. 116, n. 3. The Greek fragment has broken off by now.　　　[5] III. I. I.　　　[6] See below, p. 117, n. 4.

the points which the Church of Origen's day does preach about, it is very natural to mention the existence of angels as one of the points of preaching, without implying that so subordinate a point appears in the *summary* of the faith which a Creed is. Again, this κήρυγμα clearly is not independent of Scripture; it looks to Scripture for its support. Once again, it seems to me, we have in this word another description of what all the words and phrases we have just been mentioning imply—κανών, ἐκκλησιαστικὸς λόγος, and so on—and that is, the interpretation of her tradition in preaching and teaching by the Church of Origen's day. And by Origen's day, this was, so all the evidence suggests, precisely equivalent to the Church's interpretation of the Bible. It is not, of course, exactly identical with the Bible. In preaching and teaching her tradition the Church of Origen's day did not simply read the Bible in the market-place or at the Eucharist and expect it to speak for itself, any more than the Church of to-day does. In preaching her tradition (which obviously for some time before Origen's day had been an oral tradition, though by his day it had become a written one) the Church formed it into systematic teaching and into articles of faith. She commented upon it; she elaborated it; she drew it out. This process is the κήρυγμα. No doubt the κήρυγμα is thought of by Origen's day as a more or less fixed list of articles to be derived from Scripture, whereas the other terms may be looser in their meaning. But there are no satisfactory grounds for assuming with Bardy that κήρυγμα is in Origen virtually equivalent to σύμβολον, whereas κανών has much the same meaning that I have seen in κήρυγμα.

And yet Origen can say ἐν τῷ κηρύγματι...παραδέδοται. The κήρυγμα is not only the Church's interpretation of the Bible in Origen's day; it is the Church's preaching in continuity with the Church's preaching at all periods right back to the earliest beginnings, because the Church was preaching and teaching well before a word of the New Testament was written, and did not at any point abandon her preaching based on oral tradition and start anew with a quite fresh series of points based on written teaching. What she did was gradually to crystallize out into written documents the basis and authority for her κήρυγμα. This is, as far as I can see, exactly what happened in the formation of the Canon of the New Testament, and this is, as far as I can see, exactly what we find assumed in the use of the word κήρυγμα by Origen.

This should become clearer if we examine rather more closely the relation of the rule of faith to the Bible in Origen's thought. There is a passage in the *Commentary on Matthew*[1] where Origen says that the contemporary philosophical doctrine of metempsychosis must be rejected, calling it ἀλλότριον τῆς ἐκκλησίας τοῦ θεοῦ περὶ μετενσωματώσεως δόγμα, οὔτε παραδιδόμενον ὑπὸ τῶν ἀποστόλων οὔτε ἐμφαινόμενόν που τῶν γραφῶν. This passage could conceivably be used to support a theory that Origen distinguished the Bible's tradition from a tradition handed down from the apostles independently of it, but this seems a very far-fetched interpretation of the passage, quite apart from the evidence of other places that Origen held no such theory. It is more natural to interpret the passage as meaning, 'neither handed down by the apostles [i.e. not in the New Testament], nor found anywhere in the Bible [i.e. not in the Old Testament, nor in non-apostolic parts of the New, such as the second and third Gospels, and Acts]',[2] and assume that here we have an example of Origen's citing the Bible as the authority for the Church's doctrine. In *Concerning First Principles*[3] there is a passage discussing judgement and resurrection which contains this phrase: '*secundum quod comminantur sanctae scripturae et ecclesiastica praedicatio continet.*' If the translation is faithful to the original here (and in view of what we have already said about Rufinus' habit of altering Origen's words on such points as these, we cannot take this for granted), this suggests that the two—Bible and Church's preaching— are parallel, though identical in content. In the *Commentary on Matthew*[4] he has this sentence: μαθητεύεται δὲ τῇ βασιλείᾳ τῶν οὐρανῶν γραμματεὺς κατὰ μὲν τὸ ἁπλούστερον ὅτε ἀπὸ Ἰουδαϊσμοῦ ἀναλαμβάνει τις τὴν Ἰησοῦ Χριστοῦ ἐκκλησιαστικὴν διδασκαλίαν, but he adds that the scribe is more profoundly instructed when he learns to interpret the Scriptures allegorically. This would imply that the teaching of the Church and the teaching of Jesus (presumably in the Gospels) are the same thing, and—more important—that allegorization is something one stage beyond 'ecclesiastical teaching', which is a view which we shall examine more narrowly a little later. In the same work[5] Origen states that if anybody has a difficult problem, it is a good thing

---

[1] XIII. I.
[2] Moreover Origen proceeds immediately afterwards to give Scriptural evidence that the world is perishable.
[3] II. 10. I.   [4] X. 14.   [5] XIII. 15.

to bring it to 'one of the teachers appointed in the Church by God', and he is clearly referring to problems of Biblical interpretation. Later still in this same commentary,[1] he says that to disbelieve the words of Scripture as not representing what Jesus really said would be to act contrary to the ἐκκλησιαστικὸν λόγον, which certainly suggests that the Church guarantees the Scriptures as authentic. Finally, two sections in the second part of this commentary[2] are particularly relevant. Those who say, 'Behold, he is in the wilderness' (Matthew 24. 26), Origen interprets as meaning those who produce 'secret and not generally used Scriptures'. But when heretics try to produce their doctrine from acknowledged Scriptures, then they are saying, 'Behold, he is in the inner chambers'. The Church alone, Origen goes on, does not add to nor subtract from the word and the meaning of Scripture. According to this passage, then, the Church has the right to decide what is genuine Scripture and what is not, but has no right to complement or to mutilate Scripture once she has decided that it is Scripture proper. The lately discovered *Conversation of Origen with Heracleides* seems to confirm this conclusion clearly. At one point in this *Conversation* (text, p. 144), Origen is recorded as saying, εἴ τι περὶ κανόνος λείπει, ὑπομνήσατε· ἔτι λοιπὸν εἰς τὴν γραφὴν ἐροῦμεν. Scherer interprets this: 'If any doubtful point concerning the rule of faith remains, mention it; we shall continue to give a commentary on Scripture'; and he explains in a footnote (n. 1, p. 144 of text) that Origen intends to deal with difficulties about points in the rule of faith while commenting on Scripture. The *Conversation* then goes on to record (text, p. 144) a question put by one Dionysius: εἰ ἡ ψυχὴ τὸ αἷμα; This seems to make it clear both that the κανών was considered provable by Scripture and had independent authority, and that it was not a stereotyped formula or embryonic creed, because the question of the soul's relation to the blood could not possibly be included in such a formula.

Generally, then, our investigation hitherto has tended to suggest that Origen did regard the Church's rule of faith as separate from Scripture, but not entirely dissociated from it. The Church's rule of faith was in fact the Church's handling and interpretation of Scripture, and its content must therefore be identical with and derive its support

[1] XVII. 35.
[2] Part II, 46 and 47; 46 has already been referred to above, p. 92.

from Scripture. But because the rule of faith is what the Church teaches and preaches, and because it derives in unbroken continuity from what the Church always has taught and preached from the very beginning, it cannot be precisely the same as the written books of the Bible, though it is certainly not thought to constitute a separate source of doctrine from Scripture. The rule of faith is the Church's tradition as the Church teaches it, preaches it, and hands it on to her faithful children. The Scriptures are the same tradition of the Church as it is written down to be for all Christians 'the certainty of those things wherein they are instructed', and the source of the Church's teaching and preaching. I am struck with the aptness of Mondésert's simile in which Scripture is the shepherd and what he calls tradition, but I would call the rule of faith, is the flock.[1] It is worth noting, incidentally, how very far Origen is from imitating Clement of Alexandria in his identification of the rule of faith with his esoteric tradition.

But before we begin to consider how far this rule of faith can be identified or connected with a creed in Origen's thought, there are two important points to be noted which throw some light on Origen's conception of the rule of faith. The first point is that Origen consistently claims that the allegorization of Scripture is the Church's special way of interpreting the Bible, handed down to her by the apostles. In his *Homilies on Genesis* he says: 'The Church of God therefore interprets references to births in this way, and in this way understands mention of procreations, upholds in this way the activities of the patriarchs by a respectable and decent interpretation, in this way refuses to stain the words of the Holy Spirit with futile and Jewish legends, but regards them as full of decency and full of virtue and practical value. Otherwise, what sort of profit shall we derive from reading that so great a patriarch as Abraham not only lied to King Abimelech but also betrayed the honour of his wife?'[2] Or again, in the *Homilies on Leviticus*[3] he says: 'Are we to imagine that Almighty God who was giving answers to Moses from heaven made regulations about an oven, a frying-pan, and a baking-pan?... But the children of the Church have not so learnt Christ, nor have they been so instructed in him by the

---

[1] See above, p. 38.

[2] VI. iii. I read '*partus*' in this passage for Migne's impossible '*paratus*'.

[3] V. viii. Origen is here referring to Leviticus 7.8f. There is no particular reason to suspect Rufinus' translation here.

apostles.... Nay, let us rather see by means of that spiritual interpretation which the Spirit gives to the Church....' Again, on the 'stations' of the children of Israel in the wilderness recorded in Numbers 33, he says:[1] 'And who would dare to say that the things which are written through the Word of God have no profit and can give no wholesome lesson, but simply relate the historical event which then became part of the past but now does not concern us at all if it is related? This is an irreligious opinion and one strange to the catholic faith, and belongs to that school alone who deny that the God of the law and the God of the gospel is the single wise Father of our Lord Jesus Christ.'

This association of allegorizing with the apostles and the churchman is pressed even closer elsewhere. In the *Homilies on Luke*[2] Origen says that heretics may try to allegorize the New Testament; but how inconsistent they are to allegorize the New, but not the Old. He himself, as a churchman ('*ecclesiasticus*'), which is synonymous with Christian, is more consistent. He freely attributes his own practice of allegorizing to S. Paul, who, he says,[3] delivered to the Gentile church the method of interpreting the Old Testament so as to apply it to Christ. In his *Homilies on Leviticus*[4] he suggests that Paul made an addition to the Old Testament narrative in his version of it because 'he had learnt that this was the meaning of the Lawmaker by the knowledge of truest doctrine that was handed down to him' (i.e. by allegory). Later in the same passage he says: '*Mihi autem, sicut Deo et Domino nostro Jesu Christo, ita et apostolis eius adhaerere bonum est, et ex divinis Scripturis secundum ipsorum traditionem intelligentiam capere.*' The same view is taken in the *Homilies on Joshua*:[5] 'Had not, I think, those physical conflicts constituted the type of spiritual conflicts, the books of the Jewish histories would never have been handed down by the apostles as worthy to be read in the churches by the disciples of Christ, who came to teach peace.' We have seen[6] how Origen links the spiritual understanding of Scripture with τοῦ κανόνος τῆς Ἰησοῦ Χριστοῦ κατὰ

---

[1] *Hom. on Numbers* XXVII. ii.   [2] XVI, on Luke 2. 34.

[3] *Hom. on Exodus* v. i. Cf. later in the same passage, '*qualem tradiderit de his Paulus apostolus intelligentiae regulam*', and '*videtis quantum differat ab historica lectione*' [he is referring to 1 Cor. 10. 1–4] '*Pauli traditio*'; and he goes on to say that we must follow this rule of interpretation given us by Paul, lest '*rursus ad iudaicas fabulas convertamur*'.

[4] VII. iv. He is again referring to the beginning of 1 Cor. 10.

[5] XV. i.   [6] See above, p. 92.

διαδοχὴν τῶν ἀποστόλων οὐρανίου ἐκκλησίας in the Fourth Book of *Concerning First Principles*. We can turn to his *Homilies on Psalms*[1] and find him claiming that even if the heretics do understand the Scriptures allegorically, '*in ipso autem spiritali intellectu apostolicae non teneant regulam veritatis*'. The *Conversation of Origen with Heracleides* brings out vividly both Origen's conviction that allegorization was the Church's way of interpreting Scripture, and also his uneasy consciousness that he was here on disputed ground. At one point (text, pp. 148–154) he makes a very long exordium before he reaches his real subject, showing great reluctance to speak. He even says, Ἀγωνιῶ καὶ εἰπεῖν, ἀγωνιῶ καὶ μὴ εἰπεῖν (p. 152); he fears that he may be misunderstood by his crasser hearers, because he is about to speak a λόγον μυστικόν (p. 152). This interpretation can only be understood, he adds, διὰ τοῦ φρονεῖν τὰ ἐκκλησιαστικά, διὰ τοῦ βιοῦν ἐκκλησιαστικῶς (p. 154). It is obvious that Origen expects opposition to his allegorization (see Scherer's remarks, p. 72 of Introduction, and p. 151, n. 3, of text).

That the Alexandrine Fathers[2] regarded allegorization as part of the Church's rule of faith and as handed down from the apostles has been noted by several scholars. Bigg[3] says that allegorism 'was regarded by all as one of the articles of the Ecclesiastical Canon or Tradition'. He thinks that they conceived of this tradition of allegorizing as delivered by a succession, not of bishops, but of teachers. Prat seems quite happy about this fact. 'Origen', he says,[4] 'places in the number of the Church's fundamental dogmas the existence of a mystical sense, hidden under the letter of Scripture. In this he is in agreement with the apostles and all the Christian tradition.' We have already seen how Bouyer[5] uses this fact in his argument for the existence in Origen's belief of a tradition of doctrine independent of Scripture, and even calls it 'the commonest view of tradition as such in all Christian antiquity'.

But this is in reality a conclusion to which we should not so comfortably assent. In the first place, though Origen attributes allegorism to

---

[1] *Homily* IV *on Psalm 37. 1* (*P.G.* XII, 1351).

[2] For Clement's agreement on this point, see above, p. 63 (especially n. 7).

[3] For Bigg's discussion of the whole subject, see his *Christian Platonists*, pp. 85–7.

[4] *Origène, le Théologien et l'Exégète*, p. 125.

[5] See above, p. 36.

the rule of faith of the Church, it is clear that he also supported this attribution by reference to Scripture, as his quotations of S. Paul show. And the fact that this allegorism was included in the list of articles of his esoteric doctrine[1] makes this point all the surer. In the second place, can we with easy minds agree that allegorism really is an original article of the Church's tradition, if we are to accept Origen's version of allegorism? Are we to assent to his tortuous twistings of meaning, his gross violations of the original intention of the Biblical text, his exegetical methods which may have some faint parallel in the New Testament writers' treatment of the Old Testament, but which derive much more obviously from non-Hebraic and non-Biblical sources, such as Clement of Alexandria, the *Epistle of Barnabas*, Philo, and that list of pagan allegorists which de Faye has so laboriously compiled for us? This is indeed a desperate expedient, and few modern writers would resort to it, not even, I imagine, Prat and Bouyer. But if we agree (as I think we must) that in respect to allegorizing, Origen did as he probably did with all his esoteric doctrines, that is, he himself taught and believed them, and assumed that Christ and his apostles taught and believed them, but could not prove, and never claimed that he could prove, that they had been taught and believed continuously from the apostles' day to his own independently of the Bible, then Origen's contention that allegorism was an original article of the Church's rule of faith becomes worthless. It becomes about as likely as Clement's claim to possess esoteric doctrine derived from Christ and his apostles independent of the Bible. No doubt the Church always had up to Origen's day (and indeed has regularly since then also) interpreted the Old Testament in a special sense as applying to and predicting the coming of Christ. This much is clear enough from the New Testament alone. And no doubt this interpretation did distinguish the Church's from the Jewish view of the Old Testament and that of some heretical sects. Indeed, the whole original Christian tradition demands that the Church should do precisely this. But this is not to say that we can attribute to the Church a fund of doctrine interpretative of the Bible (or of the original oral tradition which in fact crystallized out into the Bible), and independent of it, which is in fact what Bouyer and Prat are anxious to do. If we try to appeal to Origen for support in such a theory, our theory will break down for lack of any satisfactory

[1] See above, p. 82.

foundation. Two quotations from a recent book on Irenaeus put the matter in its true light:[1] 'Plainly, allegoristic exegesis is almost purely subjective. He who uses it can find in the Holy Book anything he has already in mind, so that every conceivable system of doctrine may substantiated from Scripture. Past and present Christian history clearly shows this. The acid test of the unhistorical and unscientific nature of this method is that a given writer can be found to interpret one and the same text in opposite senses in different parts of his work.' 'Historical ignorance forced the Catholic Christian into the same fast-and-loose game as the heretic, well aware though he was of the perils of religious subjectivity. If the resultant controversial frustration was to be avoided there had to be provided a set of rules for the game. Here was the motive behind the retreat to the authority of the Church. The Church roundly asserted that certain historical and certain allegorical inter-pretations, and they alone, were legitimate. For sanction in her judge-ment she appealed to her numbers, her manifest good character, her continuity in different times, and her unanimity in different places.'

The other point which is likely to throw some light on Origen's view of the rule of faith is that on several occasions he unmistakably overrides the rule of faith and prefers instead of it his own esoteric teaching. This will become clear if we make a brief examination of his use of the term ὁ ἐκκλησιαστικός. By ὁ ἐκκλησιαστικός Origen means the average churchman truly representing the mind of the Church, and he figures occasionally in Origen's writings. The significant thing is that ὁ ἐκκλησιαστικός is sometimes the average churchman who believes and thinks as the Church believes and thinks, but on other occasions the average churchman who had better leave the interpretation of Scripture to the professors. In the *Commentary on John*[2] there is quite a long discussion conducted on the question of how exactly John the Baptist was Elijah, between ὁ ἐκκλησιαστικός and somebody whom Origen calls ὁ πρότερος, and he concludes on the whole on the side of ὁ ἐκκλησιαστικός. We have seen[3] how, in his *Homilies on Luke*, he declares that '*ecclesiasticus*' is synonymous with Christian, and how such a person alone knows how to use allegorism. On the other hand, in a later chapter of the *Commentary on John*,[4] in discussing the inter-pretation of John 4. 35 ('Say not ye, There are yet four months, and

---

[1] J. Lawson, *The Biblical Theology of Saint Irenaeus*, pp. 84, 95.
[2] VI. 10–14.   [3] See above, p. 102.   [4] XIII. 44.

then cometh the harvest? behold, I say unto you, Lift up your eyes, and look on the fields, that they are white already unto harvest'), Origen gives the view (among others) of ὁ ἐκκλησιαστικός, and rejects it. In a *Fragment on Exodus*[1] there is a discussion of the meaning of the words, 'a jealous God, visiting the iniquities of the fathers upon the children' (Exodus 20. 5). This passage, he says, has disturbed everyone. Some attack the God who made these laws; others think that God really does visit sins in this way. As for ὁ ἐκκλησιαστικός, he will not take the passage literally, like the Jews, nor divide God, like the heretics, but will admit that it is rightly written, but that he does not know the meaning of what is written. He had better pray for guidance and listen to Origen.

Several other passages which do not directly mention ὁ ἐκκλησι-αστικός bear out the point that Origen is quite capable of setting aside the Church's view or the Church's rule of faith. 'Many people', he says in his *Commentaries on the Psalms*,[2] 'attempt to interpret the Scriptures, both from among churchpeople and from among those outside the church, heretics and Jews, or even Samaritans, but they do not all speak soundly. The man who has a gift for this from God is rare.' In his *Against Celsus*[3] he replies to Celsus' objection to what he calls the resurrection of the flesh by distinguishing between 'that which is described as the resurrection of the flesh' and 'the resurrection as understood more lucidly by the better-informed', and by pointing out that Scripture does not compel us to believe in the resurrection of the flesh, referring to 1 Corinthians 15. 35–8. A little later he claims that 'Behold, I tell you a mystery' (1 Corinthians 15. 51) means that the better-informed can understand the resurrection as Origen explains it (and he calls this explanation ἀπόρρητόν τι καὶ μυστικόν), whereas the other, simpler people will continue believing in the resurrection of the flesh. We should compare this passage with one in the *Commentary on Matthew*[4] where Origen is concerned to establish that the Christian can believe in the resurrection without believing in the resurrection of the flesh, which he calls τὴν ἐν τῇ ἐκκλησίᾳ πεπιστευμένην ἀνάστασιν νεκρῶν. It becomes obvious then that on this point at least, the formulation of the belief in the resurrection of the body or of the flesh,

---

[1] *P.G.* XII, 289.   [2] *P.G.* XII, 1601, on Ps. 119. 85.
[3] v. xviii, xix.
[4] XVII. 29. It is significant that the Latin translation omits this passage.

Origen held that the Church's rule of faith should be transcended and modified by the intellectual Christian.[1] Earlier in the same *Commentary on Matthew*[2] we find this sentence: 'And even that which is thought to be ecclesiastical teaching (ἐκκλησιαστικὴ διδασκαλία), if it becomes servile with the intention of flattering, or as an excuse for greed, or when someone is seeking glory from men on account of his teaching, does not carry any weight with those who are placed by God in the Church as first apostles, then prophets, and thirdly teachers.' In his *Commentary on John*[3] he interprets the 'mountain' in John 4. 21 ('neither in this mountain, nor in Jerusalem, shall ye worship the Father') as the pretended knowledge of the heretics, and 'Jerusalem' as 'the rule of faith (κανών) prevalent among the majority of the Church', which can be transcended by the man who is τέλειος and ἅγιος.[4]

There can, then, be no doubt whatever that Origen did not imitate Clement of Alexandria in identifying his esoteric teaching with the rule of faith of the Church. Though he claimed that both had certain things in common (for instance, the use of allegorism), he kept the two quite distinct in his mind. Indeed, the conclusion that by 'the rule of faith' and all similar expressions he meant simply the Church's interpretation of Scripture, as it appeared in the teaching and preaching of the Church of his day, is confirmed by this willingness of his occasionally to set aside this rule of faith. Had he meant by the rule of faith some source of original doctrine independent of Scripture, he would never have overruled it, just as he never consciously overruled Scripture.

This tendency on the part of Origen has been noted by some writers. '*Cette orthodoxie ecclésiastique à laquelle Origène tient si fortement*', says Lebreton,[5] '*n'est pas pour lui le dernier mot de la foi*'; and he quotes several instances of this tendency. And Cadiou recognizes how loosely Origen held to the rule of faith when he says:[6] '*Rarement il commençait*

---

[1] A long fragment from the *Commentary on 1 Corinthians* defends against the heretics the Church's belief (ἐκκλησιαστικὴν πίστιν) in a resurrection; it probably comes (as Jenkins, the editor of the passage, suggests) from the early work *On the Resurrection*. It does not, however, affect the discussion here on Origen's belief in the resurrection *of the flesh*. See *J.T.S.* x, p. 45, LXXXIV.

[2] XI. 15.   [3] XIII. 16.

[4] This passage has already been referred to on p. 91. Lebreton ('Les Degrés de la Connaissance', p. 271) quotes this passage but does not draw out its significance.

[5] 'Le Désaccord de la Foi', tom. 19, p. 502.

[6] *La Jeunesse d'Origène*, p. 76.

par établir la foi commune, l'unanimité des Églises, leur droit d'interpréter la Bible. Il voulait rejoindre la croyance plutôt que s'appuyer sur elle.'

Tollinton[1] has some interesting observations too upon the Alexandrian Fathers' conception of the authority which interprets Scripture. Later ages, he says, usually confined the interpretation to official authority, and in the second century this held in some Churches: 'Even to Irenaeus the succession of the episcopate was valuable principally as a guarantee of sound doctrine. But Alexandria stood for a different principle, for the place of the scholar, the doctor, the lecture-room, in determining Christian truth.' Pantaenus, Tollinton thinks, was probably a layman. Later the Church was compelled by the need for dealing with heretics and by various other pressures to confine the teaching office to bishops. 'So the scholar surrendered his rights to the bishop, and when the bishop was also a scholar, all went well. But when he was not, the surrender, though inevitable, had its dangerous consequences.' Cadiou, in his *Jeunesse d'Origène*,[2] discusses the same question. He first points out that in Origen's day '*le don de prophétie ne peut s'exercer que d'une manière conforme aux institutions religieuses et sous la direction de l'autorité*'. This may well be true, because Origen, intellectual as he was, had no particular interest in the gift of prophecy in the contemporary Church.[3] But Cadiou should find more satisfactory authority to quote than the Latin translation of the *Commentary on Matthew*, and this does not characterize all Origen's attitude to authority. We may indeed agree with Cadiou that the view of K. Mueller, which he quotes, is exaggerated—to the effect that Origen did not allow that bishops had any control over Christian doctrine, and permitted them only a purely external authority over Christian teachers. But Cadiou himself exaggerates in the opposite direction. Where his speculations were concerned, Origen acknowledged no ecclesiastical control or authority, and the very fact that he did at a critical moment in his career move from Alexandria to Caesarea confirms this conclusion. Cadiou himself later acknowledges that Origen does seem to hold the view that the bishop's functions are limited by his moral character. It is difficult to draw any other conclusion from such passages as *Commentary on Matthew* XX. 14, where Origen says that

---

[1] *Clement of Alexandria*, Vol. II, pp. 228–9. [2] Pages 382 n., 383, 387.

[3] See a passage in the *Comm. on Matthew* (*P.G.* XIII, 1669), '*qui ecclesiastice docent verbum prophetae sunt Christi*'.

those who rely on the text Matthew 16. 19, τὸν τόπον τῆς ἐπισκοπῆς ἐκδικοῦντες, should know that authority to bind and loose depends upon moral and religious achievement in confessing Peter's confession, and not on any authority conferred by the episcopal office.[1] Daniélou contents himself with remarking[2] upon this passage that Origen was an idealist in his view of ecclesiastical discipline; but with regard to a similar passage in *Concerning Prayer* xxviii, where Origen says plainly that nobody, certainly not priests, can absolve for such sins as idolatry, adultery, and fornication, he suggests that the words only apply to sins '*pour lesquels il ne suffit pas d'une absolution immédiate*'—a suggestion for which there is no particular evidence.[3]

If we are to attempt to summarize Origen's conception of the Church's rule of faith, we must first clear away some misconceptions of it which are to be found in the minds of certain modern scholars. Molland, for instance, is quite justified in quoting Kattenbusch[4] to the effect that the apostolic and ecclesiastical tradition consists for Origen in 'the body of sacred books handed down from the apostles, and in a body of doctrines which can be easily proved from these writings'. But when he claims[5] that to Origen there is not the slightest difference between 'biblical doctrine' and 'ecclesiastical doctrine', he is not justified by the facts which we have set out. Similarly, when we find Charles Williams in his very stimulating and original but occasionally inaccurate book, *The Descent of the Dove*,[6] making the following statement, we must emphatically dissent from him: 'Origen, like all intelligent readers then as now, realized that he needed a check upon

---

[1] See Daniélou, pp. 56, 57, 63; and Latko, *Origen's Concept of Penance*, Chapter IV (pp. 118–30), though I do not find his solution convincing. Cf. Ignatius, *Letter to Polycarp* I. 2 (ed. Kirsopp Lake, *The Apostolic Fathers*, Harvard University Press, 1945, Vol. I, p. 268): ἐκδίκει σου τὸν τόπον.

[2] *Origène*, p. 83.

[3] Ibid. pp. 81–2. For a very full discussion of this passage, see Latko, Chapter VI (pp. 141–55). See also *Commentaires Inédits des Psaumes*, p. 103 (CXVII, 9 a), where Origen, commenting on the phrase, 'It is better to trust in the Lord', refers to Micah 7. 5, 'Trust ye not in a friend, put ye not confidence in a guide' (LXX ἐπὶ ἡγουμένοις), and adds οὐδὲ ἐπὶ ἐπισκόποις οὖν ἐλπιστέον. A similar remark is found on p. 118 (CXVIII, 161 a), where his comment on 'Princes have persecuted me without a cause' runs: καὶ ὑπὸ τῶν ἀρχόντων τῆς ἐκκλησίας ἐστὶν ὅτε εἰκῇ τις καὶ δωρεὰν διώκεται. Cf. p. 130 (CXLI, 5 d).

[4] Molland, p. 92. He quotes Kattenbusch, *Das apostolische Symbol*, Vol. II, p. 137.   [5] Molland, p. 93.   [6] Page 38.

his own brain, and he found it, where all Christians have found it, in the universal decisions of the Church. This authority he recognized; this relationship he desired.' Our confidence in the accuracy of this statement is not increased when to support it he gives a quotation from Clement of Alexandria. Again the Migne editor[1] says that Origen '*Scripturarum auctoritati auctoritatem ecclesiasticae traditionis adiungit*', a way of describing Origen's handling of the Church's rule of faith which needs considerable modification. Prat's statement,[2] too, of Origen's definition of the faith, '*C'est la prédication ecclésiastique, c'est-à-dire le magistère vivant et infaillible de l'Église qui règle et délimite l'objet de la foi*', is quite inaccurate in view of the facts which we have set out. For similar reasons we must reject courteously but firmly Bardy's disingenuous suggestion that when about the year 212 Origen visited Rome, '*sans nul doute s'y informe-t-il surtout de la tradition apostolique, de la succession des évêques, de la règle de foi*'.[3] The only facts of which we can be sure concerning Origen's connection with Rome are that when he visited there he listened to a teacher who was later an anti-Pope, and that in mentioning the Church's rule of faith in his writings, he never makes any mention whatever of the see of Rome, or even of S. Peter. Even Denis is seriously overstating the case when he says, '*Origène se serait arrêté dès le premier pas s'il avait soupçonné qu'il sortit de la droite voie de la tradition*', and when he later speaks of '*sa soumission absolue à la tradition ecclésiastique*'.[4] Nor can we quite agree with von Balthasar's verdict,[5] '*Unité de la Parole dont l'unique Église catholique est la gardienne. C'est à elle qu'Origène adhère de toutes ses forces, d'après elle il veut être nommé,[6] c'est sa tradition qu'il veut com-*

---

[1] Preface to Vol. XII of *P.G.* The editor, however, adds that '*perraro ad Scripturae traditionisque auctoritatem recurrit, idque tantum cum generatim sensus allegorici veritas est constituenda*'. In other respects this is a good essay on Origen's interpretation of Scripture, and one worth reading.

[2] Quoted already on p. 46, n. 2.

[3] 'La Règle de Foi d'Origène', p. 167. How is it that when theologians of all ecclesiastical complexions want to make a particularly ill-supported statement, they introduce it with the word 'doubtless'?

[4] Denis, pp. 1–2.   [5] 'Le Mystérion d'Origène', p. 547.

[6] Citing *Hom. on Luke* XVI, '*Ego autem qui opto esse ecclesiasticus et non ab haeresiarcha aliquo nuncupari*', etc., and *Hom. on Leviticus* VII. 4, '*Mihi autem, sicut Deo et Domino nostro Jesu Christo, ita et apostolis eius adhaerere bonum est, et ex divinis Scripturis secundum ipsorum traditionem intelligentiam capere*'. I have already quoted this on p. 102.

prendre.' Origen professed to follow the Church's rule of faith as handed down from the apostles when he chose, but he could on other occasions encourage his disciples to ignore this rule. We must equally describe as an exaggeration the sentence of Daniélou:[1] '*Si lui-même a proposé des opinions qui ont plus tard été rejetées par le magistère, c'était, de sa part, en toute soumission à l'Église et à titre d'exercice.*' Origen on several occasions puts forward opinions which he knows perfectly well are not those of the Church, but this does not prevent his teaching them quite confidently. He did not want of course to abandon the Church's rule of faith, but he was perfectly willing to improve upon it.

The best and most useful discussion of Origen's conception of the rule of faith that I have encountered is G. Bardy's article, already quoted more than once.[2] After sketching the outlines of a Creed which he thinks he can recover from Origen's works, he says[3] that for Origen the words ἐκκλησιαστικός and εὐαγγελικός or ἀποστολικός are identical and interchangeable in their meaning. But of course to Origen the Church is the sole authoritative interpreter of Scripture to guard it against heresy. He admits[4] that '*il n'y a qu'une différence formelle entre la prédication de l'Église et celle des livres saints, l'une n'étant que le développement de l'autre*'. Then he quotes Kattenbusch[5] to the effect that the Church 'appears as the depositary of revealed truth; the Church's preaching is synonymous with true faith, and the Church's actual preaching is guaranteed in that it is the tradition of the apostles, inherited in a direct line. This theory is also clearly that of Irenaeus, as it is common to Irenaeus and to his Greek predecessors of the second century.' Finally, Bardy claims[6] that Origen knew a rule of faith inasmuch as he knew a symbol or creed, and that this was provided for him by the ecclesiastical tradition.

Though Bardy makes several important points in his essay, I join issue with him on certain aspects of the subject. Whether Origen betrays knowledge of a 'symbol' or not, he certainly did not refer to a creed when he referred to his rule of faith. He meant by this the

---

[1] *Origène*, p. 24.

[2] The earlier part of this essay has been dealt with on p. 94 above.

[3] 'La Règle de Foi d'Origène', p. 193.

[4] Ibid. p. 194.   [5] *Das apostolische Symbol*, Vol. II, p. 174.

[6] 'La Règle de Foi d'Origène', p. 195. Bardy's view is, however, as we have seen, that Origen did not call this 'rule of faith' a κανών. Origen's attitude to creeds is dealt with in the next chapter.

doctrine which the Church of his day was preaching, and he linked it very closely with the Bible. Apart from the 'symbol', Origen knows of no source of doctrine but the Bible, even of secret doctrine. The rule of faith is the Church preaching the Bible, and preaching it in continuity with the apostles. Again, Origen differs markedly both from Irenaeus and from Tertullian (and indeed, in a different fashion, from Clement of Alexandria) in never emphasizing the separateness of the rule of faith from, or its independence of, the Scriptures. He sometimes encourages his disciples to transcend the rule of faith, never to transcend the Scriptures. He never speaks of 'canonical' Scriptures or of a 'canon' of Scripture.[1] Indeed, for Origen to have possessed, as Clement imagined himself to possess, a secret tradition of doctrine independent of the Bible would have been much to his advantage, because of his theory of Reserve and esoteric teaching. Yet never does he profess to derive even advanced doctrines from anywhere but the Bible.

Von Balthasar, in the article to which I have already referred several times, 'Le Mystérion d'Origène', claims that in his use of the word μυστήριον Origen betrays his belief in a tradition of interpreting the whole Christian revelation, involving a harmony of the Old and New Testaments and a thoroughgoing allegorization of the Bible, and not merely that, but a life lived in this tradition of interpreting revelation. 'Ce n'est qu'en vivant dans une grande ἀνακεφαλαίωσις, le tradition totale du Christ, que nous serons hommes spirituels et vrais "gnostiques".'[2] We must accept the total allegorization of the whole Bible and give our allegiance to the whole movement from literal sense to Eternal Gospel, if we are to benefit from either. And from this interpretation of μυστήριον Bouyer at least draws support for his theory that Origen believed in a tradition of doctrine independent of the Bible but interpretative of it. But though Origen may well have taught that only the Church can acquire this 'total view' of the whole Christian revelation which alone expresses the will of Christ—and in this point lies the chief point of von Balthasar's article—there is no justification for saying that this guarantees to the Church a fund of doctrine independent of the Bible and interpretative of it. The evidence hitherto

---

[1] This is where Kattenbusch, whose account of Origen on the subject is otherwise illuminating, seems to have been misled.

[2] 'Le Mystérion d'Origène', p. 561.

produced has not established that Origen even thought of the Church as interpreting Scripture with any other advantages than the guidance of the Holy Ghost and common sense. And no treatment of the word μυστήριον in Origen will be of use in establishing any other conclusion.[1]

In brief, then, we may say that when Origen spoke of the rule of faith of the Church, he meant the Christian faith as it was preached and taught by the Church of his day, and as it had been preached and taught ever since the time of the apostles. He thought of this rule of faith in contrast to the versions of the Christian faith, often professing to be based on the Bible, taught by the heretics, and he even spoke of it as consisting of articles (δόγματα). He did not identify it with the Creed of the Church of his day, but he called it κανών or κήρυγμα or λόγος or γνώμη or διδασκαλία or βούλημα or κατήχησις or πρόθεσις, and he usually accompanied these words with the adjective ἐκκλησιαστικός. The content of this rule of faith was identical with that of the Bible, and indeed was proved and demonstrated from the Bible, but the rule is not identified with the Bible. The Church by preaching this rule of faith authorized and guaranteed the Bible as the source of tradition belonging to her, and not to either heretics or Jews, but she thereby was bound to the Bible, and had no authority either to add to or subtract from it. On occasion Origen is ready to encourage his pupils to ignore or overrule or transcend this rule of faith in the interests of his esoteric teaching, but he never encourages them to ignore or overrule the Bible. His rule of faith therefore cannot be identified with his esoteric teaching, as Clement's can with his.

[1] Μυστήριον for Origen really means 'dispensation', not unlike οἰκονομία. See a fragment on Ps. 78. 15 (*P.G.* XVII, 144), which says that Christ τὸ πικρὸν τῆς Μερρᾶς, τοῦ κολαστοῦ νόμου, μετέβαλεν εἰς γλυκύτητα τῇ παραδοχῇ τοῦ ξύλου τοῦ σταυροῦ, καὶ τοῦ ἐπ' αὐτοῦ μυστηρίου. For 'mystery' Origen uses ἀπόρρητον.

CHAPTER VII

THE RELATION OF RULE OF FAITH
TO CREED IN ORIGEN

W E must not leave our exploration of Origen's attitude to his secret tradition and to the rule of faith until we have dealt more fully with a subject to which we have already referred several times, namely the place of a Creed in his doctrine of tradition. We have already given some reasons for thinking that Origen did not identify either the rule of faith or his secret tradition with a contemporary Creed. But the question must be more fully examined. In the first place, there is considerable evidence that in the early Church the Creed was often treated very much as a secret tradition. Badcock[1] has an interesting note on the Creed as a *disciplina arcani*. It used to be employed, he tells us, as a watchword of orthodoxy or reliability between Christians in a time of heresy or persecution. Hence it was not often written down and was to some extent secret. Bethune-Baker[2] notes this same secrecy about Creeds, quoting Tertullian (*Apology* 7), '*omnibus mysteriis silentii fides adhibetur*', and producing some further evidence from Cyprian. But it should be noted that this secrecy, as described by Badcock and Bethune-Baker, arises from a different motive from that of Clement's and Origen's esoteric tradition. The Creed is kept secret as a precaution against betraying important matters to outsiders, heretics or pagans or direct enemies of the faith. The Alexandrian Fathers keep their doctrine secret to prevent its upsetting and bewildering the simpler sort of believing Christians. In one passage only (as has already been noticed)[3] does Origen seem to suggest that his secret teaching can be identified with a Creed, apparently equating 'the teaching given privately by Jesus to his true disciples' with the Creed and the admission to the sacraments of Baptism and Holy Communion imparted to the fully qualified catechumens. But this is, as far as I can discover, a solitary example. Kelly, indeed (*Early Christian Creeds*, pp. 87, 168–70), is

[1] *History of the Creeds*, pp. 106–7.
[2] *Introduction to the Early History of Christian Doctrine*, p. 35.
[3] On p. 78. The passage is *Against Celsus* III. lx.

confident that this *disciplina arcani* was not widely in force before the middle of the third century.

It is *a priori* unlikely that the Alexandrian Fathers should place Creeds very prominently in their doctrine of tradition, because of the place which speculation occupies in this doctrine. Lebreton has a noteworthy observation upon this point: 'It is certain', he says,[1] 'that among the Alexandrian masters the chief activity of theology was no longer directed towards the same subjects as was the common and popular faith, such as the baptismal Creed sets out: the point of departure is the same; God the Father, Jesus Christ, the Holy Spirit: but it pays little attention to the other articles of the Creed, the Church, the forgiveness of sins, the resurrection of the flesh, and substitutes for them dogmas which the Creed never mentions, concerning the nature and origin of the soul, free will and human responsibility. Owing to this fact, Christianity, which was above all a religious faith, sometimes takes on the appearance of a metaphysical doctrine.' And later[2] he points out the results of this state of affairs. The simple believers knew only Jesus Christ, and him crucified. But 'the scholars saw in the same mystery the solution of all the riddles of the world.... *Attirés sur le terrain des philosophes, les théologiens chrétiens subissent leur influence.*'

These observations are wise ones, and might serve as a salutary warning to us as we embark on the delicate task of detecting traces of Creeds in Origen's writings. We shall not, for instance, allow ourselves to make such easy generalizations as that of Denis, when he identifies[3] Origen's κήρυγμα ἐκκλησιαστικόν with '*le Credo de son temps*'. Badcock indeed, throughout his *History of the Creeds*, sees no direct connection between the rule of faith and the Creed in the Early Church (unlike Cullmann[4] he derives all Creeds from the baptismal Creed). But in fact by his account any given Creed must also have been a summary of the Church's rule of faith, that is, of the Church's preaching at the time the Creed originated. In a sense, Creeds as a class are the only survival of the rule of faith of the Church before the Scriptures of the New Testament were accepted as normative. And it is significant that neither Clement of Alexandria nor Origen provides us with a rule of faith which can be exactly equated with what we can reconstruct of the Church's normal rule of faith elsewhere.

[1] 'Le Désaccord de la Foi', tom. 20, p. 14.
[2] Ibid. p. 15.　　　[3] Denis, p. 55.　　　[4] See above, p. 39, n. 3.

There certainly are a number of passages in Origen where we can find lists of articles of Christian teaching. A most interesting one occurs in Origen's Preface to the *Concerning First Principles*.[1] This is a list of things which Christ and the apostles preached as necessary (in contrast, probably, to the esoteric teaching). These are:

One God, the Creator, God of the Old Testament.

Jesus Christ, Son of God, Who was incarnate, Who was born of a Virgin Birth, Who suffered, died, rose again, and is now glorified.

The Holy Spirit, who inspired the men of the Old Testament and the New Testament.

The Future Life and the Resurrection of the Dead.

Free will and the struggle against sin (but the manner of the soul's generation is not stated).

The existence of the devil and his angels (but how the devil became the devil is not clearly stated).

The creatureliness and final destruction of the world.

That the Holy Scriptures are inspired by the Holy Spirit and have two meanings, the second only intelligible to those who have wisdom and knowledge from the Holy Spirit; and that there is 'a spiritual law'.

The existence of angels (but their creation, and other details, are not in the κήρυγμα;[2] and whether the heavenly bodies have rational souls or not is not stated).

Later Origen says that these truths must be worked into a system ('*seriem quamdam et corpus*'), 'either by the evidence to be found in the sacred Scriptures, or by that to be discovered by the investigation of the logical consequences of the Scriptures and adherence to accuracy'.[3]

A comment on this list by Pamphilus, who reproduced it in the First Book of his *Apology for Origen*, is interesting. These articles, he tells

---

[1] Sections 4–10.   [2] A Greek fragment survives here.

[3] Section 10. I am now in a position to show that the words '*recti tenore*' (see above, pp. 51, 97) could not possibly mean 'by the rule of faith', because this list is, in all probability, Origen's version of the rule of faith itself. One sentence from Rufinus' *Liber de Adulteratione Librorum Origenis* (*P.G.* XVII, 626) clinches finally the proof of this point. He says that the fact that people such as Origen would never write anything inconsistent with the Church's rule of faith can be demonstrated, not only from Origen's own statements, but '*solo argumento ex rerum consequentia ac recti tenore*'.

us,[1] Origen in his work next proceeded to defend and discuss, '*omnibus adhibitis probamentis ex Scripturis sanctis manifestius et constantius asserens*', but for the things not stated in the Church's preaching relying on his own speculations, and, in setting forth all truth belief in which is obligatory on Christians, allowing only that which does not contradict '*apostolicis et ecclesiasticis dogmatibus*'. It is indeed obvious that this list cannot strictly be described as based on a Creed. Koetschau[2] has suggested that Origen is here deliberately calling attention to the points upon which he felt himself free to speculate. Bardy[3] allows that this list cannot be called more than '*la pensée personelle d'Origène*', and observes striking omissions and additions when he compares it with any Creed contemporary with Origen. For omissions we may instance the strange absence of reference to the Church, and for additions the mention of free will, of the existence of the devil, and of angels.[4] Cadiou believes that this passage does not quote verbally any rule of faith: '*L'expression est variable, personelle, adaptée à l'intention immédiate*', and it is full of philosophical explanations and digressions. And he notes how the authority of the Bible is throughout the work invoked to confirm the teaching and theology which Origen sets forth in it.[5]

Later in the same work[6] we find another list of doctrines. These Origen describes as the first intentions of the Holy Spirit when he introduced allegory into the Bible. He wanted to impart knowledge concerning τῶν ἀπορρήτων μυστηρίων, τῶν κατὰ τοὺς ἀνθρώπους πραγμάτων, that is to say, concerning the salvation of souls, how they need God's help, and about God and his only-begotten Son, and about

---

[1] *P.G.* xvii, 552. Cf. xvii, 605, where Pamphilus, contending that there is no official doctrine of the Church on the origin of the soul, mentions one theory, and objects to it, among other things, that no support for it can be found in Scripture. Undoubtedly he thought of the Church's rule of faith as deriving its authority and support from Scripture, and he (rightly) assumed that Origen took the same view.   [2] Introd. to *G.C.S.*, Origen v, p. cxxxviii.

[3] 'La Règle de Foi d'Origène', p. 189.

[4] There are some parallels to the mention of angels, but only in the context of Christ's Exaltation and Lordship, and not as an article by themselves or in association with devils or heavenly bodies (see Cullmann, *The Earliest Christian Confessions*, p. 60). These are 1 Timothy 3. 16, ὤφθη ἀγγέλοις; *Epistle of Polycarp* 2. 1, ᾧ ὑπετάγη τὰ πάντα ἐπουράνια καὶ ἐπίγεια, ᾧ πᾶσα πνοὴ λατρεύει; and Ignatius, *Trallians* 9. 1, βλεπόντων τῶν ἐπουρανίων καὶ ἐπιγείων καὶ ὑποχθονίων.

[5] *La Jeunesse d'Origène*, pp. 270, 272.   [6] *Con. First P.* iv. 2. 7.

several points of Christology; and as a consequence of these, know-ledge about angels, fallen and unfallen, must be included in 'the principles of the divine teaching', and about the differences of souls, the origin and nature of the world, and the origin and extent of evil. We have already shown that this can only be a list of the doctrines of Origen's secret teaching, and that Prestige's view cannot be upheld that this is an example of the Creed of Origen's day.[1] It can hardly even be the rule of faith or the preaching of the contemporary Church, because Origen refers to it as ἀπόρρητα μυστήρια, by which he cer-tainly means his esoteric teaching, and because several of the points here mentioned, such as the differences of souls and the origin and nature of the world, cannot have figured prominently (if they appeared at all) in the preaching of the Church of his day. We shall not, I think, be far wrong if we describe the former list as Origen's version of the rule of faith which the Church of his day, as far as he knew it, preached, and the second as the points of his esoteric teaching, which were not necessarily preached or taught by anyone except Origen and his teachers and his disciples. It is no hindrance to this view that the first list contains several unusual articles which have an Alexandrian savour about them, because it is very likely that something as fluid as the Church's rule of faith should vary in different parts of the Church, and in Alexandria should acquire some local variations. I do not know any reason to think that the rule of faith (as contrasted with the Creed) necessarily even consisted of a series of articles strictly so called, though different teachers may have articulated it in this fashion from time to time.[2]

Caspari in his article which we have already referred to more than once[3] points out that further light is thrown on the definition of τὰ μέγιστα in Clement of Alexandria when we compare what Origen has to say on the same subject. In his *Concerning First Principles*, a little earlier than the passages we have just been quoting,[4] he defines belief in God, in Jesus Christ, and in the Holy Spirit as belief '*in magnis et maximis*', as contrasted with '*in parvis et minimis*'. Again, in the *Commentary on John* XXXII. 3, Origen says that not to believe that there

---

[1] Though this διδασκαλία is very like what Prestige defines as διδασκαλία.

[2] As indeed Origen sometimes appears ready to do (see pp. 97–8).

[3] 'Hat die alexandrinische Kirche', p. 358. For τὰ μέγιστα in Clement, see above, p. 65.   [4] Book I, Preface, 2.

is one God of law and gospel, who created all things, would be to be lacking in τῷ μεγίστῳ τῆς πίστεως κεφαλαίῳ. Similarly in the *Commentary on Matthew*, Pt. II, 33, he speaks of '*publicis quidem et manifestis capitulis*', that is, one God of law and gospel; Jesus Christ, the firstborn of all creatures, who came at the end of the age to fulfil prophecy and took on himself truly human flesh and was born of a Virgin, and was crucified and rose from the dead and deified the nature which he had assumed; the Holy Spirit, who was in the patriarchs and prophets and was given to the apostles; the resurrection of the dead. The passage ends '*sicut evangelium docet certissime credunt et omnia quaecumque feruntur in ecclesiis*'. It is very obvious that these passages are based on a Creed. Caspari also calls attention to some passages where Origen seems to refer to a Creed repeated at baptism.[1] There is, for instance, *Homilies on Exodus* VIII. 4, where he uses the words 'when we come to the grace of baptism, renouncing all other gods and lords, we confess only God the Father and Son and Holy Spirit'; and *Exhortation to Martyrdom* xvii, τί λεκτέον διὰ τοῦ ἀρνεῖσθαι ἀθετούντων ἃς ἔθεντο πρὸς θεὸν συνθήκας καὶ παλινδρομούντων ἐπὶ τὸν Σατανᾶν, ᾧ βαπτιζόμενοι ἀπετάξαντο; and a long similar passage in *Homilies on Numbers* XIII. xii.[2]

There is another list in Origen's *Homilies on Jeremiah*.[3] Here he says that Jeremiah 4. 3 ('Break up your fallow ground, and sow not among thorns') means, when it is allegorized, 'Do not give Christian teaching until its hearers are prepared for it'. This teaching—which he calls τὰ σπέρματα τὰ ἅγια—he summarizes as: 'the doctrine concerning the Father, that concerning the Son, that concerning the Holy Spirit, the doctrine concerning resurrection, the doctrine concerning punishment, the doctrine concerning refreshment, that concerning the law, that concerning the prophets, and, in short, each of the things that are written.' This looks very like a Creed, perhaps, in view of the phrase 'each of the things that are written', a Creed thought of as a summary of Scripture, but still a Creed. No exotic doctrines compel us to regard it as Origen's esoteric teaching; no obviously non-credal articles

---

[1] See 'Hat die alexandrinische Kirche', pp. 359 (n. 1), 364.

[2] Compare what Lawson has to say of Irenaeus: 'The Rule of Truth...is received by means of baptism.' He refers to *Adv. Haer* I. 9. 4. See *The Biblical Theology of Saint Irenaeus*, p. 266.

[3] v. 13.

suggest that it is the rule of faith rather than the Creed. On the contrary, the expression τὰ σπέρματα suggests a summary rather than a full statement.

Bardy, in his article, 'La Règle de Foi d'Origène',[1] mentions four passages in particular where we may reasonably detect traces of a Creed. One is from the *Commentary on John*,[2] where Origen refers, at various points over a long passage, to God the Father, Jesus Christ, the Holy Spirit, creation, the crucifixion, and the Virgin Birth; it is a list of points at which heresy is opposed to truth. There is another passage in the *Homilies on Leviticus*,[3] which is shorter, and refers to God the Father, the Son, and the Holy Spirit. But it also refers to 'carnis *resurrectionem*', which is a likely indication (as Bardy might have observed) of Rufinus' hand. The third passage is one in the *Commentary on Matthew*, to which our attention has already been called when we were considering Caspari's views on this subject.[4] The fourth passage comes from a fragment on the Epistle to Titus,[5] and mentions only Father, Son, and Holy Spirit. We should perhaps note one more passage, which occurs in the fragments of the *Commentary on 1 Corinthians* edited by C. Jenkins (Sect. IV, p. 234). Kelly (*Early Christian Creeds*, pp. 92–3) includes it in his list (which is otherwise rather a meagre one) of Origen's references to a Creed. It refers to 'the Church's belief (ἐκκλησιαστικῷ δόγματι) about the Father and the Son and Holy Spirit, further about the Incarnation (τῆς καθ' ἡμᾶς οἰκονομίας), about the Resurrection and Judgement'. It is interesting to note that after he has given this list of beliefs, Origen adds to them καὶ τοῖς κανόσι τοῖς ἐκκλησιαστικοῖς, thereby distinguishing the rule of faith from the Creed, but putting the two on a level.

This evidence makes it clear that Origen did in his writings recognize a Creed, as distinct from the rule of faith and from his esoteric teaching. It would presumably consist of a Trinitarian formula (no doubt of much the same sort as Caspari has recovered from Clement of Alexandria) for certain, and probably a greater or lesser amount of detail under the heading of the second article, including a mention of the Virgin Birth, and conceivably (but here our evidence is tenuous) an article covering the resurrection of the dead. But, as Lebreton has

[1] Op. cit. pp. 189–92. [2] XXXII. 16. [3] V. X.
[4] Pt. II, 33 (*P.G.* XIII, 1643–4). See above, p. 119.
[5] *P.G.* XIV, 1303–4.

already reminded us, Origen does not give this Creed a prominent place in any sense, and it is likely that for him the boundary between the Creed and his particular version of the rule of faith was a tenuous one. Observe how even in an unmistakably credal statement like that quoted from the *Homilies on Jeremiah* above,[1] he slips in the phrase 'that concerning the law', which probably refers to the allegorization of the Old Testament and has no parallel in other Creeds. No doubt for him the boundary between the rule of faith and his esoteric teaching was similarly tenuous, though much clearer than it was in Clement's teaching. Origen probably regarded the Creed as a short summary of the rule of faith, designed for beginners;[2] if he did, this would amply account for his lack of interest in it. We have no evidence that he regarded the Creed as a source of doctrine independent of the Bible, so that Bardy's contention[3] that the Creed that he does know of is a rule provided for him by ecclesiastical tradition apart from the Bible is an unfounded one. If he does not regard the Church's rule of faith as independent of the Bible, it is most unlikely that he should so regard the Creed. In any case he seems to refer so seldom to a Creed that the question is not an important one. If the solitary passage[4] which attributes the Creed to his secret tradition is to be followed, Origen certainly based this Creed on the Bible, as he based all his ἀπόρρητα. But this does not seem to be at all a characteristic passage.

Before we try to summarize our findings in this examination of Origen's doctrine of the rule of faith, and of his Creed, it is worth while to return once more to his esoteric tradition. If we set out the articles of this teaching as if they were a Creed (though we are agreed that they are not) and compare them with Clement of Alexandria's similarly set out overleaf, the results may be interesting.

It will be noticed that these lists coincide in some interesting instances. In his mention of the allegorization of the Bible, of the Godhead as an

---

[1] See p. 119.

[2] See the quotation of *Comm. on Romans* IX. xxxvii, on p. 83 above, where the words '*at certe ad summam fidei satis sint*' seem to bear out this opinion.

[3] 'La Règle de Foi d'Origène', p. 196.

[4] See above, pp. 78, 114. It is, however, interesting to note that the profession of faith of Heracleides of the *Conversation* runs thus (*Conversation*, pp. 118–20 of text): πιστεύομεν ὅτι εἴληφε σάρκα ὁ Χριστός, ὅτι ἐγεννήθη, ὅτι ἀνῆλθε εἰς τοὺς οὐρανοὺς ἐν τῇ σαρκὶ ᾗ ἀνέστη, ὅτι κάθηται ἐν δεξίᾳ τοῦ Πατρὸς μέλλων ἐκεῖθεν ἔρχεσθαι καὶ κρίνειν ζῶντας καὶ νεκρούς, θεὸς καὶ ἄνθρωπος.

Origen's Secret Doctrines[1]	*Clement's Secret Doctrines* (all found on pp. 63 and 64)
The salvation of souls (78).	—
God and his only-begotten Son (78).	—
Several points of Christology (78).	—
Knowledge about angels, fallen and unfallen (79).	—
The differences of souls (79).	—
The origin and nature of the world (79).	Cosmological and theological speculations.
The origin and extent of evil (79).	—
The pre-existence of souls (79).	—
Universal salvation (80).	—
The pre-mundane Fall (80).	—
The doctrine of the Atonement. ⎫	—
Who deserves to be called God and who not. ⎪	—
The reason why the Incarnation ⎬(81). came when it did.	Christian apologetics against heretics.
The duration of Christ's reign and judgement ⎭	—
Doctrines about prayer (81–2).	Mystico-intellectual contemplation of
The resurrection of the *body*[2] (82).	divine things.
?The doctrine of the Trinity (82).	—
Allegorization of the Bible (82).	Allegorization of the Bible.

article of teaching, of doctrines about prayer, and of the origin and nature of the world, Origen is treading on ground where Clement had either gone before him, or had designed to go in his περὶ Ἀρχῶν. Again, it is clear that both lists start from something not unlike the Church's κήρυγμα or rule of faith as their groundwork (and we have noticed already that both writers claim at least one of their articles of esoteric tradition—the allegorization of the Bible—as part of the Church's rule of faith). But both writers depart, each in his own characteristic way, very far from anything which we could imagine to be the rule of faith of the Church of their day. Clement is preoccupied with the relation between the gospel and the philosophy of the Greeks. Origen is concerned to work the materials of the κήρυγμα into an

---

[1] In this list the Arabic numbers in brackets refer to the pages of this work where each article has been discussed and its context given.

[2] As contrasted with the resurrection of the flesh.

elaborate and comprehensive theological system,[1] introducing thereby a number of speculations quite exotic to the original tradition. It is noteworthy, too, that Clement, if we are to judge by the account of ordinary and Gnostic doctrine given in *Strom.* IV. i,[2] seems particularly anxious to establish the credentials and respectability of the Bible, whereas Origen takes them much more for granted, though he is even more interested than Clement in the Bible's interpretation.

Now let us compare a list given to us by Irenaeus which has several interesting similarities both with Clement's and with Origen's lists. It comes from *Adversus Haereses*.[3] In the previous chapters Irenaeus has described how the Church's faith is always the same all over the world. Then he begins to explain how the faith may appear different in different places, though not with that exotic variety which the heretical sects display:

But if certain of us possess a special knowledge (κατὰ σύνεσιν εἰδέναι) to a greater or lesser extent, this is not accounted for by our altering the whole structure (ὑπόθεσις) itself, and contriving some other God than the Creator and Maker and Sustainer of all, as if he were not sufficient, or another Christ, or another Only-begotten. It is accounted for by the process of working out the truth of those things which are spoken in parables, and assimilating it to the structure of the faith; and by the exposition of that enterprise and dispensation of God undertaken towards the human race; and by the instruction about God's patience both at the rebellion of angels who sinned, and at man's disobedience; and by the imparting of reasons for one and the same God having made some things temporary and some things eternal, some things heavenly and some earthly; and by the understanding of why, even though he is invisible, God appeared to the prophets, not in one unvarying form, but differently to different men; and by explaining why several covenants were instituted with the human race, and the character of each covenant; and by investigating why God shut up all under sin that he might have mercy upon all; and by establishing[4] why the Word became flesh and suffered, and by explaining why at the end of the times the Incarnation of the Son of God took place, that is, the beginning took place in the end, and by expounding the end and the things to come, and such things as those found in the Scriptures, and by not concealing the reason for God's having

---

[1] We have seen on p. 116 that Origen specifically states his intention of working the materials of the κήρυγμα into a system.

[2] See above, p. 64.

[3] *Adversus Haereses* (Harvey's edition, Cambridge, 1857), Book 1, cap. iv, pp. 94–7.

[4] Allowing Harvey's παριστᾶν for the text's εὐχαριστεῖν.

made the Gentiles who had no hope fellow-heirs and fellow-members of the Body and equal sharers in the holy things; and by teaching how this mortal flesh shall put on immortality and this corruptible incorruptibility; and by preaching how he shall say, That which was not a people is a people, and she who was not beloved is beloved, and how the children of her who was barren are more than those of her who has a husband. For it was concerning these matters and matters like them that the apostle cried, O the depth of the riches and the wisdom and the knowledge of God! How unsearchable are his judgements, and his ways past finding out! But this special knowledge is not arrived at by contriving above the Creator and Maker a Mother of him and of these other things, some Idea of the wrongheaded Aeon, and by going to such lengths of blasphemy; nor by falsely supposing a Pleroma above even the Mother, which is sometimes thirty and sometimes an innumerable multitude of Aeons, as those teachers say who are truly barren of divine understanding. The real Church, on the other hand, has in all its parts one and the same faith all over the world, as we said before.

The resemblance of this list of doctrines to Origen's and Clement's lists of esoteric doctrine is unmistakable. Indeed, some of the articles in it are identical with some on Clement's list and others with some on Origen's. Both Alexandrian Fathers share with Irenaeus their interest in allegory (for this is probably the meaning of Irenaeus' words, 'the process of working out the truth of those things which are spoken in parables')[1] and in cosmogony. Origen echoes his mention of the Fall, of the Atonement, of the reason for the time of the Incarnation, and of the resurrection of the body. In fact, Origen reproduces six of Irenaeus' thirteen articles.

But it must be noted that what Irenaeus is reproducing here is neither the Church's rule of faith (which is what he means, roughly speaking, by ἡ τῆς πίστεως ὑπόθεσις), nor his own private speculations. Nor does he claim to be describing a secret tradition.[2] He makes it perfectly clear what he is reproducing here. It is precisely Prestige's διδασκαλία—'the accumulating wisdom of philosophically grounded Christianity', 'an accretion, enlargement, confirmation of the faith'. It is the result of the Christian teacher's reflecting upon and expounding the consequences and ramifications of the Christian faith; it is the inevitable and necessary articulation and development of the original

---

[1] The parallel with *Comm. on Matt.* XIV. 12 is striking. See above, p. 82, n. 4.
[2] For Irenaeus' rejection of esoteric tradition in orthodox Christianity, see above, p. 87, n. 5.

Christian tradition. It is, in short, theology. But Irenaeus knows what he is doing here. He will have nothing to do with Gnostic speculations. In theory at least, he will not even tolerate Christian speculation. Lebreton[1] quotes an interesting passage later in the *Adversus Haereses*: 'If anyone says to us, How then has the Son been produced by the Father?, we shall reply to him that this production, or generation, or pronunciation, or revelation, or in short this indescribable generation, whatever name you like to call it, nobody knows, not Valentinus, not Marcion, not Saturninus, not Basilides, not the angels, nor the archangels, nor the principalities, nor the powers, but only the Father who has begotten the Son who is born.'[2]

How different is the atmosphere of this theology from that of the Alexandrian Fathers! At Alexandria, says Lebreton, the tension between simple believers and intellectuals was greater than elsewhere. '*Chez les simples croyants, les suspicions sont plus vives, et provoquent, chez les théologiens, plus d'irritation.*' This was partly, he adds (quoting a comment of de Faye upon Clement), because of the presence of a greater number of Gnostic sects there, but also partly because of the existence there of a school of Gnostic-minded Christians.[3] The only thing that restrained Origen from indulging freely in Christian speculation was his fear that the uneducated Christians might get him into trouble if he went too far; and nothing restrained Clement, except conceivably the fear that he might be thought ridiculous by the pagan philosophers.[4] That speculation was irrelevant or even unsuitable to the Christian faith—which is Irenaeus' contention—was very far from their thoughts. They both used the device—almost deliberately eschewed by Irenaeus—of pretending to a secret tradition in order to present their speculations to their chosen audiences in an acceptable form.

But it is clear that Clement and Origen developed their speculation from just such a list of Christian διδασκαλία as we found in the fourth

---

[1] 'Le Désaccord de la Foi', tom. 19, p. 485. Lebreton quotes *Adv. Haer.* II. xxviii. 4–6.

[2] Compare Cadiou's reference to Hippolytus' explicit denunciation in *Contra Noetum* of the attempt to define how the Son is generated: ἢ οὐκ αὔταρκές σοι μαθεῖν ὅτι υἱὸς θεοῦ σοι ἐφανερώθη εἰς σωτηρίαν; See *La Jeunesse d'Origène*, pp. 350–1.

[3] 'Le Désaccord de la Foi', tom. 19, p. 492.

[4] See the quotation on p. 63 above.

chapter of the First Book of Irenaeus' work. Irenaeus implies that such knowledge of the Christian faith κατὰ σύνεσιν would vary from place to place within the whole Church, and no doubt the διδασκαλία of Alexandria would from early times have been more inclined to make concessions to speculation, even to Gnostic speculation, than would that of other churches, just as, perhaps, the διδασκαλία of Rome, if we are to judge by local characteristics, would have been conservative and unimaginative, and that of Caesarea more open to Rabbinic influences. No doubt, for that matter, as we have already suggested, the κανών, the Church's rule of faith, would be rather more fluid, and rather more exposed to influences extraneous to the original Christian tradition, in Alexandria than elsewhere.

We may therefore summarize our findings hitherto made in this investigation of Origen's doctrine of tradition by saying that he derives all his doctrine from the Bible; that his conception of the Church's rule of faith is the preaching and teaching of the Church of his own day, deriving its support from and making its appeal to, but at the same time guaranteeing, the Bible, in continuity with the teaching of the Church from the earliest times; that he takes very little notice of credal forms and never implies that they have any authority independent of that of the Bible,[1] and that the esoteric tradition to which he professes to have access is in fact the normal, inevitable development and enlargement—such as we find referred to in Irenaeus—of the Church's faith, in the process of its being handled by theologians, diversified and rendered at times almost unrecognizable by private speculations matured by Origen himself or by the school of Alexandria to which he belonged.

---

[1] Cf. a passage in *Comm. on Romans* VI. iii, where he is dealing with the verse Romans 6. 17, 'Ye became obedient from the heart unto that form of doctrine whereunto ye were delivered'. In commenting upon this he seems to assume (no doubt rightly) that the words refer to the '*traditio symboli*' before Baptism, but he emphasizes the word 'form', and says that we shall only know the true doctrine in the next life.

CHAPTER VIII

THE CANON OF SCRIPTURE

WHEN we approach the subject of the Canon of Scripture in Origen, it is worth while to follow our usual procedure and examine first the attitude of Clement of Alexandria, even though in this particular matter we shall discover that Origen differs markedly from Clement.

Clement refers to no list of books officially guaranteed as inspired, and of course he never uses κανών to express this meaning. Tollinton[1] has a useful note upon Clement's attitude to the Canon which brings these points out clearly. 'His rule or canon', he says, 'is something other than a list of authoritative writings, and to a very large extent his strong preferences and affinities determine his use of the Church's literature rather than any decision of authority from without. Thus, while it is quite clear that Clement attached less weight to the Epistle of Barnabas than he did to the Epistles of S. Paul,[2] it would be going beyond our evidence to declare that this was because the latter were canonical and the former not. The grounds for the different degrees of canonicity are not explicitly declared. What the Lord had said was of primary weight. What could claim to be "Apostolic" came next in order. These distinctions were unquestioned and sufficient. Beyond them lay a domain where some questions were still undecided and unrecognized.' Mondésert[3] echoes this. Clement, he says, does not know 'une liste précise de livres officiellement reconnus comme inspirés.... Il y a des livres qui sont évidemment ceux de l'Église, d'autres qui sont évidemment hérétiques; pour ceux qui sont entre les deux, il s'en servira si besoin est, autant que de Platon, d'Homère ou de la Sybille, car partout où il y a quelque vérité celle-ci appartient de droit au vrai disciple du Logos.'

The nearest Clement approaches to a conception of a Canon of Scripture is when he refers in *Stromateis* III. iv[4] to the view of certain heretics that sexual promiscuity is legitimate for Christians, and says that they derive it ἔκ τινος ἀποκρύφου. But this is the only clear

---

[1] *Clement of Alexandria*, Vol. II, p. 175.
[2] This particular point is, as we shall see, not at all 'quite clear'.
[3] *Clément d'Alexandrie*, pp. 118–19.   [4] *P.G.* VII, 1133.

reference to apocrypha as apocrypha. In another place (*Stromateis* I. xx),[1] Clement does to some extent distinguish between the literature of Greek culture and Scripture, for he says: χωρίζεται δὲ ἡ Ἑλληνικὴ ἀλήθεια τῆς καθ' ἡμᾶς, εἰ καὶ τοῦ αὐτοῦ μετείληφεν ὀνόματος, καὶ μεγέθει γνώσεως καὶ ἀποδείξει κυριωτέρᾳ καὶ θείᾳ δυνάμει καὶ τοῖς ὁμοίοις. θεοδίδακτοι γὰρ ἡμεῖς, ἱερὰ ὄντως γράμματα παρὰ τῷ Υἱῷ τοῦ θεοῦ παιδευόμενοι· ἔνθεν οὐδ' ὡσαύτως κινοῦσι τὰς ψυχάς, ἀλλὰ διαφόρῳ διδασκαλίᾳ. This certainly acknowledges the existence of ἱερὰ ὄντως γράμματα, though he never draws up a list of them. In one fragment,[2] quoted by Eusebius as from the Seventh Book of Clement's *Hypotoposeis*, he appears to assume that there can be only four Gospels, for he says, 'John last of all, observing that the physical events (τὰ σωματικά) were explained in the Gospels, urged on by his friends and inspired by the Spirit, wrote a spiritual Gospel (πνευματικὸν εὐαγγέλιον)'. But in spite of this, Clement quotes from at least two apocryphal gospels as well as the canonical ones: from the *Gospel according to the Hebrews* once, in *Stromateis* II. ix,[3] where he does not comment upon its genuineness or spuriousness; and from the *Gospel according to the Egyptians* four times (*Stromateis* III. vi, ix [twice], and xiii).[4] In three of these last references Clement records, without comment on its genuineness, an alleged conversation between our Lord and Salome, and in one of these (III. ix) he emphasizes that the words quoted should be marked by those people who 'submit to anything rather than to the true rule of the Gospel' (τῷ κατὰ τὴν ἀλήθειαν εὐαγγελικῷ κανόνι). But in the fourth case (III. xiii) this gospel has been cited by the heretic, Julius Cassianus, against whom Clement is in this passage writing, and Clement's comment is, 'First of all, we do not have this saying in the four Gospels handed down to us, but in the *Gospel according to the Egyptians*'. Nevertheless, he goes on carefully to allegorize the passage quoted by Cassianus.[5] So on the question of the Canon of the Gospels Clement's attitude seems to be equivocal.

---

[1] *P.G.* VIII, 816.   [2] *P.G.* IX, 749, frag. ix.   [3] *P.G.* VIII, 98.

[4] *P.G.* VIII, 1149, 1168, 1194. Hilgenfeld (*Novum Testamentum extra Canonem Receptum*, edition of the fragments of lost apocryphal New Testament works, p. 43) fails to notice the reference in III. vi; he also thinks that he can find a reference to this Gospel in the *Excerpta ex Theodoto*, para. 67.

[5] Molland, *The Conception of the Gospel*, p. 14, has not noticed that there are other references to this gospel in Clement where he apparently accepts it as genuine.

The Epistle to the Hebrews he always attributes to S. Paul. 'This, indeed,' says Tollinton,[1] 'was the usual view of the Church of Alexandria, which differed here from the Churches of Rome and Carthage.' Clement does however say, in a fragment of the Sixth Book of his *Hypotoposeis* quoted by Eusebius,[2] that the letter was written by S. Paul Ἑβραϊκῇ φωνῇ, but Luke carefully translated it for the benefit of the Greeks, and that is why it has a similar style to Acts, and is not superscribed 'Paul, an apostle'.[3]

Two apocryphal or sub-apostolic works quoted by Clement deserve special mention, the Greek *Sibylline Oracles* and the *Epistle of Barnabas*. The Greek *Sibylline Oracles* is a work composed about A.D. 1 by different hands, the latest oracle being about the death of Herod the Great; it expected a sudden advent of the Messiah. Later Christian additions, however, were made to this collection, as late as several centuries A.D. Now Clement in his early work, the *Protreptikos*, quotes 'The Sibyl' several times. He calls her ἡ προφῆτις (*Protreptikos* III and VI),[4] and in *Protreptikos* VIII,[5] having stated that for the truth about God you must go to the prophets, he quotes three of them—the Sibyl, Jeremiah, and Isaiah! In his later works he drops altogether his allusions to her, though he is still far from abandoning her as false. In *Stromateis* VI. v,[6] in a passage differentiating between the Greek philosophers' knowledge of God and that of the Christians, he quotes some unknown apocryphal work in which S. Paul is represented as drawing attention to the testimony given to Christ by the Sibyl and by the mythical personage Hystaspes. It is noteworthy that Origen never quotes from the Sibyl, though[7] in *Against Celsus* VIII. lvi, he argues against Celsus' accusation that the Christians wrote the oracles themselves, asserting that no ancient copies of the oracles can be found which do not contain the Christian passages.

To the *Epistle of Barnabas* Clement refers eight times,[8] never throwing any doubt on its value. Eusebius tells us (*H.E.* VI. 14) that

---

[1] *Clement of Alexandria*, Vol. II, p. 226.　　[2] *P.G.* IX, 748, frag. ix.

[3] Cf. *P.G.* IX, 732, frag. i, probably also from the *Hypotoposeis*, on 1 Peter 5. 10, where a similar statement is made.

[4] *P.G.* VIII, 141, 177.　　[5] *P.G.* VIII, 188.　　[6] *P.G.* IX, 264.

[7] As H. N. Bate points out in his Introduction to the *Sibylline Oracles, Books III–IV* (S.P.C.K., 1918), p. 33.

[8] For the references see Hilgenfeld, *Novum Test. extra Canonem*, Introduction to his edition of the *Epistle of Barnabas*, p. x.

in his *Hypotoposeis* Clement discussed all the (what Eusebius calls) canonical (ἐνδιάθηκος) Scriptures, and also the Epistle of Jude, the other General Epistles, the *Epistle of Barnabas*, and the *Apocalypse of Peter*. Clement uses Barnabas mainly as a mine for suggestions about allegorizing the Old Testament Law. In *Paidagogos* II. x, for instance,[1] he quotes the apocryphal saying 'Thou shalt not eat the hare nor the hyaena' from the Epistle, and adopts its allegorization of it. In *Stromateis* II. vi and vii[2] he calls the author ὁ ἀπόστολος Βαρνάβας, and in II. xx[3] he calls him ὁ ἀποστολικὸς Βαρνάβας, and says that he was one of the Seventy and a fellow-worker with Paul. In two important passages he makes it clear that it is largely from this work that he derived his conception of γνῶσις, outlined above. In *Stromateis* V. x, Barnabas is referred to as σαφέστερον γνωστικῆς παραδόσεως ἴχνος παρατιθέμενος,[4] and he here quotes the τί λέγει ἡ γνῶσις μάθετε of the Epistle. In a fragment of the *Hypotoposeis* quoted by Eusebius,[5] he describes how ἡ γνῶσις reached 'the Seventy, of whom Barnabas was one', from our Lord.

Other apocryphal or sub-apostolic works quoted by Clement without reference to their genuineness or otherwise are: the *Preaching of Peter* six times;[6] Hermas' works four times (Mondésert has no real ground for his suggestion that Clement quotes Hermas' *Shepherd* merely as '*une façon littéraire de citer ses auteurs*');[7] the *Apocalypse of Peter* three times;[8] the *Traditions of Matthew* once;[9] the *Book of Enoch*

---

[1] *P.G.* VIII, 497. For similar adoptions of allegorizations in *Barnabas*, see Strom. II. xv, xviii; v. viii (*P.G.* VIII, 1005, 1021; IX, 81).

[2] *P.G.* VIII, 965, 969.

[3] *P.G.* VIII, 1060; but then elsewhere he calls Clement of Rome an ἀπόστολος.

[4] *P.G.* IX, 96.

[5] *P.G.* IX, 749, frag. ix. For the importance of these passages for determining the source of Clement's doctrine of secret tradition, see above, pp. 68–9.

[6] *Strom.* II. xv; VI. v, vi, vii, xv; *Ec. Proph.* lviii (*P.G.* VIII, 1008; IX, 257, 269, 280, 352, 728).

[7] *Clément d'Alexandrie*, p. 245. The references are *Strom.* I. xvii, xxix; II. ix; IV. ix (*P.G.* VIII, 800, 927, 980, 1283). But Hilgenfeld (*Nov. Test. extra C.*, Prolegomena to his edition of the *Shepherd*, p. xi) thinks he can detect more references. [8] *Ec. Proph.* xli, xlviii, xlix (*P.G.* IX, 717, 720).

[9] *Strom.* II. ix (*P.G.* VIII, 981). But Hilgenfeld (op. cit., Edition of the fragments of lost works, pp. 50–1) points out that in *Strom.* VII. xvii, Clement refers to the work as heretical, and that in *Strom.* III. iv, and VII. xiii (*P.G.* IX, 513) he prefixes it with λέγουσι. Hilgenfeld thinks the work may be quoted in a reply to Zacchaeus attributed to our Lord in *Strom.* IV. vi.

once;[1] the *Didache* once;[2] Clement of Rome he quotes or refers to several times,[3] never making any qualification of his authority. We have seen already how Clement of Alexandria refers in *Stromateis* VI. v to some unknown apocryphal work in which S. Paul is represented as drawing attention to the testimony given to Christ by the Sibyl and Hystaspes. This work may be the *Preaching of Peter*. Hilgenfeld[4] thinks he can detect several more references to this work in Clement.

Besides the unplaceable legal ordinance cited from the *Epistle of Barnabas* in *Paidagogos* II. x, Clement quotes five apocryphal sayings, two of which are attributed to our Lord. In *Stromateis* I. xxiv[5] he quotes as our Lord's, αἰτεῖσθε τὰ μεγάλα καὶ τὰ μικρὰ ὑμῖν προστεθή- σεται, a logion which is cited by Origen also and has a ring of genuine- ness about it. Then in *Quis Dives* xl he ascribes to Jesus the saying (found also in Justin Martyr's *Dialogue with Trypho*): ἐφ' οἷς ἂν εὕρω ὑμᾶς, ἐπὶ τούτοις καὶ κρινῶ.[6] The other three sayings are: σὺ γάρ εἶ κιθάρα καὶ αὐλὸς καὶ ναὸς ἐμός (*Protreptikos* I,[7] which may be a fragment of an early Christian hymn); the saying 'Those who draw ropes and weave nothing', which he describes in *Stromateis* I. viii[8] as ἡ γραφή, though nobody can place it satisfactorily; and the expression τέτοκε καὶ οὐ τέτοκε, applied to the Blessed Virgin Mary (*Stromateis* VII. xvi),[9] and also called ἡ γραφή. Tertullian quotes this saying in his *De Carne Christi*, and attributes it to Ezekiel. Mondésert[10] quotes as an 'agraphon' the ἐξέλθετε ἐκ τῶν δεσμῶν οἱ θέλοντες of *Stromateis* VI. vi. But this may be a conflation of two texts. The Migne editor, for instance, refers to Isaiah 49. 8, 9.

There is in *Excerpta ex Theodoto*[11] a saying of our Lord presented thus: διὰ τοῦτο λέγει ὁ Σωτήρ· σώζου σὺ καὶ ἡ ψυχή σου. It is difficult to say whether we are to regard this as an uncanonical saying to be found in Clement or not, because it is not certain whether we are to attribute

---

[1] *Ec. Proph.* liii (*P.G.* IX, 724).

[2] *Strom.* I. xx (*P.G.* VIII, 817), where he quotes *Didache* iii. 5, without naming it, as ἡ γραφή.

[3] See Hilgenfeld (op. cit., Prolegom. to his Edition of Clement of Rome's *Epistle to the Corinthians*, p. xxii) for the references.

[4] Op. cit., Edition of the fragments of lost works, pp. 62–5.

[5] *P.G.* VIII, 905.   [6] *P.G.* IX, 645.   [7] *P.G.* VIII, 60.

[8] *P.G.* VIII, 737.   [9] *P.G.* IX, 529–30.

[10] *Clément d'Alexandrie*, p. 244. The place in Migne is *P.G.* IX. 265.

[11] Casey's edition, p. 40.

the *Excerpta* to Clement or not. Mondésert's comment on them is just and worth quoting.[1] '*Une couleur gnostique*', he says, '*très prononcée*' is visible in them. '*À chaque pas, on rencontre les personnages allégoriques: Sigê, Bathos, Sophia, Topos; ou ces êtres plus concrets que sont le Père, la Mère, le Fils, les Puissances, les Éons, les protoctistes, les anges, le Démiurge, etc. Quelques-uns de ceux-ci ne sont pas inconnus du fidèle orthodoxe, mais ils apparaissent ici un peu perdus dans une cosmogonie et une sorte de théogonie, qui, à première vue, peuvent lui paraître à tout le moins bizarres. Un lecteur qui ne connaît le gnosticisme que de nom, trouvera même cela déconcertant et rébarbatif.*' But Mondésert is nevertheless quite sure that the *Excerpta* are by Clement and he says that scholarship is virtually unanimous upon the point. If we are to conclude that the *Excerpta* are from Clement's pen, we may be pardoned if we agree with Cadiou that they do not necessarily represent his own opinions. Cadiou[2] calls them '*ce cahier d'école où Clément avait laissé des notes de lecture qu'il pensait réfuter, et plus souvent encore mettre habilement en œuvre dans ses Stromateis*'. On this understanding, then, we may admit this saying as an apocryphal logion quoted by Clement.

Clement refers also to a few traditions independent of the Bible, without naming his sources for them, some of them genuine-seeming, and some of them not. He tells us, for instance, in *Paidagogos* II. i,[3] that the apostle Matthew ate only seeds and berries, and vegetables, and no meat, and (as we have had occasion to note more than once) that Barnabas was one of the Seventy.[4] He says that 'the story goes' (φασί γ' οὖν) that S. Peter at his wife's execution encouraged her with comforting words. Hilgenfeld thinks that this comes from the *Acts of Paul* or the *Acts of Peter and Paul*.[5] He records in a fragment quoted from the Fifth Book of the *Hypotoposeis*[6] that Christ is said to have baptized Peter only, and that Peter baptized Andrew, Andrew James and John, and these two the rest of the apostles. There is also in *Quis Dives* xlii[7] the charming story of John the apostle (whom he clearly identifies with

---

[1] *Clément d'Alexandrie*, p. 254. See also p. 255.

[2] *La Jeunesse d'Origène*, p. 135.

[3] *P.G.* VIII, 404–5.   [4] *Strom.* II. xx (*P.G.* VIII, 1060).

[5] *Strom.* VII. xi (*P.G.* IX, 488). See Hilgenfeld, op. cit., edition of the fragments of lost works, p. 73.

[6] *P.G.* IX, 745, frag. ix.   [7] *P.G.* IX, 648.

the author of the Apocalypse, as he describes him as leaving Patmos) reclaiming the young robber. It is noteworthy that he calls this story μῦθον, ἀλλ᾽ οὐ μῦθον, ἀλλ᾽ ὄντα λόγον περὶ Ἰωάννου τοῦ ἀποστόλου, παραδεδομένον καὶ μνήμη πεφυλαγμένον, which makes it clear that he set a definite value even by this sort of non-Scriptural tradition.

This evidence should surely be enough to convince anyone that Clement of Alexandria has almost no conception of what we mean by the Canon of Scripture, in the sense of a list of books guaranteed as authentic tradition in contrast to others whose genuineness is not certain. The most we can say is that he seems to assume that the Canon of the Gospels is closed, though even here he apparently is ready on occasion to admit exceptions. He shows no sign at all of wanting to call in the judgement of the Church to decide the genuineness of any work which may be Scripture; but he can sometimes brand a book as heretical. It may well be that Clement's attitude is not typical of the attitude of the Church of his time in other parts of the world. Irenaeus, for instance, had a much more definite conception of the finality of the Canon of the Gospels at least. But it is likely that Clement's attitude was the attitude of the Church of Alexandria, and therefore no doubt the attitude which Origen inherited. We must now turn to see what we can discover concerning Origen's conception of the Canon of Scripture.

We have already had occasion to examine Origen's use of the word κανών.[1] He never uses it to mean what we mean by the phrase 'Canon of Scripture'. Indeed, according to H. Oppel, who has written a monograph upon the word, κανών does not occur meaning 'the list of the writings acknowledged by the Church as documents of the divine revelation' until we reach Athanasius.[2] It is remarkable that in the whole of his *Letter to Africanus*, which is entirely devoted to discussing the canonicity of the History of Susanna, Origen does not use the word κανών once.

The question of the Old Testament Canon was forced upon Origen's notice by the fact that he could not help observing in the course of his studies that the LXX contained a considerable amount of material which the Jews, who only accepted twenty-two books,[3] did not

---

[1] See above, pp. 91–5.
[2] 'KANΩN', pp. 70, 71. He derives his information for the ecclesiastical meanings of the word from Zahn's *Grundriss der Geschichte des Neutestament-lichen Kanons.*   [3] See *Comm. on Psalm 1 (P.G.* xii, 1084).

recognize as canonical. He discusses the whole question most fully in the *Letter to Africanus*. He states quite frankly that if we are to reject all the parts of the Old Testament not extant in Hebrew, then—ὥρα ἀθετεῖν τὰ ἐν ταῖς ἐκκλησίαις φερόμενα ἀντίγραφα, and, generally, to tell Christians to abandon the copies of the Bible they now possess, and to go begging to the Jews for purer versions. But he agrees that in arguing with the Jews we should use only the parts of the Old Testament which they allow, so that they may not disregard our arguments on the ground that they are based on false documents. His reason for compiling the Hexapla, he says, was to prevent anybody's accusing the Church of using spurious evidence.[1] In this Letter, of course, he is quite sure of the genuineness of the History of Susanna, and presumably he remained so to the end of his life, for in the *Commentary on Matthew*[2] he quotes from it, adding the comment that he is 'not unaware that it does not appear in the Hebrew Scriptures', but he uses it 'because it is received in the Churches'. It is worth noting, however, that much earlier in his career Origen had had doubts about the genuineness of this work. In a fragment from the Tenth Book of Origen's *Stromateis* preserved in Jerome's *Commentary on Daniel*, cap. xiii,[3] he leaves as an entirely open question the problem of the puns upon the names of trees in the History of Susanna 54, 55, 58, 59, and whether they could represent a Hebrew original, saying that we shall have to agree with those '*qui Graeci tantum sermonis hanc volunt esse pericopen*'. Whether this refers to the History as a whole or only to the passage containing these puns is not clear, but at any rate this is a much more hesitant attitude than the confident and smooth way in which he explains these difficulties in the later *Letter to Africanus*. Similarly, in the same fragment[4] he expresses himself as uncertain about the authenticity of the History of Bel and the Dragon.

It is quite clear, however, that Origen held that apocryphal traditions, even outside those books which the Hebrew Bible lacked and the LXX contained, might be quite genuine ones. In his *Letter to Africanus*[5] he says that the Jews made a practice of excising from their books anything discreditable to judges, elders, or rulers, and that these excised portions sometimes appear ἐν τοῖς ἀποκρύφοις. And he adds the childish accusation that the Jews deliberately inserted unworthy matter

---

[1] *Letter to Africanus* 4 and 5.   [2] Part II, 61.
[3] *P.G.* XI, 104.   [4] *P.G.* XI, 105.   [5] Sect. 9.

into the ἀπόκρυφα in order to make that material in them appear spurious which was in fact quite genuine, but discreditable to those in authority among the Jews. In his *Commentary on Matthew* X. 18, he admits that the story of Isaiah's being sawn asunder occurs in an apocryphal book, but supports the authenticity of the story by reference to Hebrews 11. 37, where it is mentioned.[1] Similarly he believes that our Lord's statement in Matthew 23. 35, that Zachariah was slain between the porch and the altar, must have been derived from a passage ἐν τῷ ἀποκρύφῳ. Later in the same work,[2] he accounts for the attribution of a passage of Zechariah to Jeremiah in Matthew 27. 9, 10, by suggesting that either it is a copyist's error, or there is some apocryphal writing of Jeremiah not known to the general public, but in the possession of Matthew, from which this quotation is taken. He says that S. Paul knew of secret writings unknown to us and quoted them, and he instances 1 Corinthians 2. 9 ('what eye hath not seen nor ear heard'), and 2 Timothy 3. 8 ('as Jannes and Mambres withstood Moses'). Presumably it is on this principle that he uses Jewish apocalyptic works written after the Jewish Canon was virtually closed. In the *Concerning First Principles*,[3] he quotes the *Ascension of Moses*, but adds in defence of it that the passage is quoted in the Epistle of Jude. In the *Homilies on Joshua*[4] he refers to the *Assumption of Moses* without naming it. In two places (a fragment of the *Commentary on Genesis* quoted in *Philocalia* XXIII. 15[5] and *Commentary on John* II. 31) he refers to a work which he calls *The Prayer of Joseph*. In his edition of the *Philocalia*, J. Armitage Robinson suggests *Testament of Asher* 7 as the source for the passage quoted in the *Commentary on Genesis*.[6] But there is no satisfactory parallel to this passage anywhere in the *Testament of Asher* or in any part of the *Testament of the Twelve*

---

[1] He mentions the same story again in *Commentary on Romans* VIII. vi; *Hom. on Jeremiah* XX. 9; *Homilies on Isaiah* I. v; and *Letter to Africanus* 9. It is known that there was in existence in early times a book whose Latin title was *De Prophetarum vita et obitu*, and an anonymous treatise on this subject is found in the Codex Marchalianus of the LXX. See Lake and Cadbury, *Beginnings of Christianity*, Vol. IV, p. 82.

[2] Part II, 117.   [3] III. 2. 1.

[4] II. i. We cannot be sure that the phrase '*licet in canone non habeatur*' which follows the reference to the book is not Rufinus' addition.

[5] Page 204 in J. A. Robinson's edition.

[6] The editor of the *Comm. on John*, A. E. Brooke, makes the same unwarranted assumption (Vol. I, p. 16), presumably following Armitage Robinson.

Patriarchs, nor yet to the much longer passage from this *Prayer of Joseph* quoted in the *Commentary on John*. This particular quotation is prefaced by the phrase, εἰ δέ τις προσίεται καὶ τῶν παρ' Ἑβραίοις φερομένων ἀποκρύφων τὴν ἐπιγραφομένην Ἰωσὴφ Προσευχήν, and followed by the comment, εἰκὸς γὰρ τούτων ἀληθῶς ὑπὸ τοῦ Ἰακὼβ λεγομένων καὶ διὰ τοῦτο ἀναγεγραμμένων. Perhaps the fact that Origen sees fit here to defend his use of this apocryphal *Prayer of Joseph*, whereas in the *Commentary on Genesis* he quoted it without comment, reflects a growing caution in referring to non-canonical books which we shall see reproduced more clearly elsewhere. But, since the composition of the Second Book of the *Commentary on John* cannot have been much later than that of the Third of the *Commentary on Genesis*, this suggestion can be at best only tentative. He quotes from the *Testament of the Twelve Patriarchs* in *Homilies on Joshua* XV. vi. From unnamed apocryphal works he has derived the name of Joseph's wife given him by Pharaoh, Asenath;[1] a story about an angel named Ananehel giving favour to Esther;[2] a phrase, ἐπὶ τὰ κλίματα τῆς ψυχῆς ἐπισκηνοῖ ὁ Σατανᾶς, from a work dealing with Zacharias, father of John;[3] and a reference in *Homilies on Luke* XXXV (on Luke 12. 59) to two opposing angels fighting over Abraham's body.

The case of the *Book of Enoch* deserves special consideration, for here we can actually observe Origen's judgement altering in course of time. Three times in *Concerning First Principles*[4] he quotes it without comment upon its genuineness. Once in the *Commentary on John*[5] he refers to the book, adding the phrase, 'if anyone cares to receive the book as holy'; in *Against Celsus* he refers to a notion taken from the book as 'a thing neither spoken nor heard in the Churches of God';[6] and in the *Homilies on Numbers* he mentions the books of Enoch, but refuses to quote them as an authority, because 'These books do not seem to be thought authoritative among the Hebrews'.[7]

---

[1] *Fragments on Genesis*, *P.G.* XII, 136. Perhaps this argues a knowledge on Origen's part of some ancestor of the work we know as *Joseph and Asenath*. Asenath was the name given to the daughter of Dinah by Shechem in Rabbinic tradition. See E. W. Brooks' Introduction to his Translation of *Joseph and Asenath* (S.P.C.K. 1918), p. xiii.   [2] *Comm. on Romans* IX. xi.

[3] *Comm. on Ephesians* XX, p. 554, on Eph. 4. 27. Several of these instances are noted by Daniélou, *Origène*, p. 178.

[4] Once in I. 3. 3, and twice in IV. 4. 8.

[5] VI. 42.   [6] v. lv.   [7] XXVIII. ii.

In his attitude to the Canon of the Old Testament, then, Origen seems to us to-day to attempt to have it both ways, that is, he acknowledges the right of the Jews to decide their own Canon, and yet he also recognizes the authenticity of any tradition outside the Jewish Canon that appeals to him. But in fact this only means that Origen is adopting the very loose attitude to canonicity which he inherited from Clement, and modifying it by the respect for the Hebrew Bible which his Biblical scholarship—so much sounder than Clement's—taught him.

His attitude to the Canon of the New Testament is stricter. There is indeed for him no official imposition of canonicity. But he recognizes quite clearly the finality of the four Gospels. He makes this clear by a passage in the *Homilies on Luke*, for which a Greek fragment survives:[1] πολλοὶ ἐθέλησαν γράψαι, ἀλλ' οἱ δόκιμοι τραπεζῖται οὐ πάντα ἀνέκριναν, ἀλλὰ τὰ τέσσαρα μόνα ἐπελέξαντο. Then he mentions gospels which are not genuine: τὸ κατ' Αἰγυπτίους εὐαγγέλιον, and τῶν Δώδεκα εὐαγγέλιον, and τὸ κατὰ Θωμᾶν εὐαγγέλιον, and κατὰ Βασιλίδην εὐαγγέλιον, and κατὰ Ματθίαν, καὶ ἄλλα πλείονα, τὰ δὲ τέτταρα μόνα προκρίνει ἡ θεοῦ ἐκκλησία. These gospels were written by people who only 'took in hand' to write, but the Four were inspired by the Holy Spirit. We may compare a fragment of the *Commentary on Matthew* quoted by Eusebius (*H.E.* VI. 25): μαθὼν περὶ τῶν τεσσάρων εὐαγγελίων ἃ καὶ μόνα ἀναντίρρητά ἐστιν ἐν τῇ ὑπὸ τὸν οὐρανὸν ἐκκλησίᾳ τοῦ θεοῦ. And yet even here we do not find Origen quite exclusive; Prat is not quite accurate when he says[2] that Origen 'recognized only four canonical Gospels, because tradition recognized no more besides'. The tradition received by Origen from Clement at least would not have been as exclusive as this, and in fact, as we shall see, Origen does sometimes quote from other gospels than the Four. Moreover Koetschau[3] points out that Origen quotes sayings of our Lord which do not appear in the canonical Gospels,[4] and he makes the interesting suggestion that Origen set very little store by S. Mark's Gospel, for he shows little familiarity with it, and in one passage in

---

[1] *Hom. on Luke* I (on Luke I. 1–4), *P.G.* XIII, 1801. The δόκιμοι τραπεζῖται, I now think, must be the evangelists and not, as I suggested in my article 'Origen's Doctrine of Tradition' in *J.T.S.* (Vol. xlix, no. 193–4 [1948]), the Christian *élite*.

[2] *Origène, le Théologien et l'Exégète*, p. 8.

[3] Introduction to his Edition of *Against Celsus* (*G.C.S.*, Origenes I), Section III.

[4] See below, p. 145.

Against Celsus seems to have forgotten it altogether. There is no justification for Lawson's statement[1] that Origen (among others) permitted the non-canonical gospels to be read in private, though not in public worship.

In his *Commentary on John*[2] he divides the books claiming to be inspired into γνήσιον, νόθον, and μικτόν; but (as is true, indeed, of his threefold division of the allegorical senses of Scripture), he does not often keep to this division. His most characteristic phrase for describing books as what we should to-day call 'canonical' is αἱ φερόμεναι ἐν ταῖς ἐκκλησίαις τοῦ θεοῦ γραφαί,[3] or κατὰ τὰ ἀναντίρρητα τῶν ἀναφερομένων βιβλίων θεοπνεύστων.[4] In other words, the conception of an official *list*, which the word Canon suggests to us, is as entirely absent from Origen as it is from Clement. The general judgement and use of the Church is his approximate (but not exclusive) guide.[5]

In a passage in the *Commentary on Matthew*,[6] he mentions the *Gospel of Peter* and seems inclined to believe a tradition which he finds in it. In a fragment of the *Commentary on John*[7] Origen discusses the authenticity of several books. Of the Second Epistle of Peter he says ἀμφιβάλλεται. He says that the author of the Fourth Gospel and the First Epistle of John is the author of the Apocalypse; and of 2 John and 3 John he says, οὐ πάντες φασὶ γνησίας εἶναι ταύτας.[8] He mentions the *Gospel according to the Hebrews*, with a qualification, in the *Homilies on Jeremiah*,[9] and without comment in *Commentary on John* II. 12, and

---

[1] *Biblical Theology of Saint Irenaeus*, p. 45.   [2] XIII. 17.

[3] *Against C.* VI. xx; cf. *Comm. on John* XIX. 23, ὡς ἐν τῇ φερομένῃ Ἰακώβου ἐπιστολῇ; *Against C.* VI. xxvi, τῶν ἐν ταῖς ἐκκλησίαις φερομένων εὐαγγελίων; *Letter to Africanus* I, τῆς ἐν τῷ Δανιὴλ φερομένης ἐν ταῖς ἐκκλησίαις Σωσάννης.

[4] The phrase is in this context applied to the O.T. Canon. See *Comm. on Ps. 4. 2 (P.G.* XII, 1140).

[5] I need hardly emphasize by now that the Latin translations of Origen come within the circle of suspicion in their references to the Canon and must be used with great discrimination. Yet many scholars have quite failed to realize this.

[6] X. 17. He may be here identifying the *Gospel of Peter* with the *Book of James*, or (though this seems to me less likely) he may mean that the story is to be found in one of these two books. His phrase is τοῦ ἐπιγεγραμμένου κατὰ Πέτρον εὐαγγελίου ἢ τοῦ βιβλίου Ἰακώβου.

[7] Frag. 107 in A. E. Brooke's edition.

[8] The statement, therefore, of Blackman (*Marcion and his Influence*, p. 37) about 2 John, that by the end of the second century we find it (among others cited) 'in the canon of most churches', must not be applied to include the Church of Alexandria.   [9] XV. 4; the qualification is εἰ δέ τις παραδέχεται.

again (Hilgenfeld adds)[1] in *Against Celsus*,[2] and in the *Commentary on Matthew*.[3] The *Preaching of Peter* (Πέτρου κήρυγμα or *Petri Doctrina*) he describes in the *Concerning First Principles* as 'not counted among the ecclesiastical books', though he also tries to explain away the argument based upon it on other grounds,[4] and in *Commentary on John* XIII. 17 he mentions it as quoted by Heracleon, and seems most uncertain about its genuineness. In the *Commentary on Matthew*[5] Origen remarks that '*in quibusdam scripturis non publicis*' the conversion of Pilate's wife is recorded. This is a reference to *The Acts of Pilate*, and he clearly has no confidence that they are genuine. Earlier in the same work[6] he has quoted the *Clementine Recognitions* without comment as to their authority. Clement of Rome's *Epistle* he quotes four times,[7] on no occasion hinting anything as to its unfitness to be called Scripture. He accepted the *Epistle of Barnabas* as genuine without question (though he is not nearly as much interested in it as is Clement), for he quotes from it three times[8] without comment on its genuineness. He certainly regarded it as Scripture because in one of these references (*Against Celsus* I. lxiii) Celsus had apparently quoted it, and Origen would have hastened to disown it, had he thought it suspect. Instead he calls it τῇ Βαρνάβα καθολικῇ ἐπιστολῇ.[9] Hilgenfeld is surely not overstating when he says of Origen's use of this work, '*inter sacras scripturas quodam modo numeravit*'.

Then there are two works where we can with some confidence trace a cooling of Origen's approval concerning them. One of these is the *Shepherd* of Hermas. Six times he refers to it without commenting on its inspiration.[10] There are two other passages in the *Concerning First*

---

[1] *Nov. Test. extra Can.*, Introd. to fragments of lost works, p. 6.

[2] v. lxi.　　　　　　　　　　　　[3] XVI. 12.

[4] *Con. First P.*, Origen's Preface, 8.　　[5] Part II, 122.　　[6] Part II, 77.

[7] *Con. First P.* II. 3. 6; *Comm. on John* VI. 36; *Hom. on Joshua* III. iv; and Fragments on Ezekiel (*P.G.* XIII, 767–836), on Ezekiel 8. 3. See Hilgenfeld, op. cit., Prolegomena to his edition of Clement's *Epistle to the Corinthians*, xxii–xxiii.

[8] *Con. First P.* III. 2. 4; *Comm. on Romans* I. xviii (on Rom. 1. 24); *Against C.* I. lxiii. See Hilgenfeld, op. cit., Prolegomena to his edition of the *Epistle of Barnabas*, x.

[9] Koetschau (*G.C.S.*, Origenes I, Introduction, Section III) points out that in this passage the quotation from *Barnabas* is immediately followed by one from Luke and from 1 Timothy, so that *Barnabas* can, in Origen's estimation, stand beside the εὐαγγέλιον and the ἀπόστολος.

[10] *Con. First P.* I. 3. 3; III. 3. 4; *Comm. on John* I. 17; *Hom. on Joshua* X. i; *Hom. on Ezekiel* XIII. iii; Frag. on Hosea (*Philoc.* VIII. 3).

Principles, one (II. 1. 5) where he quotes Hermas and then says that he supports the view he is contending for '*ex Scripturarum auctoritate*', and the other (IV. 2. 4) where he describes the *Shepherd* as τῷ ὑπό τινων καταφρονουμένῳ βιβλίῳ, but it is obvious that he himself is not among these despisers. *Concerning First Principles* I have dated about 225. In the *Homilies on Luke*[1] (*c.* 233–4), he is still very sure of the inspiration of the work; for, having quoted an apocryphal work which he knows may be disputed, he adds that if this work offends anybody, he can find the same doctrine in Hermas' *Shepherd*, as if it were a much more widely-acknowledged source. In the *Commentary on Romans* he calls it 'a work which seems to me very useful, and, as I believe, divinely inspired'.[2] In the *Commentary on Matthew* (which I have dated 246) he describes it as φερομένης μὲν ἐν τῇ ἐκκλησίᾳ γραφῆς, οὐ παρὰ πᾶσι δὲ ὁμολογουμένης εἶναι θείας;[3] we may therefore conclude that we have original comments of Origen, and not additions of his translators, in the '*si cui placeat illum legere librum*' of *Commentary on Matthew*, Pt. II, 53, the '*si cui tamen Scriptura illa recipienda videtur*' of *Homilies on Numbers* VIII. i (dated 246–55), and the '*si cui tamen libellus ille recipiendus videtur*' of *Homily* I *on Psalm 38*, Section I (dated 247–8), all of which suggest a more hesitant attitude to the *Shepherd* later in Origen's life.[4] What precisely occasioned Origen's hesitation we do not know. It can hardly have been the objection raised against it by the Muratorian Canon, that it was composed '*nuper temporibus nostris*',[5] for Origen must always have known the approximate date of its author. Perhaps it was a gradual realization that the book was not as widely accepted among Churches generally as he had supposed when he wrote the *Concerning First Principles*.[6]

[1] Homily xxxv (on Luke 12. 59).

[2] *Comm. on Romans* x. xxxi. I have dated this Commentary 245 on pp. 16–17, 26.

[3] XIV. 21.

[4] Hilgenfeld (op. cit., Prolegomena to his Edition of the *Shepherd*, p. xi) finds another reference in the *Comm. on Matthew*, which I have not checked. But he has not noticed the references in the *Homily on the Psalms* or the *Commentary on Romans*. For the passage in the *Homily on the Psalms*, see *P.G.* XII, 1372.

[5] See Blackman, *Marcion and his Influence*, p. 34, n. 1.

[6] Irenaeus called it ἡ γραφή, but this does not necessarily imply that he regarded it as what we should now call 'canonical', any more than Origen's use of this word for the *Shepherd* implies that he did. See Lawson, *Biblical Theology of Saint Irenaeus*, p. 50.

The other work where we may trace a similar process working is the *Acts of Paul*. In *Concerning First Principles*[1] he quotes this book with evident belief in its genuineness; but in the *Commentary on John* XX. 12 (which must have been composed at the earliest in 233) his verdict on the book becomes εἴ τῳ δὲ φίλον παραδέξασθαι.

Origen's attitude to the Epistle to the Hebrews is the most revealing of all for a study of his views on canonicity. In the vast majority of his references to the book he assumes without question that it was written by S. Paul. Once[2] he admits the possibility of its not having been written by Paul (though he tells us that he himself believes in the Pauline authorship), once[3] he calls it ἡ πρὸς Ἑβραίους ἐπιστολή only, and once, in a well-known fragment of his *Homilies on Hebrews* preserved by Eusebius,[4] he discusses the whole question fully. The passage is important enough to be set out at some length. It runs thus:[5]

'The nature of the style of the Letter inscribed "To the Hebrews" has not the Apostle's unskilful diction, for he confessed that he was unskilled in word, that is in style. But anyone who understands how to distinguish one style from another would agree that the Letter displays better Greek in the composition of its expressions. On the other hand anyone who has read the Apostle's writings attentively would assent also to the opinion that the ideas of the Letter are magnificent, and not inferior to the acknowledged works of the Apostle.' And later: 'If I were to give my opinion, I would say that the ideas are those of the Apostle, but the style and the composition of one who

[1] I. 2. 3.   [2] *Comm. on Matt.*, Pt. II, 28.
[3] Fragment of a Commentary on Psalm 40. 6 (*P.G.* XII, 1409).
[4] *H.E.* VI. 25.
[5] Ὁ χαρακτὴρ τῆς λέξεως τῆς πρὸς Ἑβραίους ἐπιγεγραμμένης ἐπιστολῆς οὐκ ἔχει τὸ ἐν λόγῳ ἰδιωτικὸν τοῦ ἀποστόλου, ὁμολογήσαντος ἑαυτὸν ἰδιώτην εἶναι τῷ λόγῳ, τουτέστι, τῇ φράσει. ἀλλά ἐστιν ἡ ἐπιστολὴ συνθέσει τῆς λέξεως ἑλληνικωτέρα, πᾶς ὁ ἐπιστάμενος κρίνειν φράσεων διαφορὰς ὁμολογήσαι ἄν· πάλιν τε αὖ ὅτι τὰ νοήματα τῆς ἐπιστολῆς θαυμάσιά ἐστι καὶ οὐ δεύτερα τῶν ἀποστολικῶν ὁμολογουμένων γραμμάτων, καὶ τοῦτο ἂν συμφήσαι εἶναι ἀληθὲς πᾶς ὁ προσέχων τῇ ἀναγνώσει τῇ ἀποστολικῇ....

Ἐγὼ δὲ ἀποφαινόμενος εἴποιμ' ἂν ὅτι τὰ μὲν νοήματα τοῦ ἀποστόλου ἐστίν, ἡ δὲ φράσις καὶ ἡ σύνθεσις ἀπομνημονεύσαντός τινος τὰ ἀποστολικά, καὶ ὡσπερεὶ σχολιογραφήσαντός τινος τὰ εἰρημένα ὑπὸ τοῦ διδασκάλου. εἴ τις οὖν ἐκκλησία ἔχει ταύτην τὴν ἐπιστολὴν ὡς Παύλου αὕτη εὐδοκιμείτω καὶ ἐπὶ τούτῳ. οὐ γὰρ εἰκῇ οἱ ἀρχαῖοι ἄνδρες ὡς Παύλου αὐτὴν παραδεδώκασι. τίς δὲ ὁ γράψας τὴν ἐπιστολήν, τὸ μὲν ἀληθὲς θεὸς οἶδεν. ἡ δὲ εἰς ἡμᾶς φθάσασα ἱστορία, ὑπὸ τινων μὲν λεγόντων ὅτι Κλήμης ὁ γενόμενος ἐπίσκοπος Ῥωμαίων ἔγραψε τὴν ἐπιστολήν, ὑπὸ τινων δὲ ὅτι Λουκᾶς ὁ γράψας τὸ εὐαγγέλιον καὶ τὰς Πράξεις.

is relating from memory the apostolic teaching and as it were interpreting what had been said by the teacher. If therefore any Church finds this Letter attributed to Paul, let it treat it as authentic even because of this attribution, for the men of old did not hand it down as Paul's for nothing. As for who wrote the Letter, God knows the truth. The information which has come down to us consists of some sources which say that Clement who was bishop of the Romans wrote the Letter, and others, that Luke did who wrote the Gospel and the Acts.'[1]

This frank statement makes perfectly clear what we might infer from Origen's references to other works whose authority was disputed, that the question of authorship was not the only test, in his eyes, of a book's authority. In this case the Letter's νοήματα θαυμάσια commend it to him, and it is likely that this was true of Hermas' *Shepherd* too. Secondly, the tradition current in the Church concerning a book was something which, in Origen's view, should be given its true weight, but was not by any means decisive. Thirdly, the final standard of judgement in this matter was the fluctuating and indefinite one of the use of any book in question in the Church of Origen's day, and Origen was content to leave it so without betraying any signs of wanting an official list of books of the New Testament Canon. These words even go far to modify the theory that it was owing to a mistaken critical judgement of the early Church that the Epistle to the Hebrews was allowed into the New Testament Canon at all.[2] Origen's grounds for accepting this Epistle are independent of the question of its apostolic authorship, the uncertainty concerning which he does not attempt to disguise.

We must not, however, overlook the fact that Origen does show noticeably more definiteness about the New Testament Canon than Clement. He is more concerned to distinguish genuine tradition from that which is uncertain or spurious, he takes far more notice of the verdict of the Churches in general. He is, as we have seen, quite willing to admit apocryphal books as profitable, or as containing profitable portions, but he insists upon exercising a critical judgement upon them. In one passage in the *Commentary on Matthew*[3] he says that he knows

---

[1] Observe that Origen's theory is really a modified version of Clement's. See above, p. 129.

[2] See the remark of W. F. Howard in *The Bible in its Ancient and English Versions*, p. 68, quoted by Blackman, *Marcion and his Influence*, p. 34, n. 2.

[3] Part II, 28 (*P.G.* XIII, 1657).

very well that many apocryphal writings are composed by heretics in order to convey false doctrine, and may even have been deliberately circulated by the Jews, and that a well-trained critical mind is necessary to distinguish valuable apocryphal matter from falsehoods. The passage (which is extant only in Latin) goes on to say '*nemo uti debet ad confirmationem dogmatum libris qui sunt extra canonizatas scripturas*'. Quite apart from the fact that Origen himself clearly breaks this rule, the phrase '*canonizatas scripturas*' betrays the addition or alteration of the unknown translator of this Commentary, and we can base no argument upon this sentence, though Cadiou (who should know better) does.[1] Later in the same work[2] Origen distinguishes between heretics who produce '*secretas et non vulgatas scripturas*' and those who argue from '*canonicas scripturas*'. We do not know, of course, the original Greek of either of these terms,[3] but the passage does obviously imply a distinction between recognized and not recognized writings which Clement would hardly have understood.

In summarizing Origen's attitude to the Canon we can say without qualification that he regards the Canon of the Gospels as closed in a more final sense than did Clement, and that he displays a greater desire for definiteness than he, and a more sensitive appreciation of the possibilities of documents' being spurious. But fundamentally Origen's attitude to the Canon is the same as Clement's; he will accept as Christian evidence any material that he finds convincing or appealing. Neither of them shows any signs of being conscious of the existence of a *list* of canonical works, apart from the list of four Gospels recognized as more authoritative than any others. Clement's promiscuous acceptance of any work, no matter how doubtful its relevance to the Christian dispensation, which appealed to his curious and comprehensive intellect is in Origen's case modified by the accuracy of a scholar and the experience of a traveller. But that is all. It is quite possible that the

---

[1] *La Jeunesse d'Origène*, p. 79. We have seen this translator introducing alterations already. See above, p. 43. Perhaps this passage may be used as evidence to date the translation at the earliest somewhere in the fourth century. The only occurrences of '*canonizatus*', apart from this one, listed in the *Glossary of Later Latin* (A. Souter, 1949, p. 37) are from Ambrose and from an Arian fragment of the fifth or sixth century.

[2] Pt. II, 46.

[3] If I were to guess, I should say ἀπόκρυφας for '*secretas*' and φερομένας ἐν ταῖς ἐκκλησίαις for '*canonicas*'.

Alexandrian school were unusual in their attitude to the Canon. Blackman[1] says that 'in principle, the limits of the canon were fixed by about A.D. 180. The struggle with Montanism rather than the struggle with Marcionitism was the decisive factor in producing the conception of a closed "apostolic canon"'; and no doubt this statement is true for other Churches than that of Alexandria. We have the evidence of the Muratorian Canon to show that in the time of Clement of Alexandria the 'closed canon' was a conception known at Rome. There is the evidence of an unknown anti-Montanist writer (c. A.D. 192–3) quoted by Eusebius[2] who uses the expression, ἐξευλαβούμενος μή πη δόξω τισίν ἐπισυγγράφειν ἢ ἐπιδιατάσσεσθαι τῷ τῆς τοῦ εὐαγγελίου καινῆς διαθήκης λόγῳ, ᾧ μήτε προσθεῖναι μήτε ἀφελεῖν δυνατόν.[3] But certainly in Alexandria in the time of both Clement and Origen the conception of 'a closed "apostolic canon"' is unknown. Bardy is quite inaccurate in saying that in Origen's time 'Une liste officielle' of Scriptures formed the point of departure for Christian teaching.[4] The verdict of Merk,[5] strangely followed by Daniélou, is a definite exaggeration. 'Das ist überall die Stellung die Origenes zu den Büchern der hl. Schrift einnimmt, ein Schwanken ist bei ihm nicht erkennbar. Er ist in der Abgrenzung der Bücher viel bestimmter als sein Lehrer und Vorgänger Clemens, wir dürfen wohl die Behauptung wagen, dass sich unter allen orientalischen Schriftstellern kaum einer findet, der mit dieser Grundsätzlichkeit und Bestimmtheit den Katholischen Standpunkt ausgesprochen hat.' We have seen several examples of vacillation in this matter on Origen's part, and if the 'Catholic view' of the Canon includes reference to a list of books authorized by any authority more official than that of their use in the average Church of Origen's day, Origen does not share the Catholic viewpoint. It is probable that these authors have been misled, as too many other scholars have, by the references to the Canon in the Latin translators of Origen's works, all of whom lived at least a century after

---

[1] *Marcion and his Influence*, p. 34. [2] *H.E.* v. 16.

[3] Blackman, op. cit. p. 34, n. 1, refers this to the Canon of Scripture. I do not see why it should not be as suitably referred to the κανὼν ἐκκλησιαστικός, the Church's version of what the Gospel and N.T. are.

[4] 'La Règle de Foi d'Origène', p. 173. Later, on the same page, he quotes the phrase 'canonicae scripturae' as Origen's, from Rufinus' translation of the *Con. First P.* IV. 4. 6. I cannot consider this evidence admissible. See above, p. 143.

[5] 'Origenes und der Kanon des alten Testaments', p. 204; see Daniélou, *Origène*, p. 143.

his day, when very different conceptions of the Canon prevailed from Origen's own.

Something more remains to be said, however, on the subject of traditions outside the Canon of Scripture mentioned by Origen, and not attributed to any particular book. Like Clement, he occasionally quotes a *logion* attributed to our Lord or his apostles which has not survived in any canonical book. In *Concerning Prayer* ii. 2, he quotes a sentence which we have already found quoted by Clement,[1] αἰτεῖτε τὰ μεγάλα καὶ τὰ μικρὰ ὑμῖν προστεθήσεται, and to it he adds the corresponding verse, αἰτεῖτε τὰ ἐπουράνια καὶ τὰ ἐπίγεια ὑμῖν προστεθήσεται.[2] In the *Homilies on Numbers*[3] he quotes, without assigning it to any book of the Bible, a saying of our Lord: '*Aut non legistis quia et sacerdotes in Templo sabbatum violent et sine crimine sint?*' The Migne editor thinks that it is a vaguely remembered reproduction of John 7. 22, but it is more likely a *logion* from some apocryphal gospel which Origen thought, by a lapse of memory, was from a canonical one. And in *Homilies on Leviticus*[4] he quotes a *logion* which he calls apostolic, 'Blessed is he who even fasts in order that he may feed a poor man'.

Then we can glean a number of disconnected historical facts or guesses about characters and incidents in the New Testament, but not found in it, scattered up and down Origen's works. In *Against Celsus* I. lvi, he says that the manger where Jesus was laid, on being born, was in a cave, and that everybody knows it. In the same work he twice tells us[5] that the two disciples going to Emmaus were Simon and Cleopas. Probably the first piece of information was based on widespread popular tradition and the second on an intelligent guess. Of the same sort are the statements concerning Gaius, mentioned in Romans 16. 23, that '*Fertur sane traditione maiorum quod hic Gaius primus episcopus fuerit Thessalonicensis ecclesiae*';[6] or the tradition concerning the deaths of the apostles, that Thomas died in Parthia, Andrew in Scythia, John

---

[1] See above, p. 131.
[2] He refers to it again in *Against C.* VII. xliv, though he does not directly quote it. He does quote it again, however, *Comm. on Psalm 4, verse 3 (P.G.* XII, 1147).
[3] XXIII. iv. [4] x. ii.
[5] II. lxii, lxviii. The information is repeated in *Hom. on Jeremiah* xx. 8.
[6] *Comm. on Romans* x. xli.

in Ephesus,[1] Peter (after visiting Pontus, Galatia, Bithynia, Cappadocia, and the Jewish Diaspora in Asia) in Rome, crucified head-
downwards, and Paul also in Rome;[2] or the assumption made in
Homilies on Genesis[3] that the Magi mentioned in Matthew's Gospel
were three in number; or the information that Tabor was the mountain
upon which Jesus was transfigured, and Hermon the hill upon which
was situated the city called Nain.[4] The story of the death of Zacharias,
father of John the Baptist,[5] is probably a piece of tradition of the same
sort.

There is one copious and unusual source of this extra-Scriptural
occasional tradition about which we have so far said little, and which
we must now examine more carefully; that is, contemporary Jewish
scholarship. It is very clear that Origen was in quite close touch with
Rabbinic scholarship for most of his life, and from this source he
derived a varied collection of elaborations upon the narrative of the
Old Testament, exegetical and philological suggestions, and Midrash
generally. The habit of elaborating upon the Old Testament stories he
must have learnt primarily from Philo (who was of course indebted in
his turn to the Jewish schools of his day). Philo is perfectly capable of
expanding his account of an Old Testament incident without any
particular source to justify him, from sheer desire to make his account
more readable or more elegant. For instance, in his *De Josepho*[6] he puts
into the mouth of Jacob, when tempted by Potiphar's wife, a long and
most amusingly inappropriate speech about the sources of moral
action. This is, of course, not Midrash, but an attempt to follow the
tradition which had long existed in the writing of secular history, that
the historian composes suitable speeches to put into the mouths of his
characters. He is also inclined to improve a narrative in order to make
it more elegant. In his account of Joseph's adventures he 'improves'
the phrase 'and he shaved himself' of Genesis 41. 14,[7] and he has

---

[1] But in *Comm. on Matt.* XVI. 6 he says that the Roman Emperor exiled John
to the island of Patmos, and seems to imply (but we cannot be certain) that he
died there.

[2] Quoted by Eusebius, *H.E.* III. 1, from the Third Book of Origen's *Commentary on Genesis.*

[3] XIV. iii.   [4] *Comm. on Psalm 89, verse 12 (P.G.* XII, 1548).

[5] For the references see above, p. 42, n. 2.

[6] *De Josepho* IX.

[7] *De Josepho* XX. The phrase becomes καὶ τἆλλα φαιδρύνοντες.

previously represented Joseph as behaving rather like an Elizabeth Fry to the other prisoners while he was in prison.[1] Similarly, in his description of Balaam's encounter with the ass, he cannot bring himself to call the creature anything as homely as ὄνος but calls it merely ὑποζύγιον, and he omits the incident of the ass speaking, probably because he thought it would sound ridiculous to Greek readers.[2] We find, however, more definitely derived and traditional elaborations on the Biblical narrative than these in Philo. In the *De Vita Mosis*[3] he tells us that sources for Moses' life are the Scriptures and the information 'of the elders'; this latter he calls τὰ λεγόμενα, so it is presumably oral tradition.[4] Again he says, of a most unconvincing gloss to the effect that the sacrifice of the Passover was made by heads of families and not by the priests, because the Israelites were originally in such a hurry to leave Egypt that they could not wait for the priests to do the sacrificing, ταῦτα μὲν κατὰ παλαιὰν ἀρχαιολογίαν ἱστορεῖται.[5] The work *De Abrahamo* is particularly rich in these additions. Abraham's encounter with Pharaoh concerning Sarah his wife is described in exaggerated language with a wealth of new detail.[6] The account of the wickedness and destruction of Sodom and Gomorrah is full of non-Biblical elaboration.[7] Abraham's exploit narrated in Genesis 14 is greatly embroidered; Philo tells us that Abraham slew some of the enemy in their beds, the armed resistance of some he overcame, and he lost none of his own men.[8] And a little later on[9] he tells us that οἱ σαφέστατα διηγούμενοι relate that Abraham kept Hagar as his concubine only till she was pregnant, not till a son was born. The same Midrash is apparent, though not so frequently, in other books. He amplifies the story of Joseph's distribution of the corn in Egypt.[10] In his biography of Moses he tells us that Pharaoh's daughter wanted a child, and once pretended to be pregnant; and he adds a deal of fanciful detail about Moses' boyhood.[11] Similarly he tells us[12] that during the plague of water turned into blood, great heaps of carcasses of men

---

[1] Ibid. xvi.   [2] *De Vita Mosis* I. xlviii, xlix.   [3] I. i.

[4] T. W. Manson (*The Teaching of Jesus*, p. 290, n. 2) tells us that 'Along with the written Law Moses was believed to have received other oral instructions which were handed down through the authorities listed in the Mishnah'.

[5] *De Specialibus Legibus* II. xxvii.

[6] *De Abrahamo* xix.

[7] Ibid. xxvi–xxvii.   [8] Ibid. xl.   [9] xliii.

[10] *De Josepho* XLIII.   [11] *De Vita Mosis* I. v.   [12] Ibid. I. xvii.

killed by the plague lay about the cross-roads, and elsewhere[1] that all the ancestors of the wives of priests must have attained the standard of purity laid down for their wives in Leviticus 21. 7—a refinement which is not to be found in the Bible itself.

Clement of Alexandria was not at all interested in, or (except that he mentions that one of his teachers was a Hebrew from Palestine)[2] closely in touch with, contemporary Jewish thought. He must have known some Midrash, for he records[3] that Moses' name at his circumcision was Ioakeim, and in heaven, after his assumption, Melchi. This may have been derived from Philo, or possibly from an apocryphal work. And, as we have seen,[4] he refers to people called οἱ μύσται from whom he may have derived a little further information of this sort. But he had little or no respect for Jewish tradition or scholarship. He calls the literal interpretation of the Bible the 'Jewish' one,[5] and he wrote a book called κατὰ 'Ιουδαϊζόντων, of which only a small fragment survives.[6]

In contrast with Clement, Origen is well acquainted with contemporary Jewish scholarship, and shows its influence on many occasions. That there did exist traditions among the Jews independent of the Bible but concerned with its interpretation or supplementation he must have known from Philo. Indeed in one place[7] he quotes what he calls a χαριεστάτην παράδοσιν from someone whom he calls ὁ 'Εβραῖος to the effect that the difficult parts of Scripture have their solution in other parts of it. It is quite possible that this Hebrew is Philo.[8] In the *Commentary on Matthew*[9] he conjectures that the chief priests and elders might have had secret traditions about the question of authority

---

[1] *De Specialibus Legibus* I. xix. He is supported by Josephus, *Contra Apionem* I. 31, here.

[2] *Strom.* I. i (*P.G.* VIII, 697–704). See p. 53 above.

[3] *Strom.* I. xxiii (*P.G.* VIII, 889).   [4] See p. 54 above.

[5] *Paid.* I. vi (*P.G.* VIII, 292); he uses 'Ιουδαϊκῶς meaning 'in the literal sense'. This indeed seems to have been a widely-accepted usage of the word. Origen uses it.

[6] See frag. xvii, *P.G.* IX, 768.

[7] *Comm. on Psalms, Book I*; *Philoc.* II. 3; *P.G.* XII, 1080.

[8] Otherwise Origen refers to Philo directly or indirectly thirteen times: *Against C.* I. xv; IV. li; V. lv; VI. xx; VII. xx; *Comm. on Matt.* X. 22; XV. 3; XVII. 17; Pt. II, 69; Frag. on Genesis 2. 2 (*P.G.* XII, 97); *Hom. on Exodus* IX. iv; XIII. iii; *Hom. on Jeremiah* XIV. 3.

[9] XVII. 2.

which our Lord posed to them in reply to their question to him in Matthew 21. 23. In the *Homilies on Numbers*[1] he makes the suggestion that the Magi derived their knowledge of the significance of the star from the writings of the school of Balaam's disciples, who wrote down the words attributed to Balaam in Numbers 23 and 24, and especially 24. 17 ('There shall come forth a star out of Jacob'). The Magi, he says, learnt this information ἐκ πατρικῆς παραδόσεως καὶ διδαχῆς. That both Clement and Origen imagined that the Jews under the Old Testament had access to secret traditions we have already seen in our examination of the doctrine of secret tradition of both these writers.[2]

We can give many examples of how this sort of non-Scriptural material was reproduced by Origen.[3] He has, in the first instance, plenty of experience of controversy with Jewish scholars on points of Christian doctrine. In the *Commentary on John*[4] he tells us that to the Christian claim that Christ in his Entry into Jerusalem fulfils the prophecy of Zechariah 9. 9 Jewish writers object, asking how Christ fulfilled the verse next after 9. 9, 'I will cut off the chariot from Ephraim and the horse from Jerusalem, and the battle bow shall be cut off'. And again, they ask, why did Jesus use animals for so short a journey? And how did he manage, according to Zechariah's account, to sit on two animals? In *Against Celsus*[5] we learn that Jewish scholars maintained that the Suffering Servant passage, Isaiah 52. 13–53. 12, was written about the whole people 'which experienced the Dispersion and was afflicted, in order that many might become proselytes by reason of the dispersal of the Jews among the other races'. Later in the same work[6] Celsus adopts what is clearly the stock argument of the Jews against Jesus—that he established his reputation by γοητεία. In the *Homilies on Genesis*[7] the Jews are represented as asserting '*allegoriae non superest locus*', a line of argument which probably accounts for the use of the adjective Ἰουδαϊκός by Clement and Origen. And in the *Homilies on Leviticus*,[8] commenting on Leviticus 6. 18, 'Whosoever

[1] XIII. vii. The conjecture is repeated (perhaps indeed the passage is reproduced) in a fragment from Catenae, *P.G.* XVII, 24.

[2] See pp. 56, 58, 80, above.

[3] For this subject see also Bardy, 'Les Traditions Juives dans l'Œuvre d'Origène', in the *Revue Biblique*; Cadiou, *La Jeunesse d'Origène*, pp. 56–61; Daniélou, *Origène*, pp. 176–9.

[4] X. 27.   [5] I. lv.
[6] III. i.   [7] III. vi.   [8] IV. vii.

toucheth them [the offerings of the Lord] shall be holy', Origen says that if you take this ordinance literally, it outrages the moral sense. But when he asks the Jews about it, all they can reply is, 'That was what the Law-maker decided; nobody argues with his Lord'.

But Origen's acquaintance with Rabbinic schools is by no means confined to controversy. He reproduces several times glosses on the Old Testament which are obviously akin to midrash and sometimes tells us something of the source of the information. In *Homilies on Genesis* II. ii, Origen replies to the objections made by the heretic Apelles to the smallness of the ark by producing a theory which, he says, ἐμάθομεν δὲ ἡμεῖς ἀπό τινος τῶν παρ᾽ Ἑβραίοις ἐλλογίμων. In the *Homilies on Jeremiah*,[1] commenting on Jeremiah 20. 7, 'Thou hast deceived me, O Lord, and I was deceived', a passage which clearly had given the Rabbis trouble as well as Origen, he says: 'I will first make use of a Jewish tradition which comes to us from a man who was a refugee because of his faith in Christ and because he had risen superior to the Law and had reached the point where we are.' The suggestion is in fact an unimpressive one to the effect that God first induced Jeremiah to become a prophet who would declare woe to all nations, and then, to the prophet's chagrin, included the Jews in this declaration. In the *Homilies on Isaiah*,[2] commenting on Isaiah 6. 5, 'Mine eyes have seen the King, the Lord of Hosts', Origen says: 'Why should we not relate at this point a certain tradition of the Jews which is like the truth, and yet not true, and why should we not find an answer to the problem it presents?' He then relates a tradition that Isaiah was sawn asunder on a charge of blasphemy because he had said that he had seen God. Origen accepts the fact of Isaiah's martyrdom, but defends him from the charge of blasphemy. In the Ninth Book of the same work[3] he gives an explanation of Isaiah's reluctance to prophesy (on much the same lines as that given about Jeremiah's in the *Homilies on Jeremiah*) derived, he says, 'from a certain Jew'. In the *Homilies on Ezekiel*[4] he quotes the explanation (an impossibly ingenious one) given by 'a certain Jew' of why Ezekiel refers (14. 14) only to Noah, Daniel, and Job. In a number of Fragments on Ezekiel[5] he quotes from somebody whom he calls ὁ τῶν Ἑβραίων διδάσκαλος, who was apparently

---

[1] XX. 2.   [2] I. v.   [3] IX. i; on Isa. 6. 8, 9.   [4] IV. viii.
[5] *P.G.* XIII, 767–826. This fragment is on Ezek. 5. 10, and the later one on 9. 4.

commenting on 1 Samuel 2. 30, a theory concerning God's function of punishing which is very consonant with Origen's own theories of punishment.[1]

In a later fragment of this series a most interesting piece of information appears. Origen points out that for the 'mark' which is to be set upon the foreheads of the people of Jerusalem Aquila and Theodotion have σημείωσις τοῦ θαῦ, and that when he asked 'the Hebrews' if they have any πάτριον μάθημα about this 'tau', he received three different answers. One said that as 'tau' was the last letter of the Hebrew alphabet, it signified the perfection of those who were thus marked. The second said that it was a sign of those who kept the Law, for ת stood for תּוֹרָה. A third (who was a Christian Jew) answered him that as the 'tau' in old Hebrew characters was like a cross (X), this was a prophecy of the sign that Christians would make on their foreheads, as they do make the sign now when they begin any undertaking such as praying or reading Scripture. This last piece of information is particularly interesting, as it may well lie behind the account of the faithful being sealed on their foreheads in Revelation 7. 3, 4. The author of Revelation may have assumed that the 'tau' in Ezekiel 9. 4 (for he obviously has this passage in mind here) was a prefiguring of the X of Christ. The old Hebrew characters were still used in some circles in his day, because they appear upon coins minted during the rebellion of Bar-Cochbar (132–5), which must have been after his day.[2]

In his Preface to the *Commentaries on the Psalms*[3] Origen follows the opinion of a certain Ἰουλλος, 'the patriarch, one who was held to be a wise man by the Jews', whom he tells us he had himself consulted upon the subject, to the effect that Psalm 90 and the ten Psalms following it were by Moses. Bardy[4] says that Ἰουλλος may be a corruption of Hillel, though no Rabbi Hillel contemporary with Origen is known. Graetz conjectured that another Rabbi whom Origen is known to have

---

[1] See also *Comm. on John* VI. 14, where he tells us, ὡς ἐν ἀπορρήτοις, οὐκ οἶδα πόθεν κινούμενοι οἱ Ἑβραῖοι παραδιδόασι that Phineas the son of Eleazar was Elijah himself, and the peace that was promised him in Num. 25. 11–13 really meant a promise of immortality. Apparently it was the mention of Phineas in Judges 20. 28 that prompted this theory.

[2] It is noteworthy that the author of Revelation does not call the 'mark' set on his people by the Beast a σημεῖον, but a χάραγμα (13. 16). The σημεῖον was a consecrated sign, the Cross. See above, p. 68, n. 1.

[3] *P.G.* XII, 1056.   [4] 'Les Traditions Juives', pp. 223–4.

consulted is to be identified with Rabbi Hoschaya Rabba, who lived at Caesarea. There are a number of less interesting pieces of information to be found in Origen's works which nevertheless clearly come from Rabbinic sources. He says in the *Commentary on Matthew*[1] that Ἑβραῖοι παραδιδόασι that the body of Adam was buried at Golgotha, and he seems inclined to believe this tradition. In his *Commentary on Romans*[2] he quotes a tradition '*a patribus rationabiliter tradita, his scilicet qui ex Hebraeis ad Christi fidem venerunt*', to the effect that the three sons of Korah mentioned in Exodus 6. 24, Assir, Elkanah, and Abiasaph (all of whose names he allegorizes, but not, I think, from this tradition), separated themselves from the sons of Korah destroyed in the regrettable incident recorded in Numbers 16, and composed instead the Psalms which are headed 'Of the sons of Korah'. In a fragment on Genesis 2. 8,[3] he tells us that the Hebrews have a tradition that the place was called Eden before God planted a garden there, and that it is the centre of the world. In a later fragment of the same series, on Genesis 41. 8, Origen asks the very reasonable question, how did Pharaoh know that the magicians of Egypt were not interpreting his dreams, when he could not remember the interpretation? And he gives the answer of one whom he calls ὁ Ἑβραῖος, that Pharaoh had seen the interpretations when he had seen the dreams, but had forgotten the interpretations—an answer which should surely satisfy any modern psychologist. Obviously in the same category is the tradition recorded in the *Homilies on Genesis*[4] that there was a place set aside in the ark for the animals' dung. Scripture, Origen adds, is silent about this because it was not fit for allegorization. Possibly we should assign to the same category the story, mentioned in the *Fragments on Ezekiel*,[5] that Nebuchadnezzar fried alive (ἀπετηγάνισε) the sons of Zedekiah the King of Judah.

Origen displays also some knowledge of Jewish custom and practice, and of Rabbinic glosses on the Law and etymologies and translations. In his Preface to the *Commentaries on the Song of Songs*,[6] he says, on the subject of the danger of interpreting the book carnally: 'For they say that it is a custom even among the Jews that nobody should be allowed even to hold this book in his hands unless he had reached a full and

---

[1] Part II, 126.   [2] X. vii.
[3] *P.G.* XII, 100. The later fragment is in *P.G.* XII, 133.
[4] II. i.   [5] *P.G.* XIII, 767–824, on Ezek. 4. 3.   [6] *P.G.* XIII, 63.

ripe age of life. Indeed, we gather that this is a custom of theirs too: although it is usual with them for all the Scriptures to be given to their children by their teachers and wise men, and at the same time those writings which they call δευτερώσεις, yet these four works are kept to the last, namely the beginning of Genesis in which the creation of the world is described, and the first part of the prophet Ezekiel in which an account is given of the cherubim, and his last part which contains the building of the Temple, and this book of the Song of Songs.' In *Concerning First Principles* IV. 3. 2, commenting on the prohibition in the Law against leaving the house (Ex. 16. 29) or carrying burdens on the sabbath (Neh. 13. 19), he tells us that Jewish exegetes try to explain this away without allegorizing, 'alleging futile traditions' (φέροντες ψυχρὰς παραδόσεις). They say, for instance, that 'house' means a radius of two thousand cubits. Others, 'of whom is Dositheus the Samaritan', say that the command means that everyone is to remain in the same state of mind during the sabbath. Similarly οἱ 'Ιουδαίων διδάσκαλοι say that the burden not to be carried on the sabbath means a certain kind of shoe, or a sandal with nails, or that the burden is to be carried on one shoulder, but not on two. In the *Homilies on Jeremiah*[1] he tells us that Jerusalem was originally called Iebous, and 'Ιεβούς φασιν Ἑβραίων παῖδες ὅτι ἑρμηνεύεται πεπατημένη. In a *Commentary on Psalm 105, verse 31*,[2] where the LXX has εἶπεν καὶ ἦλθεν κυνόμυια, Origen explains that the κυνόμυια was interpreted by the Hebrews to mean a miscellaneous herd of wild and carnivorous beasts. In his *Fragments on Ezekiel*,[3] when he is commenting on Ezekiel 9. 2, where, for the words 'writer's inkhorn', the LXX has the mistaken translation ζώνη σαπφείρου, Origen points out that here Aquila reads κάστω γραμματέως (for Hebrew קֶסֶת הַסֹּפֵר) and that one of the Hebrews used to say that κάστω meant καλαμάριον. Here he has picked up a piece of genuinely useful information. In *Against Celsus*[4] he quotes a Jewish opinion that circumcision was instituted to prevent a hostile angel from injuring the Jews, and when circumcised they were invulnerable to him. In support of this is quoted Exodus 4. 24–6, and the claim is made that the Hebrew, literally translated 'a bridegroom of blood', is here more correct than the LXX rendering, ἔστη τὸ αἷμα τῆς περιτομῆς. Here once more Origen has recovered a better translation through his knowledge of Rabbinic tradition.

[1] XIII. 2.   [2] *P.G.* XII, 1564.   [3] *P.G.* XIII, 767–824.
[4] v. xlviii.

His *Letter to Africanus* affords us another glimpse of his relations with the Jews. In a much earlier work, the *Stromateis*, Book x,[1] he had recorded a tradition which he had derived from a Jew concerning the names of the two elders who tempted Susanna. But he was there doubtful as to whether this is a certain tradition. Similarly in the *Stromateis* he was by no means sure that the punning on the names of trees in the History of Susanna represented a Hebrew original. But by the time he writes the *Letter to Africanus* (which we placed in 243), his doubts have vanished. He accepts the History as quite genuine, and is even prepared to believe that the puns may be reproducing an original Hebrew. One of the chief reasons for this change is that he has in the interval between the *Stromateis* and the *Letter to Africanus* consulted Jewish scholars. About the puns, he says[2] that he asked many Jews about this point, and even, at their request, showed them the trees in question. The only reply he records is that the names of these trees do not appear in the Hebrew Bible, so that his informant could not tell him for certain whether the Hebrew could bear the same double meaning as the Greek. His informant could only say the names of these trees in Aramaic (φωνῇ τῇ Συριακῇ). But this certainly argues quite a close and friendly familiarity, in at least this period of his life, with Jewish scholars. Origen's own phrase is 'the Jews with whom I associated' (Ἑβραίοις οἷς συνέμιξα).

One other point has to be recorded. We have had occasion to see several times how Origen will sometimes attribute a tradition of this sort to 'the Hebrew', not merely to 'a Hebrew' or to the Hebrews generally. The same phrase occurs in the Hexapla, as a source to which a number of readings are attributed. They appear especially in the margin of the LXX column for the books of Genesis, Job, and Ezekiel, and are often very good readings, though sometimes quite different from the Hebrew text, and sometimes paraphrases rather than transla-

---

[1] *P.G.* xi, 101, 104. These fragments are preserved in Jerome's *Commentary on Daniel* xiii.

[2] *Letter to Africanus* 6. Incidentally, this would mean that we cannot place the composition of the *Stromateis* much earlier than 222, because it was during Caracalla's reign that Origen studied Hebrew under a Jewish master (see above, p. 9). Caracalla died in 217, and when the *Stromateis* were written Origen cannot have been in close touch with Jewish scholars, or presumably he would have consulted them upon this point then.

tions.[1] Field thinks that this 'Hebrew' is a Rabbinic scholar whom Origen knew or whose text or readings he had consulted. It is possible that it is to this man that Origen is referring when he sometimes attributes a tradition to 'the Hebrew'. If so, we may conjecture that part at least of this store of Rabbinic tradition came from a single Rabbi whom Origen knew personally, either in Alexandria, in his later days there (when he would be composing the *Commentary on Genesis*), or in Caesarea.[2]

We have not here gone into the question of Origen's knowledge of Hebrew (he must have had some, but cannot have had much), or of his derivation of the interpretations of place-names from Jewish sources, both of which subjects might further illuminate our study. But it is clear from the evidence set out above that Origen at least had quite a full acquaintance with schools of Jewish scholarship (and not only Jewish-Christian circles), not merely for purposes of controversy, but even for the sake of common study of difficulties in the Old Testament, study conducted in a friendly spirit. Some scholars have been ready to represent the breach between Judaism and Christianity after the Fall of Jerusalem as complete and virtually unbridged. 'Hostilities between Christian and Jew,' says R. H. Snape,[3] 'intolerant alike, prevented any mutual understanding; any parallelism of thought depended, it would seem, on the interpretation of the Old Testament by men under similar circumstances.' In the same vein Dom Gregory Dix can say:[4] 'However strong the Jewish influence which might still be exerted upon Christian thought and polity by its origins and by the retention of the Jewish scriptures as "inspired", after A.D. 70 there are

[1] E.g. Job 2. 5, בָּרֵךְ, ὁ Ἑβραῖος, βλασφημήσει σε (which is obviously the original, though it does not appear in the Massoretic text); Ezekiel 13. 18 (about pillows for the elbows of women), ὁ Ἑβραῖος, οὐαὶ ταῖς ποιούσαις φυλακτήρια, καὶ κρεμαζούσαις ἐπὶ τοῖς βραχίοσιν αὐτῶν, καὶ ἐπιτιθεμέναις αὐτὰ ἐπάνω κεφαλῆς ἑκάστης ἡλικίας. See Field, *Origenis Hexaplorum Quae Supersunt*, Prolegomena, pp. lxxvi–lxxvii.

[2] If I am to guess at the identity of this person, I would choose Rabbi Simeon ben Lakish, who lived c. A.D. 250 in Palestine, and one of whose remarks about God's deceiving people bears a striking resemblance to one of Origen's favourite doctrines. See C. G. Montefiore and H. Loewe, *A Rabbinic Anthology* (London, 1938), Cap. xxvi, p. 532.

[3] Excursus II, on 'Rabbinical and Early Christian Ethics', in *A Rabbinic Anthology*, pp. 638–9.

[4] *The Apostolic Ministry* (London, 1946), p. 228.

no direct contacts with contemporary Judaism save hostile ones.' This view must be modified by the undoubted fact that Origen, the greatest scholar of his day, was able to maintain friendly association with contemporary Jewish scholars and learn from them and reproduce in his own writings a number of traditions, glosses, and guesses, which are, indeed, largely valueless, but which sometimes genuinely help him to interpret a passage correctly, and are certainly indications that he valued the place from which they came as a source of no contemptible tradition.

CHAPTER IX

REVELATION OUTSIDE THE BIBLE

W E have already seen some indications that Clement at least believed that there was a tradition of genuine doctrine to be found somewhere in Greek pagan literature, quite outside the teaching of the Bible or of near-Scriptural or apocryphal works. It now remains to inquire into this subject, and to see how far Origen built upon what he must have learned from Clement in the matter and how far he departed from him.

It must first be made clear that Clement believed firmly that the Greek philosophers had had access to the Scriptures of the Old Testament. In this he was, of course, only following many predecessors. He himself quotes as his authorities for this view Tatian in his work πρὸς Ἕλληνας and Casianos in his Ἐξηγητικά;[1] also Philo, Megasthenes the historian, who lived under Seleucus Nicator, and Aristobulus;[2] in particular, the last described Plato as learning the philosophy of Moses in Egypt, and another writer, Numenius the Pythagorean, said, as Clement quotes him, τί γάρ ἐστι Πλάτων ἢ Μωϋσῆς ἀττικίζων;[3] That Philo was in the habit of attributing the doctrines of Greek philosophy to Moses we can easily discover from his works. He tells us, for instance, in commenting upon Genesis 15. 10, that the truth attributed to Heracleitus as its author that 'opposites are formed from the same whole, to which they stand in the relation of sections or divisions', was known long before to Moses;[4] and that Zeno learnt an opinion of his from Moses in Genesis 27. 40.[5] Molland says[6] that

---

[1] *Strom.* I. xxi (*P.G.* VIII, 820).

[2] *Strom.* I. xv (*P.G.* VIII, 781) and v. xiv (*P.G.* IX, 145).

[3] *Strom.* I. xxii (*P.G.* VIII, 893). Numenius of Apamea in Syria was a Pythagorean Platonic philosopher who probably belonged to the age of the Antonines. He was highly esteemed by Plotinus and his school as well as by Clement and Origen. His object was to trace the doctrines of Plato up to Pythagoras and at the same time to show that they were not at variance with the doctrines of the Brahmins, Jews, Magi, and Egyptians. Considerable fragments of his works have been preserved in Eusebius' *Praeparatio Evangelica*. He wrote a περὶ Ἀφθαρσίας Ψυχῆς; see *Against Celsus* v. lvii.

[4] *Quis Rerum Divinarum Heres* xliii.   [5] *Quod Omnis Probus Liber Sit* viii.

[6] *The Conception of the Gospel*, p. 60.

Clement follows Aristobulus' theory that there existed a translation of the Hebrew Old Testament older than the LXX, which Plato knew. Certainly Clement gives the most fanciful version of the story of the composition of the LXX itself, saying: 'The work was indeed a device of God deliberately designed to reach a Greek audience; for it was not inappropriate to the inspiration of God that he who gave the prophecy should also bring to life the translation to serve as prophecy for the Greeks.' And he goes on to record the absurd story that Ezra was inspired to write miraculously all the other Scriptures lost during the Exile.[1] His contention, based on the prior antiquity of Moses to the philosophical writings of the Greeks, is that the philosophers stole their material from the Hebrew prophets and changed it a bit, added a bit of their own, and claimed it as their own.[2]

But his claims for Greek philosophy extend much further than this.[3] He frequently quotes the poets and dramatists (even the comedians) of Classical Greek literature to support his point, on the grounds, as far as one can see, that they were in a general way inspired by God. In *Protreptikos* VII[4] he says that the poets received some knowledge of the true God, as part of that general achievement by the Greeks of τὰ μάλιστα ἐναύσματά τινα τοῦ λόγου τοῦ θείου. These quotations abound in the *Protreptikos*, Clement's earliest known work, more than in others, but they still continue present through all his writings. For instance in *Paidagogos* III. viii,[5] he quotes several lines from Hesiod and applies them to Abraham, to the apostles, and to people who will not believe in Christ. In *Stromateis* II. xix,[6] he says καί μοι δοκεῖ τὸν πιστὸν προμαντευόμενος Ὅμηρος εἰρηκέναι Δὸς φίλῳ; and in *Stromateis* IV. xxii,[7] he calls a reference in the *Odyssey* to people washing themselves before prayer ἡ εἰκὼν τοῦ βαπτίσματος ἡ ἐκ Μωῦσεως παραδεδομένη τοῖς ποιηταῖς. The climax of absurdity is reached when he sees, in the reply of the Cyclopes in the *Odyssey* to Polyphemus' complaint that Noman has injured him, doctrine concerning the Father and the Son.[8]

As we have said, he sometimes suggests that the knowledge that the Greek philosophers had of God was stolen or betrayed. *Stromateis* VI.

---

[1] *Strom.* I. xxii (*P.G.* VIII, 893).   [2] See *Strom.* I. xvii (*P.G.* VIII, 801).

[3] For this subject see also Tollinton, *Clement of Alexandria*, Vol. II, p. 233, and Molland, *The Conception of the Gospel*, caps. 5 and 6.

[4] *P.G.* VIII, 184.   [5] *P.G.* VIII, 613.   [6] *P.G.* VIII, 1048.

[7] *P.G.* VIII, 1352.   [8] *Strom.* V. xiv (*P.G.* IX, 173).

vii[1] has the following passage: 'Part they stole, part they misunderstood; and in other respects some things they said under inspiration, but did not completely work out, and some relying on human speculation and reason, and in these they made mistakes.' In *Stromateis* v. i[2] a graver charge appears. In previous books of the *Stromateis* he has accused the Greeks of stealing from Moses and the prophets. But now he will go further and say that some of the higher angels sinfully repeated 'the secret things' to women, such secrets, that is, as their unfallen brethren were preserving till the Lord's coming, and as a result the Providence of God revealed certain higher truths to the Greeks. The result is the system of Greek philosophy which has some understanding of truth but is astray in other respects, because they do not understand the necessity of allegorizing the prophecies. These different accounts of how the Greeks derived their special knowledge of God are a little confusing, but Molland[3] gives a convincing account of how these ideas developed in Clement's teaching. 'The four alternatives which Clement puts forward', he says, 'form a climax. He begins with the possibility that the truth contained in philosophy is to be ascribed to an accident involved in God's providential economy. He continues with explanations attributing the element of truth in philosophy to the general revelation, or even making the Greek philosophers prophets similar to those of the Old Testament. And he ends by indicating that philosophy owes its existence to a reflection of the eternal truth itself, and that the philosophers have beheld God—an imperfect, vague, unclear yet true vision.' But Molland believes that Clement's own theory, which is not stated here, is that the Greeks stole their philosophy from the Hebrews. He finds, too, yet one more theory of the origin of Greek philosophy in Clement[4]—that the Son, the Teacher of all created beings, taught the first generation of men, and they handed on the teaching, though it became corrupted in course of time with human teaching. Whether we are to call this natural or revealed knowledge of God it is difficult to say. He is certainly referring to a type of knowledge which we to-day should call natural, but he sometimes seems to treat it almost as if it had been revealed. The distinction between the two types of knowledge, however, was very much blurred in such a theologian as Clement, so indefinite are the

---

[1] *P.G.* IX, 277.
[3] *The Conception of the Gospel*, p. 52.
[2] *P.G.* IX, 24.
[4] Ibid. p. 57.

limits of his Scriptures and so great is his admiration for the Greek philosophers.

The content of this revelation is occasionally more closely defined. In *Protreptikos* 11,[1] he says: ἦν δέ τις ἔμφυτος ἀρχαία πρὸς οὐρανὸν ἀνθρώποις κοινωνία, ἀγνοίᾳ μὲν ἐσκοτισμένη, ἄφνω δέ που διεκθρώσκουσα τοῦ σκότους καὶ ἀναλάμπουσα. This 'kinship with heaven' was displayed in the refusal of the 'atheist' philosophers to worship the false gods of paganism, and the vague but noble addresses of such poets as Euripides to the sky as a god. In *Stromateis* v. xiv,[2] the nature of the knowledge of himself revealed by God to the Greeks is explained: ἐν μὲν πεπιστευκόσιν ὁ Υἱὸς Πατέρα μηνύων, ἐν δὲ τοῖς Ἕλλησι τὸ θεὸς ποιητής; he quotes in this passage Malachi 1. 11, a favourite proof-text for Christian writers of the second and third centuries; Justin Martyr uses it also.

About philosophy as a preparation and education (παιδαγωγία) leading to the Gospel for the Greeks Clement speaks much. Philosophy, he says in *Stromateis* I. ii,[3] is 'the clear image of truth, given as a divine gift to the Greeks', which is the strongest statement that he makes upon the subject. Later in the same book[4] he says that Greek philosophy did at least stumble upon part of the truth, and he disagrees with those who believe that the whole thing was inspired by devils: ἀλλ' οὖν [ὁ Λόγος] προκατασκευάζει τὴν ὁδὸν τῇ βασιλικωτάτῃ διδασκαλίᾳ. Later still in this book[5] he says that philosophy is like the first rungs of a ladder to Christianity. It is useful for apologetic purposes and against the heretics. It is a useful addition, but not essential.

He sometimes speaks of philosophy as the Greeks' Old Testament. For instance, in *Stromateis* I. v,[6] he has this passage: ἦν μὲν οὖν πρὸ τῆς τοῦ Κυρίου παρουσίας εἰς δικαιοσύνην Ἕλλησιν ἀναγκαία φιλοσοφία· νυνὶ δὲ χρησίμη πρὸς θεοσέβειαν γίνεται, προπαιδεία τις οὖσα τοῖς τὴν πίστιν δι' ἀποδείξεως καρπουμένοις...πάντων μὲν γὰρ αἴτιος τῶν καλῶν ὁ θεός· ἀλλὰ τῶν μὲν κατὰ προηγούμενον, ὡς τῆς τε διαθήκης τῆς παλαιᾶς, τῶν δὲ κατ' ἐπακολούθημα, ὡς τῆς φιλοσοφίας. And philosophy 'was a schoolmaster' to the Greeks as the Law was to the Jews. Just as

---

[1] *P.G.* VIII, 93.
[2] *P.G.* IX, 200.
[3] *P.G.* VIII, 709.
[4] Cap. xvi (*P.G.* VIII, 795).
[5] Cap. xx (*P.G.* VIII, 816).
[6] *P.G.* VIII, 717.

τὰ ἐγκύκλια μαθήματα are a preparation for philosophy, so philosophy is a preparation for Christianity.[1] In *Stromateis* VI. v[2] a distinction is drawn between the Christians' and the philosophers' knowledge of God. The two peoples worship the same God, but the philosophers 'have not learnt the tradition given through the Son according to a perfect knowledge'. He speaks of God as known ὑπὸ μὲν Ἑλλήνων ἐθνικῶς, ὑπὸ δὲ Ἰουδαίων ἰουδαϊκῶς, καινῶς δὲ ὑφ' ἡμῶν καὶ πνευματικῶς. And 'the same God who was the provider of both covenants was also the giver of Greek philosophy to the Greeks, by which the Almighty is glorified by the Greeks'. So he can speak of 'three peoples', and he repeats the analogy of the philosophers' being to the Greeks what the prophets were to the Jews. He refers finally to the Sibyl, who of course illustrates his fancy admirably. In *Stromateis* VI. viii,[3] he says that philosophy was given to the Greeks οἷον διαθήκην οἰκείαν, and later in the same book[4] he has this sentence: εἰκότως οὖν Ἰουδαίοις μὲν νόμος, Ἕλλησι δὲ φιλοσοφία μέχρι τῆς παρουσίας, ἐντεῦθεν δὲ ἡ κλῆσις ἡ καθολικὴ εἰς περιούσιον δικαιοσύνης λαόν.

Clement has a special admiration for Plato. In *Protreptikos* VI,[5] for instance, he states that as Plato learnt geometry from the Egyptians, astronomy from the Babylonians, certain wholesome spells from the Thracians, and some things even from the Assyrians, so from the Hebrews he learnt νόμους τοὺς ὅσοι ἀληθεῖς καὶ δόξαν τὴν τοῦ θεοῦ. Twice in the *Paidagogos* (I. viii and II. x)[6] he describes Plato as learning one of his doctrines from Moses, in the first place a conception of God's proving of us, and in the second a passage in the *Laws* which he thinks is based on Leviticus 18. 20. In another part of the *Paidagogos*[7] he quotes Plato's *Sophist* alongside of the Epistle to the Romans. He claims in the *Stromateis*[8] that in his *Theaetetus* Plato speaks of 'the Christian life'. He also uses the most extravagant language to describe Plato. He calls him ὁ τὴν ἀλήθειαν ἐζηλωκὼς τῶν φιλοσόφων Πλάτων, τὸ ἔναυσμα τῆς Ἑβραϊκῆς φιλοσοφίας ζωπυρῶν (*Paidagogos* II. i);[9] ὁ ζηλωτὴς Μωῦσεως ὁ πάντα ἄριστος Πλάτων (ibid. III. ix);[10] ὁ ἐξ

---

[1] The first statement is taken from Philo, the second repeated by Origen in his *Letter to Gregory* (see *Philocalia* XIII. 1).

[2] *P.G.* IX, 260–4.   [3] *P.G.* IX, 288.

[4] Cap. xvii (*P.G.* IX, 392).

[5] *P.G.* VIII, 176.   [6] *P.G.* VIII, 332, 505.

[7] I. ix (*P.G.* VIII, 348–9).   [8] v. xiv (*P.G.* IX, 428).

[9] *P.G.* VIII, 405.   [10] *P.G.* VIII, 628.

Ἑβραίων φιλόσοφος Πλάτων (*Stromateis* I. i);[1] and ὁ φιλαλήθης Πλάτων οἷον θεοφορούμενος (ibid. I. viii).[2]

The point at which the philosophers went wrong he does sometimes admit to be in their idolatry, but he is not nearly as strong on this point as Origen. For instance, in *Protreptikos* IV,[3] he says that the philosophers are right when they confess that the heavens were made for man to contemplate, but wrong when they worship the visible works in the heavens. But elsewhere he takes a different view. In *Stromateis* I. vii[4] he says that the philosophers had knowledge, but not faith. It was a difference between 'a guess at truth and truth itself, between resemblance and reality. 'The former comes by learning and practice, the latter by power and faith. The teaching of reverence towards God (θεοσέβεια) is a gift, but faith is grace.' And (like Origen after him)[5] he specifically excepts the Stoics, as imagining that God has a body, and the Epicureans, as denying divine Providence, from possession of 'the divine tradition' of philosophy. In the *Protreptikos*, indeed, he takes the traditional Christian attitude to the gods of paganism, partly ridiculing their anthropomorphism and crudity, and partly warning against their cult as attracting real and evil demons.[6] But elsewhere he is not so severe, and in *Stromateis* v. vii he gives a description of the gods of Egypt, not railing at the idolatry associated with them, but pointing out their symbolic meaning with a good deal of interest. For the myths associated with them he has nothing but scorn. They are μῦθοι κενοί (*Protreptikos* I),[7] and we have seen how in *Quis Dives* xlii he is careful to call his story of S. John and the robber μῦθον, ἀλλ' οὐ μῦθον, ἀλλ' ὄντα λόγον.[8]

Such then was the teaching which Origen must have inherited upon this subject, so generous in its concessions to pagan philosophy, so

---

[1] *P.G.* VIII, 696.   [2] *P.G.* VIII, 737.

[3] *P.G.* VIII, 164. The same thought is repeated *Protrep.* VIII (*P.G.* VIII, 192); *Strom.* VI. v, vi, xiv (*P.G.* IX, 260–4, 265, 333).

[4] *P.G.* VIII, 733.

[5] See *Stromateis* I. xi (*P.G.* VIII, 749); Origen's *Comm. on John* II. 3; and Gregory's *Panegyric on Origen* xiii (*P.G.* X, 1088).

[6] See *Protreptikos* II, and *passim*.

[7] *P.G.* VIII, 53.

[8] *P.G.* IX, 648. See above, p. 133. Cf. Philo, *De Legatione ad Gaium* 2 and 32, where he calls the stories of Cronos' Golden Age and of the Gorgon's Head πλάσμα μύθου.

ingenious in its reasons for subordinating the Greeks to the Hebrews. That Origen was well read in pagan philosophy is beyond doubt. De Faye, indeed, in the Introduction to the second volume of his great work, claims that Origen was the last Christian thinker of importance to understand contemporary Greek philosophy, and that after him Christian theology (in such things as the Logos doctrine) no longer used or understood philosophy; and that it was for this reason that the Church long after his death called him a heretic.[1] We get a glimpse of the course of philosophical reading set by Origen to his pupils in Caesarea when we read Gregory's *Panegyric on Origen*. He encouraged his pupils, Gregory tells us,[2] to read all sorts of pagan philosophy and poetry, Greek or barbarian, except that which was atheist, and that which denied a Providence. He tied them down to no one philosophy, but guided them through all, sifting the good in each system from the bad. This indeed is significant of the whole of Origen's attitude to pagan philosophy. '*Origène*,' says Denis,[3] '*pour parler son langage allégorique, est, à l'égard de la philosophie, dans la même position qu'Abimelech à l'égard d'Isaac, tantôt ami, tantôt ennemi.*' He is often a friend, because he finds so many affinities between Christianity and philosophy; and often enemy because each single system has several features in it which are in flagrant contradiction to the Christian tradition.

Origen emphasizes the prior antiquity of Moses to any of the Greek philosophers as strongly as does Clement, though he is not nearly so uncritical a believer in the virtues of the LXX as is Clement.[4] Origen, for instance, tells us in the *Commentary on John*[5] that Moses had learned in Egypt the mystical significance of numbers. When Celsus claims

[1] The whole of Volume II of de Faye's work is an exhaustive and classical study of the philosophical sources of Origen's thought. For the subject of revelation outside the Bible in Origen, see also Koetschau, Introduction to *G.C.S.*, Origenes I, Section IV; Molland, *The Conception of the Gospel*, pp. 86ff.; and Daniélou, *Origène*, pp. 30–2 (though in my opinion he there exaggerates the extent of the concessions made by Origen to pagan philosophy).

[2] *Panegyric* xiii, xiv (*P.G.* x, 1088, 1093).

[3] *De la Philosophie d'Origène*, p. 680.

[4] This is not the occasion to explore Origen's estimate of the comparative merits of the LXX and Hebrew Bible (I hope to set forth the evidence on the subject in a later work). Suffice it to say that Origen is not nearly so blind an adherent of the LXX as many scholars have represented him.

[5] xxviii. 8.

that the Christians derived their doctrine that God will judge the world through fire from the theory of cyclic recurrences of floods and fires held by Greek historians, Origen[1] appeals to Josephus to support him in the view that Moses and some of the prophets, who taught of God's judgement through fire, were older than any Greek historian. And he uses exactly the same argument a little later in the same work[2] in reply to Celsus' similar charge of plagiarism against the Christians in their stories of the Tower of Babel and the destruction of Sodom and Gomorrah. Later still[3] Origen has to meet Celsus' argument that the Christian doctrines of the devil and Anti-Christ are derived from Greek myth. He replies, as we should expect, that the writers in the Old Testament who mention the devil are earlier than the composition of any Greek myths. Indeed, he seems to think that the Greek myths reproduced some information derived from the Bible. Pherecydes mentions a mythical antagonist of Cronos called Ophioneus, and Origen says that he derived this story from the snake of Genesis 3. But Origen is not content to attribute Greek philosophical ideas to Moses alone among the Old Testament characters. He builds up a picture of Solomon also as the archetype of everything that a Greek philosopher should be. In the Preface to his *Commentary on the Song of Songs*[4] he says that the three divisions of philosophy, moral, natural, and speculative, are dealt with by Solomon in his three books of Proverbs, Ecclesiastes, and the Song of Songs, and that the Greek philosophers probably learnt these divisions from Solomon, '*utpote qui aetate et tempore longe ante ipsos prior ea per Dei spiritum didicisset*', and then reproduced them as their own. In a fragment on the Song of Songs found in a Catena,[5] on the phrase in the LXX version, ἐὰν μὴ γνῷς σεαυτήν, ἡ καλὴ ἐν γυναιξίν (R.V., 'If thou know not, O thou fairest among women'), he claims that we have here the origin of the famous saying of the Delphic oracle, Γνῶθι σαυτόν. His words are: τὸ πολυθρύλλητον δὲ παρ' Ἕλλησιν ἐπίφθεγμα προείληπται παραδοθὲν ἐν τῷ σοφῷ Σολομῶντι, τὸ Γνῶθι σαυτόν.

This does not of course imply that Origen has no use for and attaches no value to the philosophers. On the contrary, he makes it clear that he considered that they had achieved some important truths

[1] *Against C.* IV. xi, xii.　　[2] IV. xx, xxi.
[3] VI. xlii, xliii.　　[4] *P.G.* XIII, 73.
[5] *P.G.* XVII, 256, on Song of Songs 1. 8.

about God, and (as one might expect) he is clearer in his definition of the boundary between the philosophers and the inspired men of the Old Testament than Clement is. He admits that certain passages in the philosophers are very like some parts of Christian teaching. He does not dispute Celsus' assertion, for instance,[1] that a passage in Plato's *Crito* contains sentiments very like Christ's teaching, but in reply he lays down two general rules about what he calls ἡ ταυτότης τῶν δογμάτων between the Bible and pagan writers. In the first place, such an identity is no discredit to the Bible, especially if the Old Testament (an older work than any Greek philosophical book) can be shown to contain the view in question. In the second, the Bible can be shown to derive superior merit from the comparison, as it appeals to a far wider public than the Greek philosophers did. It is in his *Letter to Gregory* (written from Caesarea about 243) that he uses his famous analogy of the Israelites' spoiling the Egyptians to describe the approach which he takes to pagan philosophy.[2] In the *Commentary on John* he grades various schools of thought and degrees of attainment of truth among both Christian believers and heathen philosophers.[3] He starts with the text Deuteronomy 4. 19, where the sun and moon are described as allotted to other nations. Origen said that this state of affairs came about 'because those who were not able to attain to the Intellectual Nature had their sentiments concerning the Godhead aroused through the medium of sensible gods and gladly took their stand on these, and did not descend to idols and demons'. These are they who 'have wandered from God indeed, but their error is far superior to and more creditable than that of those who call the works of men's hands gods, gold and silver, the products of art'. He goes on to say that in relation to the Logos there are four classes: 'Thus some partake of the Word which was in the beginning himself, and the Word who was with God, and the Word of God, such as Hosea and Isaiah and Jeremiah, and anybody else who so fitted himself that the Word of the Lord or the Word became with him. The next are those who "know nothing except Jesus Christ and him crucified", thinking that the Word who became flesh is the whole content of the Word, and know only Christ

---

[1] *Against C.* VII. lix.

[2] *Letter to Gregory* 2 (*P.G.* XI, 88–90).

[3] *Comm. on John* II. 3. Cf. the passage from *Strom.* I. xi referred to above, p. 162, n. 5.

after the flesh; of this sort is the majority of those who are accounted believers.[1] The third class are those who have pinned their faith to words which have some share in the Word in the belief that these are superior to every word, and perhaps these are those who adhere to the respectable and superior schools of philosophy among the Greeks. Coming fourth after these are those who believe in words which are altogether pernicious and godless, those who deny a Providence, unmistakable and almost palpable though it be, and who believe in any other final cause which conflicts with that which is right.' We have already had occasion to look at a very similar passage in the *Homilies on Jeremiah*[2] where he says that the philosophers 'talk sense' (σωφρο-νίζουσιν), but their talk is not directed towards God, and it does not avail them much. In *Against Celsus*[3] he admits that philosophy is a positive assistance to Christianity. He speaks of those who have received a philosophical education, and says: 'Regarding them as already equipped with a general education and the principles of philosophy, I will try to bring them on to that wonderful and lofty enlightenment which expounds the profoundest doctrines of the Christians not perceived by the majority. For the Christians contend and demonstrate and establish, when they discuss the greatest and most vital subjects, that these were treated philosophically by the prophets of God and the apostles of Jesus.' Here he is approaching Clement's more hospitable view of the philosophers, but it is noteworthy that he is much more cautious than Clement.

The whole question of how far the philosophers attained to truth by the providence of God is discussed in some detail in the Sixth Book of *Against Celsus*, and one passage in particular has been very judiciously picked out by the compilers of the *Philocalia* as characteristic.[4] In the first place, Origen does not deny that God revealed truth to the philosophers. 'Certainly Plato the son of Ariston may explain the subject of the Original Good', he says,[5] 'in one of his Letters, and may say that the Original Good is completely ineffable, but arises from

---

[1] It is this sort of doctrine which makes anyone who has studied Origen at all carefully suspect that for him the Incarnation was ultimately an unfortunate necessity rather than something to be gloried in.

[2] v. 14. For the Greek of the passage, see above, p. 91, n. 4.

[3] III. lviii.

[4] See *Philoc.* xv, sections 5–8.   [5] Sect. 5.

frequent association, and is suddenly kindled in the soul, as light, as if from a flame leaping up. When we hear these statements (for we are careful to disagree with no rightly stated fact, and even if those who are outside the faith state facts rightly, not to attack them for the sake of argument nor to try to misrepresent anything that is sound), we agree with them because they are rightly stated; for God revealed these facts, and anything which is rightly stated, to them.' He goes on to say that the difference between this revelation and that which is in the Bible lies in the results produced by each. The philosophers did not worship God as they should have. The test is a religious, and indeed a moral, one. 'Therefore those who understood truth about God and yet did not practise that worship which was proper to the truth known about him, we declare to be liable to the punishment of sinners....And though[1] they formed conceptions of the unseen things of God and the Ideas from the creation of the world and of perceptible things, from which they proceeded to argue to the things which are known, and though they perceived not inadequately his unseen power and Godhead, none the less they became vain in their reasonings, and their heart, as if it knew nothing, wandered in darkness and ignorance about the worship of the divine....Observe then the difference between that which is rightly said by Plato about the Original Good and the things which are said in the prophets about the light of the blessed. And observe that the truths found in Plato about this matter not only did not help the average man to worship properly, but did not even help Plato, great man though he was, when he speculated about the Original Good. But the vulgar diction of the divine writings has produced a love of God in those who search it properly; and in their souls is nourished that light by that which is called oil in a certain parable, feeding the light of the lamps in the case of the five wise virgins.'

We can recover from Origen's works several examples of the particular doctrines which he thought the philosophers had had revealed to them in this way, as well as the teaching of Plato about the Original Good which has already been mentioned. He speaks in *Against Celsus*[2] of the argument for the immortality of the soul 'so well stated by the Greeks', and also[3] of 'those doctrines which cannot be lightly dismissed taught by the Greeks or barbarians concerning the immortality of the soul, or its survival, or the immortality of the mind'.

---

[1] Sect. 6. [2] III. xxii. [3] III. lxxx.

He means apparently the Pythagoreans and Platonists. In the same work,[1] he says that there is a universal intellectual inclination (κοινὴ ἔννοια) against idolatry, which fits in with the Christian revealed command against it. Still in the same work,[2] he admits that many who were strangers from the faith have written well about the living of a good life, because the incentives for this—final punishment for the bad and reward for the good—are sufficiently clear from the order of the universe. In *Concerning First Principles*,[3] having stated that the end of the whole universe is to become as like God as possible, he says that several philosophers realized this, but they took it out of holy Scripture, Genesis 1. 26, 27. In the *Homilies on Genesis*,[4] he claims that Abimelech stands for 'the scholars and savants of the world', '*qui philosophiae operam dantes, licet non integram et perfectam regulam pietatis attigerint, tamen senserunt Deum patrem et regem esse omnium*'.

Molland is therefore too sweeping in his statement[5] when he says that Origen 'condemns philosophy *en bloc*'. On the contrary, he finds many valuable things in pagan philosophy, though he does not imagine that it has anything to *add* to the faith of the Church derived from the Bible; and he even finds some use for it for the Christian. It is, however, already obvious that he is much less enthusiastic about the achievement of pagan philosophy than was Clement, and much more critical of it. We must now pay rather more detailed attention to this criticism.

In the *Against Celsus*[6] he goes through a list of the philosophic schools, Epicureans, Peripatetics, and Stoics, and shows how well justified the exponents of the Christian faith are in leading people away from their errors and perversions of truth. He regards Christianity as the best philosophy among all philosophies, and sees something false and wrong in all these others, but it is significant that he omits Platonism from this list. A little later in the same book[7] he gives us the final test by which he judged all schools of philosophy, even those of whose views he generally approved: 'But do not imagine that in my attack on Celsus I interpret those philosophers who expound the immortality or survival of the soul without relating them to the Christian system. For, though we have some things in common with

[1] III. xl. [2] VIII. lii. [3] III. 6. 1.
[4] VI. ii. [5] *The Conception of the Gospel*, p. 86.
[6] III. lxxv. [7] Cap. lxxxi.

them, we shall establish at a more opportune moment that the blessed existence which is to come will be for those only who accept the religion of Jesus (τὴν κατὰ Ἰησοῦν θεοσέβειαν) and the correct and pure worship of the Creator of all things, undefiled by any relation to a created thing.' He then asks the reader to compare the τέλος of the Christian faith with the τέλος of any 'philosophical school among Greeks or barbarians, or any profession made by the mysteries', and he concludes that whereas the others are confessedly 'human systems', Christianity makes its professions from God's inspiration. His main test is, as before, religious, θεοσέβεια or εὐσέβεια. Intellectual tests are not ignored, but they are only secondary. In the *Commentary on Romans*[1] he says that 'the wrath of God is revealed from heaven' (Romans 1. 18) applies particularly to '*sapientes huius mundi, et eos qui philosophi nominantur*', for the very reason that though endowed with wisdom they continued to worship idols.[2] We can see the teaching of his master echoed by Gregory in his *Panegyric* where he sees the great failure of pagan philosophy in its inability to worship rightly:[3] οἱ δ' ἔν τε τοῖς ἄλλοις ἔσφηλαν τοὺς ἔχοντας, καὶ δὴ καὶ τοῦ πάντων μεγίστου καὶ ἀναγκαιοτάτου, τῆς περὶ τὸ θεῖον γνώσεως καὶ εὐσεβείας.

In the *Commentary on the Song of Songs*[4] he implies that even about what truth it had received pagan philosophy was uncertain. The Queen of Sheba, he says, came to receive the solution of certain questions from Solomon: '*atque ab ipso de agnitione Verbi Dei, et de creaturis mundi, vel de immortalitate animae, et iudicio futuro, quod apud eam et apud doctores eius gentiles dumtaxat philosophos incertum semper aut dubium manebat, absolvitur.*' And in the *Commentary on Romans*[5] he

---

[1] I. xvi, xvii.

[2] Compare with this a passage in *Against Celsus* (VII. xlvi), where he agrees fervently with a very Greek distinction made by Celsus between 'being' and 'becoming', 'intelligible' and 'visible', and, in the course of his demonstration that this distinction is to be found in Scripture, makes the following remark: 'Although God in his love for mankind revealed the truth and that which may be known of himself not only to those who surrender themselves to him, but also to some of those who are outside the right worship of God and his reverence, yet some of those who in the providence of God have reached the knowledge of such great things, because their behaviour is not worthy of this knowledge, cast aside their reverence and hold down the truth in unrighteousness, and can have no ground for excuse in the sight of God, considering their knowledge of such great things.'

[3] *Panegyric* xiv (*P.G.* x, 1092).

[4] Book II, on Song of Songs 1. 5.

[5] IX. xxiv.

suggests that the self-sufficiency of pagans is one of their faults: '*Sunt autem et nonnulli gentilium compositis moribus et honeste institutis qui tamen hoc ipsum quod habent non ad Deum referunt nec ab ipso sibi datam gratiam confitentur; sed aut propriae industriae adscribunt, aut super magistris et institutoribus gloriantur.*' He will not concede anything to the mystery cults of the contemporary world, though these were clearly, even in the view of Christians, a cut above the sacrificial cults of the official gods. Celsus suggests that Christian teaching about the soul's approach to God owes something to the Mithraic mysteries.[1] Origen repudiates this, and claims that such passages as Ezekiel's description of the doors of his ideal Temple, or John the Divine's account of the heavenly city, or the account in Numbers of the position of the tribes round the camp, will all, mystically interpreted, give a similar and quite independent symbolism of the soul's approach to God. In a later passage in the same work[2] he refers to these mystery cults again. It is true, he says, that they do teach about punishments in the next life. But the difference between them and both Christianity and Judaism is that the devotees of the latter 'suggest by the lives they live that these [punishments] really do exist'.

Against the sacrificial cults of the official gods of the Graeco-Roman world he is implacably hostile. This is not, perhaps, surprising, because in Origen's own day nobody tried to force the Christians on pain of death or imprisonment to adopt Greek philosophy or be initiated into the mystery-religions, whereas if a persecution were to arise he and every Christian knew that they might have to face the alternatives of sacrificing to these gods or execution, torture, exile, or imprisonment. He adopts the view which we have found in Clement's *Protreptikos* even more emphatically than Clement, that the gods worshipped in this way are no gods but evil demons taking the form of gods to lead men astray. In *Against Celsus*[3] he takes the view that Asclepius was a demon who had the power (which connoted no moral goodness) of healing, if he chose, and of foretelling the future, and he goes on to describe his theory that the gods of paganism are evil spirits who have persuaded men that they are gods in their greed for sacrifices and their self-indulgence, and that this is the reason why they incite their worshippers to oppose Christianity. This is merely traditional Christian doctrine on the subject, echoing, perhaps a little more sharply, what Clement

[1] *Against C.* VI. xxiii.   [2] VIII. xlviii.   [3] III. xxv, xxix.

has already said.[1] Origen often refers to the oracles at pagan shrines, which probably formed a major argument in contemporary paganism's defence of its religion, and provided some difficulty for Christians. In the same work[2] he says that the pagan oracles, and especially Delphi, were inspired by no divine spirit but by filthy and hostile demons. Later[3] he calls the miracles and oracles of pagan shrines ἀναπλάσματα μυθικά, and in the *Homilies on Numbers*[4] he admits that the oracles' predictions may be fulfilled (and he instances the prophecies of Balaam and of Caiaphas as analogies), but affirms that they certainly are inspired by demons. His disciple Gregory reproduces his master's views when he refers to the Delphic oracle as δαιμόνων τῷ μαντικωτάτῳ.[5] Origen has no more respect for heathen statues. In *Against Celsus*[6] he imagines the demons as inhabiting statues and temples because they are too impure to dwell in more holy abodes.

We have already seen that he tends to be more lenient towards Plato and Platonists in his judgement of the pagan philosophers, but he is nothing like the enthusiastic admirer of Plato that Clement often appears to be. He tends, rather ungallantly, to ascribe those parts of the Platonic doctrine with which he is in agreement to the Old Testament writers. For instance, he thinks that Plato derived a thought about jewels on earth having some distillation of jewels in the 'better land' from Isaiah 54. 11, 12, though he admits that this is mere speculation.[7] He follows several predecessors of his, he says,[8] in suggesting that Plato took a passage in the *Phaedrus* from the Jewish writers. But he can be more generous. He will admit[9] that Plato states very rightly that man cannot find God in any circumstances, except possibly the very intellectual man. Plato, he says, wrote such a sentiment μεγαλοφυῶς καὶ οὐκ εὐκαταφρονήτως. Men can only find God through the Word of God given them by God, and this applies even to the very intellectual man. He cannot help adding that if the finding of the

---

[1] E.g. *Protrep.* II (*P.G.* VIII, 121 ff.): pagan gods are all demons anxious to injure their worshippers, and attracted by the smoke and smell of sacrifices.

[2] VII. iii.   [3] VIII. xlv.

[4] XVI. vii. Cf. *Hom. on Jeremiah* v. 3, where he does not deny the existence of such things, but calls them σημεῖα καὶ τέρατα ψεύδους.

[5] *Panegyric* xi (*P.G.* x, 1084).   [6] III. xxxv.   [7] *Against C.* VII. xxx.

[8] Ibid. VII. xix. The predecessors are probably Numenius, Philo, Clement, and perhaps Josephus.

[9] Ibid. VII. xlii.

true God had been possible to Plato or any of the Greek philosophers, 'they would not have reverenced, or called upon as God, or worshipped, something other than God'. On other occasions, however, he can entirely repudiate even Plato. He believes, for instance, that the devil himself inspired Plato to give his picture of the army of gods and demons in the *Phaedrus*.[1] Here he is in almost direct contradiction to Clement, who, as we have seen, rejects the view that Greek philosophy could have been inspired by devils.[2]

It is therefore incorrect to speak of Origen as believing in anything comparable to a separate tradition of doctrine to be derived from pagan philosophy, though he inherited a theory not unlike this from Clement. At the most he will admit that God revealed to the philosophers some truths which the men of the Old Testament had known long before. And he is more inclined than Clement to assume that what of truth they had realized was found by them in the Hebrew Scriptures. It is difficult to say whether we are to think of their apprehension of truth as the reception of revelation. As with Clement, so with Origen, the distinction between natural and revealed knowledge which we to-day might draw is far from clear. In their view all truth comes from God through his Word, and their conviction that the prophets and godly men of the Old Testament had known Christ in a way not at all unlike that in which the Christians of their own day knew him did not tend to make them draw any very marked distinction between knowledge of God before the Incarnation and knowledge of him after the Incarnation, or, as a consequence, between the pagan's knowledge of the pre-incarnate Christ and the Christian's knowledge of the incarnate Christ.

But Origen's consistent emphasis upon the pagan philosopher's failure to worship God as his knowledge of God should have led him to worship must not be underestimated. It is basically a very sound emphasis, and we can even see in it a deliberate intention to modify Clement's too great readiness to baptize the philosophers into the Christian faith without a proper conversion or repentance. Origen's emphasis here is Hebraic, not Greek, in its insistence upon the moral and religious consequences of philosophies as that by which they must be judged, and not their intellectual content. He has put his finger upon what is in fact the decisive line of demarcation between any Christian

---

[1] *Against C.* VIII. iv.
[2] *Strom.* I. xvi (*P.G.* VIII, 795). See above, p. 160.

knowledge of God and any non-Christian apprehension of him. He has realized (though he may not have explicitly said so) that in the Christian tradition knowledge of God is not a purely intellectual matter but means experiencing God and submitting to him with the whole personality. And in so doing he has demonstrated, in a manner which is all the more impressive for being only partly conscious, his fundamental respect for the Christian tradition of doctrine.

CHAPTER X

INSTITUTIONAL TRADITION

'INSTITUTIONAL TRADITION' is an expression which I have coined to express one form of tradition which we have found in Prestige's work, *Fathers and Heretics*.[1] Prestige tells us that 'there survives definite evidence that the meaning of the Bible was consciously sought in relation to its context in Christian institutions', in its relation, that is to say, to the other great formative contributions of the apostolic and sub-apostolic Church to spiritual order and discipline, to such things as the sacraments, the creeds, and the episcopate.[2] This tradition, he says later,[3] was derived from the Christian cultus too; Basil claims that a number of customs connected with prayer have apostolic authority; Chrysostom[4] confines this tradition to practical matters and actions. In short, 'the voice of the Bible could be plainly heard only if its text were interpreted broadly and rationally, in accordance with the apostolic creed and the evidence of the historic practice of Christendom'.[5]

Now this is a very bold and important claim to make. If the claim went no further than to assert that the Fathers often refer to certain customs, actions, and practices within the Church connected with her ordering of her worship and similar matters, and look upon them as deriving from the apostles independently of the Bible and possessing thereby an authority independent of it, this would be a comparatively minor point. But this is not what Prestige claims. He suggests that it was the general assumption of the Fathers that in certain circumstances these customs or institutions might be a source of interpretation of the Bible and consequently, of course, a potential means of supplementing it or modifying it in matters doctrinal. It becomes therefore important to examine how far this view can find support in the two writers with whom this work is concerned, Clement of Alexandria and Origen.

Clement does of course refer in his writings occasionally to Christian institutions, but he generally seems more anxious to derive an allegorical meaning from them than to take them as evidence for original Christian

---

[1] See p. 33 above.   [2] *Fathers and Heretics*, pp. 31, 32.
[3] Ibid. p. 40.   [4] Ibid. p. 42.   [5] Ibid. p. 43.

doctrine interpretative of or independent of the Bible. For instance, in the *Paidagogos*[1] he attacks contemporary celebration of the Agape on the grounds that it pollutes 'the fine and redeeming work of the Word, the sanctified Agape, with soup and gorging'; and he thinks that the feast as an institution should be taken allegorically, not literally, as ἐπουράνιος τροφή, ἑστίασις λογική. Later in the same work[2] he says that the Holy Kiss must not be abused, as it is intended to be μυστικόν. Again, in the *Stromateis*[3] he gives the reason for Christians' turning to the East for prayer; his reason is based on grounds of common sense and expediency, and he does not hint at either Biblical support or justification by ecclesiastical tradition.[4]

Earlier in the *Stromateis*, however, he comes nearer to expressing the sense of Prestige's 'institutional tradition', when he says[5] that everyone must decide on his own about writing Stromateis, just as the individual Christian is free to take his share in the Eucharist or not as they are distributing it, according to whether he thinks himself worthy or not: ἢ καὶ τὴν εὐχαριστίαν διανείμαντες, ὡς ἔθος, αὐτὸν δὴ ἕκαστον τοῦ λαοῦ λαβεῖν τὴν μοῖραν ἐπιτρέπουσι. And he quotes, very shortly afterwards, 1 Corinthians 11. 27, 28: 'Wherefore whosoever shall eat the bread or drink the cup of the Lord unworthily, shall be guilty of the body and blood of the Lord. But let a man prove himself, and so let him eat of the bread and drink of the cup.' Then in *Stromateis* I. xix[6] he speaks of heretics' being referred to in Proverbs 9. 16, 17, and he describes them as ἄρτῳ καὶ ὕδατι κατὰ τὴν προσφορὰν μὴ κατὰ τὸν κανόνα τῆς ἐκκλησίας χρωμένων. This makes it quite clear that Clement believed that the Church had the right to determine such things as the ordering of its Eucharist without any specific reference to Scripture, because, as we have seen, he conceives of his κανὼν τῆς ἐκκλησίας as independent of Scripture and interpretative of it.

But when we have gathered all the evidence available in Clement, we find ourselves with only a very meagre stock of material from which to

---

[1] II. i (*P.G.* VIII, 384).   [2] III. xi (*P.G.* VIII, 660).
[3] VII. vii (*P.G.* IX, 461).
[4] When Origen comes to deal with the custom of turning East for prayer, in exactly the same way he relies entirely on such arguments, and not on ecclesiastical tradition. See *Concerning Prayer* xxxii.
[5] I. i (*P.G.* VIII, 692).
[6] *P.G.* VIII, 813. The passage has already been referred to above on p. 60. See also Caspari, 'Hat die alexandrinische Kirche', p. 370, n. 1.

argue that for Clement 'the meaning of the Bible was consciously sought in relation to its context in Christian institutions'. In fact, for establishing this particular point the reader will easily see that we have no definite and unambiguous evidence at all. We are not justified, if we are to be faithful to the facts, in assuming that Clement believed, in the matter of Christian institutions, more than that in practical matters, such as the celebration of the Agape, the managing of the Holy Kiss, the methods of saying prayers, and the ordering of the Eucharist, the Church had freedom to follow a traditional custom without reference to the Bible.

Origen's references to Christian institutions in his works are on the whole not very frequent, and to the Christian cultus surprisingly rare. He sometimes uses them to provide analogies. In the *Homilies on Ezekiel*[1] he takes an example '*de ecclesiastica consuetudine*': if a deacon or presbyter is degraded from his order, he may start a schism, or he may accept it humbly. Or he allegorizes some details in the Old Testament to mean Christian institutions. When we are told that the Queen of Sheba saw 'the sitting of the retinue' of Solomon, this means, Origen believes,[2] bishops and presbyters; 'the attendance of his ministers' means deacons; 'their apparel', baptism; 'his cupbearers', teachers 'who mingle the word of God and teaching as it were wine for the peoples'; his 'burnt-offerings',[3] 'the mysteries, no doubt, of prayers and intercessions'. In the *Homilies on Psalms*[4] he mentions the sad fate of those who fall into grievous sin '*post illuminationem, post traditionem doctrinae*'; and in *Against Celsus*[5] he is very careful to distinguish both from contemporary pagan abstinence from food for ritual or philosophical reasons, and from the Jewish prohibition of unclean animals, the Christian custom of abstinence from food for the sake of mortification.[6] But references such as these, though undoubtedly interesting, are of very little profit if we are to determine whether Christian institutions

---

[1] x. i.

[2] *Comm. on Song of Songs* II (on Song of Songs I. 5); the immediate passage he is referring to is I Kings. 10. 5.

[3] So LXX and Vulgate for R.V. 'ascent'.

[4] *Homily* I on *Psalm 38*, sect. 6 (*P.G.* XII, 1380).   [5] v. xlix.

[6] For Origen's references to the penitential practices of the Church, see Latko's *Origen's Concept of Penance*, and for Christian prayers which can be recovered from Origen's works, see F. E. Warren, *The Liturgy and Ritual of the Ante-Nicene Church* (second edition, London, 1912), pp. 161–2.

were of interpretative value in Christian doctrine for Origen. Generally, it is worth noting, the Alexandrian Fathers do not seem anxious to dilate upon the details of Christian institutions or worship. This is, in the case of Origen at least, partly because his greatest interests lay elsewhere. Cadiou observes[1] that though echoes of baptismal and eucharistic liturgies can be found in Origen, he did show a marked preference for the content of the faith rather than '*les rites de salut*' in his attitude to Christianity. But there was also in the Christian Platonists a tendency to associate sacraments at least with their secret tradition, and therefore to be somewhat reserved about them. Cadiou notes this tendency too.[2] For them sacraments and perhaps ministry are '*voilés d'ombre, et comme rattachés immédiatement à l'Église céleste. La méthode de l'allégorie les entoure de périphrases où il n'est pas toujours aisé de les reconnaître*'.

In many cases where Origen does mention Christian institutions he presumes them to be derived from rules to be found in the Bible. It is an astonishing fact, but in his little work *Concerning Prayer* he takes all his examples of prayer from the Bible, and bases the rules he makes for its ordering entirely on the Bible, without once appealing to Christian tradition. He rules out, for instance, praying to the Father and the Son in the plural number because that is not found in the Bible;[3] he gives what he thinks is the best order for a Christian's prayer—praise, thanksgiving, confession, intercession, and finally the Doxology (because of his views on the futility of asking for τὰ ἐπίγεια, petition is virtually excluded)—but he appeals for support only to the Bible, and to no traditional order.[4] Lebreton notes an even more curious fact in this work,[5] and that is that Origen discourages prayer to Christ.[6] It is perfectly clear, as Lebreton observes, that prayer to Christ was a contemporary practice. Origen condemns it as ἰδιωτικὴν ἁμαρτίαν κατὰ πολλὴν ἀκεραιότητα διὰ τὸ ἀβασάνιστον καὶ ἀνεξέταστον ἁμαρτανόντων τῶν προσευχομένων τῷ υἱῷ, εἴτε μετὰ τοῦ Πατρὸς εἴτε

---

[1] *La Jeunesse d'Origène*, p. 384. [2] Ibid. p. 388.
[3] xv. 1. [4] xxiii. 1.
[5] 'Le Désaccord de la Foi', tom. 20, pp. 19–24.
[6] In xiv. 6 he has said that we are certainly to give thanks to Christ and to intercede with him, as Stephen did in Acts (7. 60); but in xv. 1 he modifies this, saying that perhaps (μή ποτε) we ought really to pray only to God the Father: λείπεται τοίνυν προσεύχεσθαι μόνῳ τῷ θεῷ τῷ τῶν ὅλων πατρί, ἀλλὰ μὴ χωρὶς τοῦ ἀρχιερέως.

χωρὶς τοῦ Πατρός.[1] And Lebreton insists[2] that Origen is not in this passage trying to lead the people back to the example given in liturgical prayer of praying only to the Father, for he takes all his examples from Scripture, and in the context he can be referring only to individual prayer. We have here, it appears, something very like a deliberate ignoring of the authority of tradition in Christian prayer. Again, in the *Commentary on Romans* he calls the necessity of Baptism 'ecclesiastica regula',[3] and he speaks of the Holy Kiss being 'handed down as the Church's custom'.[4] But it is clear that to him the Church's authority was in the first case John 3. 5, and in the second Romans 16. 16.

We do, however, find a few passages even in Origen in which Christian customs and institutions are regarded unmistakably as a source of authoritative tradition. In the *Commentary on Romans*[5] he says that 'although according to the figure handed down to the Churches we have all been baptized in these visible waters and in visible chrism', yet the truly baptized person receives an invisible baptism from above. And later he says that in S. Paul's day, 'it was not only, as we see is the custom now, the figure (*typus*) of the mysteries that was given to those who were being baptized, but the power and rationale (*virtus et ratio*) were handed on'. He goes on, '*pro hoc et ecclesia ab apostolis traditionem suscepit etiam parvulis baptismum dare*', because they knew of the existence of original sin. Here he makes no attempt to find Scriptural justification for infant baptism, but appeals simply to the tradition of the apostles. He does not, however, seem interested in the rite of baptism as a rite, and this is characteristic of him. Similarly in the *Homilies on Isaiah*[6] he argues that our Lord's command to his disciples to wash one another's feet could not have been intended literally, because nobody in the Church obeys it literally, which constitutes an appeal to ecclesiastical tradition, and ecclesiastical tradition as interpreting the Bible, though not, it is true, in a very important particular.

---

[1] *Concerning Prayer* xvi, 1.

[2] Op. cit. p. 23 and note. Incidentally, he also notes the μὴ δεῖν εὔχεσθαι τοῖς εὐχομένοις, in reference to prayers addressed to saints, of *Concerning Prayer* xv. 2, and *Against C.* v. xi, and remarks (p. 24): '*En tout cela il faut reconnaître l'influence d'une théologie savante faisant violence au culte chrétien pour le plier à ses lois.*' For Lebreton this is the supreme example of the '*désaccord*' between the intellectual's doctrine and the simple believer's faith.

[3] II. vii. I do not think that we can impugn the integrity of the translator here.

[4] x. xxxiii.   [5] v. viii, ix.   [6] vi. iii.

There are three passages, however, where Origen deals with this subject much more specifically. In the *Homilies on Numbers*[1] he says that in the case of many church customs most of those who observe them do not know the reason for them—such customs, for instance, as turning to the East for prayer, kneeling to pray, the manner of celebrating the Eucharist, or the words, actions, questions, and replies in baptism. But people do them all the same, 'according to the way in which they have been handed down and entrusted by the Great High Priest and his sons'. The phrase 'the Great High Priest and his sons' probably means Christ and his bishops, and this certainly implies an 'institutional tradition' independent of the Bible. Origen goes on to say that there are, of course, some who do know the reasons for these things, corresponding to Aaron and his sons; but he does not tell us who these people are. It is highly likely that the people who understand these things are, in Origen's opinion, the Christian intellectual *élite* who can allegorize them in order to obtain what he would consider suitable truths from them. The second passage is an even more interesting one. It is a fragment recovered from a Catena,[2] on Proverbs 1. 8, 'My son, hear the instruction of thy father, and forsake not the law of thy mother'. It runs thus: πατρὸς μὲν ἀκούομεν λόγους τῆς Γραφῆς· μητρὸς δὲ τὰς ἀγράφους παραδόσεις τῆς ἐκκλησίας, ὁποῖον τὸ νηστεύειν ἐν παρασκευαῖς, καὶ ἕτερα τοιαῦτα. ὥστε φησί· Μὴ πάντα θέλε ἀπὸ γραμμάτων ἀκούειν. ἔστι δὲ καὶ τοὺς φυσικοὺς νοεῖν πατέρας, ἢ καὶ τοὺς πνευματικοὺς νοεῖν διδασκάλους. καὶ γὰρ τούτων μήτηρ ἡ ἐκκλησία.
It clearly chimes in with a passage which we have already had occasion to refer to, and indeed explains it: *Against Celsus* VI. vi, where Origen says that Jesus spoke some things privately to his disciples, and some things he spoke which have not been written. Some things were 'not to be written', and others 'not to be spoken'.[3] The fragment on Proverbs enlightens us as to what these unwritten things were—'fasting on Fridays, and other things like them'. Finally, there is a most interesting passage in the *Conversation with Heracleides*,[4] where Origen is recorded as emphasizing the importance of praying rightly and consistently in the *prosphora*. You must, he says, address God as one God once, as θεῷ διὰ θεοῦ, not twice, as two gods. When you are praying, it is essential ἐμμένειν ταῖς συνθήκαις; otherwise chaos and

---

[1] v. i.   [2] *P.G.* XVII, 157.   [3] See p. 76 above.
[4] Pp. 129–30 of text.

anarchy ensue. And he tries to support his contention with a quotation of Lev. 19. 15. The passage half-way through becomes hopelessly corrupt, but it is clear enough that Origen is much concerned to ensure right doctrine in prayer and to prevent influential local people, bishops, presbyters, and laymen, from using prayer to pervert doctrine. He obviously respects ecclesiastical tradition about prayer, but is anxious to control it by right doctrine based on Scripture. The meaning of ταῖς συνθήκαις is not immediately obvious. Scherer[1] thinks that the meaning is '*les conventions, les engagements qui vont constituer la conclusion pratique du débat*'. If this is so, then it is clear that at that time and in that place the bishop could to some extent compose the prayer in the Eucharist for himself, and Origen does not want the local bishops to use this privilege in order to propagate false teaching. On any interpretation, indeed, the freedom of the bishop to improvise in the Eucharist seems to be evidenced here.

It is clear, then, that Origen did believe that there were a number of traditions connected with Christian institutions and Christian worship which derived from our Lord or his apostles and had come down to his own day independently of the Bible, and, in as far as they go and in as far as he finds it necessary, he will supplement the tradition contained in the Bible from them. But we must severely modify this conclusion by two important considerations. The first is that the points concerning which he allows this tradition are not very important ones, and none of them involve any significant modification of Biblical doctrine. In fact, the evidence we can derive from Origen suggests strongly that what he really looks for from this tradition is a guide, not to doctrine, but to actions and practical matters, such as what posture to take for prayer and when to fast; and this is a conception of 'institutional tradition' which, according to Prestige, is reproduced in other patristic writers. It is, indeed, a very likely and natural conception. And even then, Origen seems quite ready, as we have seen in dealing with his words in *Concerning Prayer*, to abandon ecclesiastical tradition in favour of the Bible in such things as ways of prayer when it suits him, just as he is ready to abandon the Church's rule of faith when it suits him. And to say that included in this tradition are creeds, or a doctrine of the ministry, is, as can readily be seen from the evidence we have reviewed, quite unjustifiable.

[1] *Conversation with Heracleides*, p. 131 of text, notes.

The second consideration is that we cannot be sure that what Origen describes as an apostolic institution really is one. Very few scholars, for instance, would confidently defend infant baptism as an apostolic institution. And when Origen suggests, as he does in the passage from the *Homilies on Numbers* quoted above, that Christian intellectuals know the allegorical meanings of a number of traditional customs, the likelihood of his having genuine and accurate information about them seems remoter. Lawson points out[1] that whenever Irenaeus gives examples of tradition of a similar sort to this, his examples turn out to be unfortunate guesses, such as the authorship of the First and Fourth Gospels, and the statement that our Lord attained the age of fifty years. We may even go so far as to say that by the end of the second century and certainly by the third century patristic writers have fallen into the habit of describing as 'apostolic' any custom whose immediate origin they could not trace and which they knew to be widely diffused throughout the Church.

The evidence therefore in Clement of Alexandria and Origen is quite insufficient for us to conclude that either of these writers regarded Christian institutions or sacraments or worship as capable of providing a fund of doctrine from which the Bible could be interpreted or modified to any important extent. We certainly must not ignore the fact that the life of the Christian Church was continuing uninterruptedly before the New Testament was written, while it was being written, and afterwards, when Clement and Origen were producing their works; indeed they must have implicitly assumed its existence and importance and did not maintain in their minds a clear separation between the evidence of Christian institutions and the evidence of the Bible such as the theology of a later day has tended to make. But if this study has made anything clear, it is that for Origen at least the Bible was his primary and only essential source of doctrine, which he would not consciously modify for any consideration, either the Church's rule of faith or the tradition of Christian institutions; and that, though Clement was clearly ready to modify Biblical doctrine by a secret tradition of teaching of his own, we cannot in all honesty associate with this secret tradition any fund of doctrine genuinely derived from very early times through Christian institutions.

[1] *The Biblical Theology of Saint Irenaeus*, pp. 90–1.

CHAPTER XI

ORIGEN'S DOCTRINE OF TRADITION

WE may summarize Origen's doctrine of tradition by saying that to him the primary and only indispensable source of tradition is the Scriptures of the Old and New Testaments. He is ready to use the books extant only in Greek in the LXX, though he is aware that in theory the Old Testament Canon ought to be confined to books originally written in Hebrew and Aramaic. He knows of no officially fixed list of the canonical books of the New Testament, except that of the Four Gospels. As his life went on, he became more cautious about admitting as Scripture books which he discovered the general judgement of the Church of his day did not endorse, but otherwise his standards of judgement of canonicity were the apparent antiquity of a book and the intrinsic value of its contents. He admitted freely any isolated traditions connected with the Old or the New Testament, provided they appeared valuable to him, and especially those which he had derived from Jewish sources. He believed that he was in possession of a tradition of secret teaching designed for the intellectual Christian, and consisting in fact of a number of theological speculations which appealed to his own mind, as well as a system of allegorizing Scripture which had been greatly developed, but not invented, by himself. But he did not profess to derive this tradition from any source except the Bible itself. He allows that the Bible must be interpreted in a way which shall not conflict with the rule of faith of the Church, by which he means the Christian faith as it is preached by the Church of his day, in continuity with the preaching of it since the very earliest times. He assumes that the content of this preaching is the same as, though not necessarily identical in form with, the doctrine of the Bible, and that it must appeal to the Bible for proof. He is ready at times to encourage his advanced pupils to ignore the rule of faith, but never to ignore the Bible. He shows signs of knowing of the existence of a creed, but displays no interest in it and probably regarded it as a mere summary of the rule of faith. He believes that pagan philosophers have been permitted by God to reach some knowledge of the truth, partly by having access to the Old Testament, and partly by the achievements of their own reason, but he regards the value of this as largely discounted because of their failure to worship God in the way that their knowledge of truth should have led them to worship. In the ordering of Christian institutions and practical details of Church life, he is often guided by traditional customs which he knows to be independent of the Bible and he believes to be genuinely original, but he is ready to set this tradition aside in the interests of what he thinks to be the rule laid down by the Bible.

When we survey this doctrine as a whole, there are certain points which stand out as remarkable, and we must end this work by treating each of them separately. In the first place, the comparison of Origen's doctrine with that of Clement of Alexandria, which has been maintained as consistently as possible throughout this work, enables us to see how very much Origen's theology has gained in *definiteness* compared with that of his predecessor. Even when we have traced to the best of our ability the relation of the rule of faith to the secret tradition in Clement, and endeavoured to see what authority Clement gave to each, we are still left with an uncertainty which cannot (judging from the different interpretations of it which have been given by different scholars) be attributed purely to the uncomprehending mind of the modern theologian but must in part arise from the fact that Clement had himself not clearly defined the subject in his own mind. With Origen there is—once we have cleared our mind of the dangerous habit of relying on the Latin translations of his works for primary evidence in this matter—very little confusion. Quite clearly, he does not confuse or identify the rule of faith with the secret tradition. He does not claim that the secret tradition has been handed down to him by some very unlikely independent agency apart from the Bible, as Clement does. We have said that Origen's attitude to the Canon is fundamentally the same as Clement's. But it is still a noticeably more definite one. He has his conception (though it may not have much influence upon his practice) of the 'genuine', 'spurious', and 'mixed' classes of books; he takes far more notice than does Clement of the acceptance of a book in the Church in general; he is more reticent in his use of such exotic temptations for the Christian apologist as the *Sibylline Oracles*. He is, in general, far more scholarly in his treatment of the Canon. He frankly acknowledges the uncertainties that attach to the authorship of the Epistle to the Hebrews. Again, he can and does set down specifically what doctrines are received by the Church's rule of faith and what are open for speculation by Christian theologians.

Inevitably this comparison raises a question upon which we have already touched,[1] the relation between Origen and Clement. That there was a close relation of thought—so close that even without Eusebius' definite testimony we should have to assume that they had been at one time in the relation of pupil and master—is perfectly obvious to anyone who has studied their works. Even where Origen differs markedly from Clement he usually starts from Clement's presuppositions. We have already made the conjecture that the relationship between the two which we find in Origen's works goes beyond that of pupil to master; that Origen was often consciously modifying and correcting Clement's doctrine, and that the reason why he did not mention him by name, though two of his works bear the same titles as two of Clement's, was that he disapproved of the heretical tendencies in Clement's thought. This suggestion has received a little confirmation in our examination of the attitude of both these writers to revelation outside the Bible. Is not Origen in his markedly critical treatment of Plato (however much he may borrow his doctrines), and in his consistent stress upon the culpability of the pagan philosophers in not worshipping God aright, deliberately dissociating himself from Clement's almost unconditional approval of these men? Clement can speak of Plato as 'that lover of truth, inspired as it were of God';[2] Origen can say that in writing the *Phaedrus* Plato was inspired by the devil. These are two extreme statements compared with one another, but they serve to emphasize vividly a contrast which is truly striking, and which we believe to be no mere coincidence.

Another point which must impress us in Origen's doctrine of tradition is his very strong emphasis on the Bible, what Harnack called his '*unbedingten Biblicismus*'.[3] We have shown that in certain circum-

---

[1] See above, pp. 23 (and n. 5), 29 (n. 4), 90.

[2] See p. 162 above. For something approaching a direct contradiction of Clement in Origen, see p. 172 above.

[3] See p. 51 above. Von Balthasar, in his article, 'Le Mystérion d'Origène' points out (p. 542) how Origen sees the Word as almost incarnate in the Scriptures, and he quotes ἐν βιβλίῳ οἱονεὶ σωματωθῇ from *Comm. in Matt.* xv. 3 (*P.G.* XIII, 1258). To Origen (pp. 545–6), just as the humanity of Christ is the visible symbol of God's having drawn near to us and saved us, so Scripture is by analogy 'the material symbol of his Word in our inmost heart during the whole course of history'.

stances he will ignore the Church's rule of faith, but he will never professedly ignore the Bible, even for the sake of his beloved secret teaching; indeed he would claim that it was from the Bible that he derived his secret teaching. We have seen how in the interests of accurate adherence to the Bible he will not even allow Christians to address prayers to Christ either with the Father or without him,[1] in spite of the support of the devotional tradition of the Church for this practice. We have noted that he does not even pretend to find his secret tradition in any other source than in the Bible. A treatment of his interpretation of Scripture as a whole could easily show what has in fact been demonstrated by many scholars in the course of their expositions of other sides of his thought: that he worked out an elaborate system of allegory in order to make Scripture supply all his demands in the realm of metaphysics, and indeed of physics too; and that he had a greater respect for the Hebrew text of the Old Testament, and indeed for high standards of textual criticism of the Bible generally, than any Christian scholar before Jerome.[2] There is nothing like this Biblical emphasis in any scholar before him, and it can be found in very few after him. So striking is it that I venture to suggest that it points to one important conclusion concerning the history of the doctrine of tradition in the early Christian Church.

But before we outline this conclusion we must deal with one serious charge which has been laid against Origen by a distinguished authority on his thought, and which is supported by a considerable amount of evidence. De Faye would have us believe that this uncompromising loyalty to the Bible which so distinguishes Origen is a mere façade composed in order to hide the fact that Origen is composing his theological system from elements in contemporary philosophy and not from any genuine tradition of Christian thought.[3] Origen's loyalty to the Bible, says de Faye, arises more from the general respect for antiquity which was the prevailing atmosphere of the schools of Alexandria; he refused to eliminate certain Hebrew elements in his thought more because of 'son sentiment chrétien'[4] than because they

[1] See pp. 177–8 above.

[2] I hope later to produce a work dealing specifically, and not merely ἐν παρέργῳ, as has hitherto been done by most scholars, with points such as these.

[3] See de Faye, Origène, sa Vie, son Œuvre, sa Pensée, Vol. I, pp. 85–95; Vol. III, pp. 107–8, 156–63.

[4] Ibid. Vol. III, p. 107.

were consistent with the rest of his thought. And he has no real use for the Jesus of history: 'Origen's philosophy owes nothing to the Jesus who lived, spoke, acted. Let us say, if it is preferable, that neither the picture of Jesus such as the earliest Christians made it in the Gospels, nor his deeds or words, had any influence on Origen's theology. The material of the Gospels was not one of the sources of his thought.'[1] The Christian Platonists only refrained from entirely abandoning the historicity of the New Testament revelation because to do so would have been out of keeping with the intellectual atmosphere of their day. 'It is not surprising that the first Christian philosophers, exegetes, and teachers retained only those elements of the tradition which fitted in with their thought, or that they allegorized the Gospels without the least concern for the historical reality which was their foundation.' Origen and Clement did not differ from their Gnostic predecessors so much in their 'method, culture, intellectual bias', as in the difference of period and circumstance. They showed the same capacity for reading their systems into the Christian revelation.[2]

There is obviously much evidence to support this accusation against the Christian Platonists. The reader of both Clement and Origen must be constantly impressed, and even shocked, by the freedom with which they will branch off into theological disquisitions which have no serious connection whatever with the theology of the Bible, all the time claiming that they are interpreting the Bible with particular success. De Faye himself has shown with exhaustive care how much Origen owes to Greek philosophy of many schools. And to deal with the question fully or adequately would be vastly beyond the scope of this work. One or two comments, however, may be made with the design of revealing what light a study of Origen's doctrine of tradition throws upon this point.

That Origen used the materials of philosophy in order to build his theological system is undeniable. But it is worth while paying some attention to the way in which he used these materials. Gregory in his *Panegyric* suggests that he used philosophical materials very freely, without committing himself deeply to any school of thought,[3] and the evidence of Origen's works seems to bear this statement out. Cadiou is probably going too far in the opposite direction when he says that the Alexandrian Fathers were not exceptionally philosophically minded, because all thinkers of Christian antiquity were inclined to be

---

[1] De Faye, op. cit., p. 160.   [2] Ibid. p. 162.   [3] See p. 163 above.

so: '*On devenait, dans la mesure permise et même un peu davantage, platonicien ou stoïcien, romain ou athénien, comme on cède à l'usage ou comme on a recours à la culture.*'[1] Von Balthasar is more accurate when he represents Origen as using pagan philosophy in the way that a carpenter uses his tools. He finds many of its doctrines useful, but he does not allow himself to be carried away by his tools. '*Il utilise les théorèmes philosophiques de son temps en théologien, il construit avec eux comme avec des pierres taillées d'avance, il les prend comme des signes, des gestes qui montrent autre chose, et qui ne l'intéressent guère en eux-mêmes.*'[2] And it is worth pointing to the definite contrast he presents to Clement in the treatment of the attainment of the pagan philosophers to truth. It is hardly conceivable that one who was so very sparing (at least in comparison with his predecessor) of praise for the exponents of Greek philosophy should have allowed himself in fact to surrender the essential content of his theology to those very philosophers whom he criticized. It is true that his theory that the philosophers had stolen extensively from the Old Testament makes it possible for him to borrow the ideas of Greek philosophy and still persuade himself that he is merely reproducing Old Testament theology. But it cannot be insignificant that the very distinction which he draws between the pagan philosophers and the men of the Old Testament in their approach to the truth—and draws so much more emphatically than Clement, even to denouncing Clement's beloved Plato—is one which gives us an opportunity, as we have seen, of declaring Origen clearly on the side of the angels.[3] This test of worship which he applies to the philosophers and whereby he finds them so much wanting is no mere isolated tradition retained by Origen out of respect for his 'Christian sentiment', but an essential part of his attitude, consistently repeated in all his references to pagan writers. And it is at the same time an inheritance from the earliest Christian, and indeed from a pre-Christian and Hebraic, theological tradition. We might add that it is obvious to anyone who reads Origen's works that though he gravely undervalues the Incarnation as a foundation dogma of the Christian faith,[4] he never

---

[1] *La Jeunesse d'Origène*, p. 400. But we have already seen (p. 125 above) that this could hardly be applied to Irenaeus. And Tertullian has his famous 'What has Athens to do with Jerusalem?'.

[2] 'Le Mystérion d'Origène', p. 530.

[3] See p. 172 above.   [4] See p. 166, n. 1, above.

makes any attempt to ignore it, or to abandon it, in his theological system. He may regard it as an unfortunate necessity, but he does regard it as a necessity. However high his thoughts may soar in the direction of that Eternal Gospel which the intellectual Christian may understand and whereby he may transcend all earthly, literal, incarnate things, he always allows that in order to reach this desirable state even the most intellectual Christian must encounter, believe in, and be baptized into, the incarnate Christ. Again, de Faye grossly overstates Origen's rejection of historicity. Origen regards historicity in much the same light as he regards the Incarnation. He gets away from it as soon as he can, but he consistently says that in the most important things the Christian must admit its necessity.[1] The balloon of Origen's speculation may soar sublimely or extravagantly into the upper air of philosophical irrelevance, but in all important points it is in contact with the ground by the lengthy but firm cable of traditional Christian dogma.

Origen did, after all, respect the Church's interpretation of the Bible. We have had to spend a considerable time during our investigation of Origen's doctrine of tradition in establishing that we have no right to claim for Origen's conception of the rule of faith and of the Church's interpretation of her tradition many of the things that have been claimed for them, and above all we have been concerned to show that Origen knows of no authoritative fund of doctrine independent of the Bible. But still the fact remains that he did recognize the right of the Church to draw up out of her tradition a rule of faith which he was bound to recognize as the right interpretation of the Bible. It is not a rule of faith like Clement's, so much confused with a very doubtful secret tradition as to be of little use for restraining his speculative activity, but one which he distinguishes from his secret tradition (which is in fact his speculative theology). Indeed, as we have seen,[2] he is careful to note the points upon which the Church has produced no article in the rule of faith. It is true that we have found him not seldom encouraging his pupils to transcend and ignore this rule of faith, but it must nevertheless have exercised a strong sobering and modulating effect upon his tendency to speculate, and have served to keep his feet upon the ground of Biblical doctrine.

[1] I hope to set out the evidence, which has never been adequately gathered together, upon this very interesting subject in a later work.

[2] See above, p. 116.

If we have satisfied ourselves that Origen's loyalty to the Bible cannot be dismissed as simply a device to enable him to introduce a quite alien philosophical system into the middle of Christian dogma, under the guise of a Biblical theology, we can turn to consider the conclusion about the development of the doctrine of tradition in the early Church mentioned above. This conclusion is put forward only tentatively, and with the greater diffidence because it can only be substantiated or disproved by a thorough examination of the whole thought of the early Church upon the doctrine of tradition—an achievement which is very far indeed from my grasp; but this conjecture may prove of value to those who are interested in tracing the development of doctrine in the Christian Church.

It is possible that Origen may represent the final stage in the alteration of the attitude of the primitive Church, or of the writers of the primitive Church, towards oral and non-Scriptural tradition. Irenaeus and Tertullian are anxious to stress the fact that in her rule of faith the Church has a tradition of teaching which could act as a substitute for the Scriptures. Irenaeus, Bethune-Baker tells us,[1] appeals to tradition as something which, even if Scripture were not there, would serve us in good stead, as it is the tradition of the teaching of the apostles, guaranteed by the consensus of the most ancient and apostolic Churches about it. He believed, in fact, according to Lawson,[2] in an unwritten tradition handed down from the apostles, independent of Scripture, which would represent the Christian faith adequately even without the Bible. This tradition is not, however, secret: 'For if the Apostles had known hidden mysteries, which they were in the habit of imparting to "the perfect" apart and privily from the rest, they would have delivered them especially to those to whom they were also committing the Churches themselves.'[3] To Irenaeus, Lawson says later, both Scripture and tradition 'are manifestations of one and the same thing, the *apostolic truth* by which the Christian lives. The authority within the Church is all one, "*the Apostolic*", however transmitted. The truth hangs by two cords, and he can speak of either as self-sufficient without intending to deny or subordinate the other.... The whole Rule of

[1] *An Introduction to the Early History of Christian Doctrine*, p. 56.
[2] *The Biblical Theology of Saint Irenaeus*, p. 87. He refers to *Adv. Haer.* III. 4. 1–2.
[3] *Adv. Haer.* III. 3. 1 (E. T., Lawson, pp. 88–9).

Truth, in all its possible manifestations, is nothing other than "*the apostolic*". It is that which the Church preaches, and which she asserts upon her own authority to be the truth. S. Irenaeus has no idea, therefore, of a separate Rule of Faith standing over against Scripture to interpret it. The interpreter of Scripture is always described as the Church, and in particular, the company of authorized and apostolic bishops and presbyters. Certainly the Rule is, in a sense, more than the Baptismal Confession. On the one hand, the Confession is only a brief compendious formula, requiring to be expounded. On the other, it is simple scriptural language, which therefore needs to be interpreted. However, the Confession is nothing other than a manifestation of the one teaching, the Rule, and may therefore be described simply as "The Rule of Faith".[1] Tertullian is even more emphatic about the independence of the rule of faith. 'There is this distinction between Tertullian and Irenaeus,' says Blackman,[2] 'that while Irenaeus regarded Scripture as the rule of faith side by side with the rule of Christian doctrine, the Creed being a sort of digest of the most indispensable articles of Scripture, Tertullian goes further and ranks the Creed above Scripture. He was forced to this by controversy with heretics; cf. *De Praesc.* 17–20, where he complains that appeal to Scripture will never convince heretics. Heretics had their own canon of Scripture.' And Bethune-Baker[3] notes that in the same work Tertullian can say: 'Whose are the Scriptures? By whom and through whose means and when and to whom was the discipline [i.e. the teaching or system] handed down which makes men Christians? Wherever you find the true Christian discipline and faith, there will be the truth of the Christian Scriptures and expositions and all traditions.'

Irenaeus is, by this account, less confident that the rule of faith is independent of the Bible than is Tertullian, but still is ready on occasion to claim its independence. It is interesting to compare the attitude of these two Fathers with that of Clement of Alexandria. On the one hand he has the conception of a rule of faith which is independent of the Bible and interpretative of it, but on the other he identifies it with his

[1] Lawson, pp. 103–4.

[2] *Marcion and his Influence*, p. 94, n. 1. I doubt whether Blackman is justified in identifying the rule of faith with the Creed.

[3] Op. cit. pp. 57–8. See p. 35 above, where this passage has already been quoted.

secret tradition, deriving it from a line of teachers of esoteric doctrine and giving it a pedigree and credentials in which we cannot believe. He does not, however, at any point claim the rule of faith as a substitute for the Bible. On the contrary, he speaks at times (as we have seen in chapter III) as if the Bible were the sole source of his doctrine. He is therefore genuinely the representative of a middle stage between Irenaeus and Tertullian, who give to the rule of faith autonomous authority, and Origen.

In Origen there is no evidence for a source of doctrine independent of the Bible. The rule of faith is only independent in as far as it is the Church preaching and teaching her faith in continuity with the faith which has from the earliest times been taught and preached by the Church. But he assumes that this preaching and teaching derive their material and evidence from the Bible. He makes no emphatic or frequent appeal to the witness of the apostolic succession of the bishops as a proof of the genuineness of the rule of faith. Where we do find such an appeal in Origen's works, it is usually in those which have survived only in Latin, and it is precisely on such a point as this that we should expect his translators to have altered or supplemented his words. Indeed, we have been able to see examples of their doing something very like this.[1] Or else he appeals to apostolic authority for his use of allegory.[2] But he hardly ever refers to the bishops as trustees of the faith in the way in which Irenaeus did. Origen had had unhappy experiences with bishops. Nor do we find any hint in Origen that the rule of faith could be a substitute for the Bible. We have noted already several times that though he can encourage his advanced students to transcend the rule of faith, he never suggests that they should transcend the Bible. Though he can, when he wants to, use the aid both of the tradition conveyed in Christian institutions and of isolated traditions derived from sources outside the Bible, he gives them no position that could make them serious rivals to the Bible as his sole important source of doctrine. In short, in the matter of tradition outside the Bible, Origen differs markedly from Irenaeus and Tertullian, and definitely, though not so markedly, from Clement of Alexandria.

Does this change of attitude which we can trace in these four Fathers of the late second and early third centuries represent the final disappearance of oral tradition from the Church's official ken? Tradition, in its

[1] See pp. 45, 46, above.   [2] See pp. 101–5, above.

largest sense, must of course have been originally oral. And even when it came to be written down in the Scriptures of the New Testament, a certain amount of oral tradition must for a time have survived, as John 21. 25 testifies. It is perhaps the consciousness of the existence of this oral tradition that makes Irenaeus and Tertullian so confident of their rule of faith, and it may be that this too contributed to persuade Clement that he was in possession of a tradition of doctrine independent of the Bible. We have seen that he clearly regards this tradition as not written.[1] But by the time that we reach Origen the possibility of oral tradition of any important kind surviving is virtually ignored. Clement was in many ways a looser and less systematic thinker than Origen, and certainly Origen was a much greater devotee and student of the Bible than Clement. But even when this has been allowed for, it may be that Origen's more rigid attitude towards what is fluid in Clement may be characteristic, not merely of Origen's personal thought, but of the thought of the Christian writers of his age.

We are accustomed to being told by scholars that the third century sees a hardening in the attitude of the Church to such things as the Canon, the ministry, and the definition and articulation of Christian doctrine; and in so far as we have seen an increased definiteness in Origen's thought over Clement's, we have been able to bear out this observation in this study of Origen's doctrine of tradition. It may be that what contributed to this hardening was, not merely the natural process of the development of doctrine, but the gradual disappearance of the possibility of the survival of oral tradition. If this were so, we should have in Clement of Alexandria and Origen the, so to speak, watershed of this process. In Clement the possibility of oral tradition is taken seriously, even though it results in some rather fantastic consequences, and in this he is apparently in continuity with Irenaeus, his predecessor, and Tertullian, his contemporary. But with Origen, who belongs to the next generation, the continuity is broken. He no longer seriously reckons with the possibility of the survival of oral tradition. Of all the aspects of Origen's doctrine of tradition with which we have been concerned in this work—his secret teaching, his attitude to the Canon, his evaluation of institutional tradition, his conception of the rule of faith, his consistent reference back to the Bible, his eager championship of allegory—this is perhaps the most important.

[1] See p. 57 above.

BIBLIOGRAPHY

In Origen's and Clement's works I have generally followed the order in Migne (except that in Origen's case I have prefixed those works read in more modern editions); in Philo's works I have followed the order of the Loeb edition; and the rest I have arranged alphabetically.

I. THE WORKS OF ORIGEN

Philocalia. Edited by J. Armitage Robinson. Cambridge, 1893.

The Commentary on S. John's Gospel. Edited by A. E. Brooke. 2 vols. Cambridge, 1896.

The Eight Books Against Celsus. Edited by P. Koetschau. (Origenes, Vols. I and II, of the series *Die Griechischen Christlichen Schriftsteller der ersten drei Jahrhunderte.*) Leipzig, 1899.

Concerning First Principles. Edited by P. Koetschau. (Origenes, Vol. V, of the series *G.C.S.*) Leipzig, 1913.

The Commentary on S. Matthew's Gospel. Edited by E. Klostermann. (Origenes, Vols. X–XII, of the series *G.C.S.*) This includes both the part extant in Greek and the *Commentariorum Series* extant only in Latin (with a few Greek fragments) which I have consistently referred to as *Commentary on Matthew*, Part II. Leipzig, 1935.

The Exhortation to Martyrdom. Edited by P. Koetschau. (Origenes, Vol. I, of the series *G.C.S.*) Leipzig, 1899.

Concerning Prayer. Edited by P. Koetschau. (Origenes, Vol. II, of the series *G.C.S.*) Leipzig, 1899.

The Homilies on Jeremiah, Commentary on Lamentations, and Fragments on the books of Samuel and Kings. Edited by E. Klostermann. (Origenes, Vol. III, of the series *G.C.S.*) Leipzig, 1901.

Fragments of the Homilies on Acts. Migne, *Patrologia Graeca*, Vol. XIV, cols. 829–30.

The Commentary on Romans. P.G. XIV, 831–1292.

Fragments from works on Galatians, Colossians, 1 *Thessalonians, Titus, Philemon, and the Epistle to the Hebrews. P.G.* XIV, 1293–1308.

The Commentary on Genesis. P.G. XII, 91–144.

The Homilies on Genesis. P.G. XII, 145–280.

Fragments of the Commentary on Exodus. P.G. XII, 281–96.

The Homilies on Exodus. P.G. XII, 297–394.

Fragments of the Commentary on Leviticus. P.G. XII, 395–404.

The Homilies on Leviticus. P.G. XII, 405–572.

Fragments of the Commentary on Numbers. P.G. XII, 573–82.

The Homilies on Numbers. P.G. XII, 583–804.

Fragments on Deuteronomy. P.G. XII, 805–18.

Fragments on Joshua. P.G. XII, 819–24.

The Homilies on Joshua. P.G. XII, 825–948.

Fragments on Judges. P.G. XII, 949–50.

The Homilies on Judges. P.G. XII, 951–90.

Fragments on 1 and 2 Samuel. P.G. XII, 991–1030.

Fragments on Job. P.G. XII, 1031–52.

The Commentaries on Psalms. P.G. XII, 1053–1684. Included in the middle of these (pp. 1320–1409) are five *Homilies* on Psalm 37 (LXX and Vulgate 36), two on Psalm 38 (LXX and Vulgate 37), and one on Psalm 39 (LXX and Vulgate 38).

Fragments of Commentaries on Proverbs. P.G. XIII, 17–34.

Fragments on the Song of Songs. P.G. XIII, 35–6.

The Homilies on the Song of Songs. P.G. XIII, 37–58.

The Commentary on the Song of Songs. P.G. XIII, 62–197.

Fragments on the Song of Songs from Procopius. P.G. XIII, 198–216.

Fragments of a Commentary on Isaiah. P.G. XIII, 217–18.

Homilies on Isaiah. P.G. XIII, 219–42.

Homilies on Ezekiel. P.G. XIII, 663–766.

Fragments on Ezekiel. P.G. XIII, 767–826.

Homilies on Luke. P.G. XIII, 1801–1900.

Fragments on Luke from Macarius. P.G. XIII, 1901–10.

The Letter to Africanus. P.G. XI, 48–86.

The Letter to Gregory. P.G. XI, 87–92.

Fragments of On the Resurrection. P.G. XI, 92–101.

Fragments from Catenae. P.G. XVII, 11–370.

The Commentary on the Epistle to the Ephesians. Fragments printed by J. A. F. Gregg in the *Journal of Theological Studies*, vol. iii (1902), pp. 233–44, 398–420, 554–76.

The Commentary on Romans. Greek fragments edited by A. Ramsbotham in the *Journal of Theological Studies*, vol. xiii (1912), pp. 209–24, 357–68, and vol. xiv (1913), pp. 10–22.

The Commentary on 1 Corinthians. Fragments edited by C. Jenkins in the *Journal of Theological Studies*, vol. ix (1908), pp. 231–47, 353–72, 500–14, and vol. x (1909), pp. 29–51.

Commentaires Inédits des Psaumes. Étude sur les Textes d'Origène contenus dans le Manuscrit Vindobonensis 8. R. Cadiou. Paris, 1936.

Entretien d'Origène avec Héraclide et les Évêques ses Collègues sur le Père, le Fils, et l'Âme, édité par Jean Scherer. Imprimière de l'Institut Français d'Archéologie Orientale, Cairo, 1949.

Die Scholien-Kommentar des Origenes zur Apokalypse Johannis, entdeckt und herausgegeben von Constantin Diobouniotis und Adolf Harnack (No. 38 of *Texte und Untersuchungen*). Leipzig, 1911.

II. ORIGINAL SOURCES OTHER THAN ORIGEN'S WORKS

CLEMENT OF ALEXANDRIA

Protreptikos. Migne, *Patrologia Graeca*, Vol. VIII, cols. 49–246.

Paidagogos. P.G. VIII, 247–684.

Stromateis. P.G. VIII, 685–1382 (Books I–IV); IX, 9–602 (Books V–VIII).

Quis Dives. P.G. IX, 603–52.

Excerpta ex Theodoto. P.G. IX, 653–97.

Eclogae ex Scripturis Propheticis. P.G. IX, 698–728.

Fragments. P.G. IX, 729–76.

PHILO

In the Loeb edition, of which Vols. I–V are edited by F. H. Colson and the Rev. G. H. Whitaker, and Vols. VI–IX by F. H. Colson alone:

Vol. I: Introduction by the Rev. G. H. Whitaker. *De Opificio. Legum Allegoria.*

Vol. II: *De Cherubim. De Sacrificiis Abelis et Caini. Quod Deterius Potiori Insidiari Soleat. De Posteritate Caini. De Gigantibus.*

Vol. III: *Quod Deus Immutabilis Sit. De Agricultura. De Plantatione. De Ebrietate. De Sobrietate.*

Vol. IV: *De Confusione. De Migratione Abrahami. Quis Rerum Divinarum Heres? De Congressu.*

Vol. V: *De Fuga et Inventione. De Mutatione Nominum. De Somniis I. De Somniis II.*

Vol. VI: *De Abrahamo. De Josepho. De Vita Mosis I. De Vita Mosis II.*

Vol. VII: *De Decalogo. De Specialibus Legibus I. De Specialibus Legibus II. De Specialibus Legibus III.*

Vol. VIII: *De Specialibus Legibus IV. De Virtutibus. De Praemiis et Poenis.*

Vol. IX: *Quod Omnis Probus Liber Sit. De Vita Contemplativa. De Aeternitate Mundi. In Flaccum. Hypothetica vel Apologia pro Judaeis. De Providentia* (all extant fragments).

In the *Tauchnitz* edition (Vol. VI, Leipzig, 1853), *De Legatione ad Gaium.*

OTHER ANCIENT AUTHORS

AFRICANUS: *Letter to Origen.* Migne, *P.G.* Vol. XI, cols. 41–8.

BARNABAS: *Epistle of.* Edited by T. Crafer. London, 1920.

EUSEBIUS: *Ecclesiastical History.* Edited by W. Bright. Oxford, 1881; 2nd ed.

GREGORY: *Panegyric on Origen.* P.G. X, 1049–1104.

13-2

HERACLEON: *Fragments of.* Edited with introduction by T. Armitage Robinson. Cambridge, 1891.

IGNATIUS: *Epistles.* Edited by Kirsopp Lake in *The Apostolic Fathers*, Vol. I, pp. 166–277. Harvard University Press, 1945.

PAMPHILUS: *Apology for Origen.* Book I, trans. by Rufinus. *P.G.* XVII, 521–615.

PORPHYRY: *Life of Plotinus*, in *Plotini Enneades*, Vol. I. Ed. by H. F. Mueller. Berlin, 1878.

RUFINUS: *Liber de Adulteratione Librorum Origenis. P.G.* XVII, 615–32.

III. MODERN AUTHORS

A. BOOKS

BADCOCK, F. J. *The History of the Creeds.* London, 1938; 2nd ed.

BATE, H. N. *The Sibylline Oracles III–IV* (translated). Introduction. London, 1918.

BETHUNE-BAKER, J. F. *An Introduction to the Early History of Christian Doctrine.* London, 1933; 5th ed.

BIGG, C. *The Christian Platonists of Alexandria.* Oxford, 1886; R.P. 1913.

BLACKMAN, E. C. *Marcion and his Influence.* London, 1948.

BROOKS, E. W. *Joseph and Asenath* (translated). London, 1918.

BUTTERWORTH, G. W. *Origen on the First Principles* (translated). Introduction. London, 1936.

CADIOU, R. *La Jeunesse d'Origène.* Paris, 1935.

CASEY, R. P. *The Excerpta ex Theodoto of Clement of Alexandria.* Edited with translation and notes. Introduction. London, 1934.

CHARLES, R. H. *The Testaments of the Twelve Patriarchs* (translated). London, 1917.

CULLMANN, O. *The Earliest Christian Confessions.* (English translation.) London, 1949.

DANIÉLOU, J. *Origène.* Paris, 1948.

DENIS, J. J. *De la Philosophie d'Origène.* Paris, 1884.

DE FAYE, E. *Origène, sa Vie, son Œuvre, sa Pensée.* 3 vols. Paris, 1923.

FAIRWEATHER, W. *Origen and Greek Patristic Theology.* Edinburgh, 1901.

FIELD, F. *Origenis Hexaplorum Quae Supersunt, Praefatio et Prolegomena.* Oxford, 1875.

FOAKES-JACKSON, F. J. *Christian Difficulties in the Second and Twentieth Centuries.* A study of Marcion and his relation to modern thought. London, 1903.

GIBBON, E. *Decline and Fall of the Roman Empire* (caps. V–XI). Edited by J. B. Bury. London, 1920–5.

HILGENFELD, A. *Novum Testamentum extra Canonem Receptum.* Leipzig, 1866.

HORT, F. J. A. *The Ante-Nicene Fathers*. Chapter on Origen. London, 1895.

KAHLE, P. E. *The Cairo Geniza*. Relevant passages. Oxford, 1947.

KELLY, J. N. D. *Early Christian Creeds*. London, 1950.

KENNEDY, H. A. A. *Philo's Contribution to Religion*. London, 1919.

KLOSTERMANN, E. & BENZ, E. *Zur Überlieferung der Matthäusklärung des Origenes. (Texte und Untersuchungen zur Geschichte der altchristlichen Literatur*, 4. Reihe, 2. Band, 2. Heft.) Leipzig, 1931.

KNOX, W. L. *Saint Paul and the Church of the Gentiles*. Cambridge, 1939.

LATKO, E. F. *Origen's Concept of Penance*. Faculté de Théologie, Université Laval, Quebec, Canada, 1949.

LAWLOR, H. J. & OULTON, J. E. L. *Eusebius' Ecclesiastical History and Martyrs of Palestine* (translated with an introduction and notes). Vol. II. London, 1928.

LAWSON, J. *The Biblical Theology of Saint Irenaeus*. London, 1948.

MOLLAND, E. *The Conception of the Gospel in Alexandrian Theology* (written by the author in English). Oslo, 1938.

MONDÉSERT, C. *Clément d'Alexandrie*. Paris, 1944.

MONTEFIORE, C. G. & LOEWE, H. *A Rabbinic Anthology*. Excursus II on 'Rabbinical and Early Christian Ethics', by R. H. Snape; Chapter xxvi, on Peace; and the List of Rabbis and their generations appended. London, 1938.

PATERSON, W. P. *The Rule of Faith*. Relevant passages. London, 1912.

PRAT, F. *Origène, le Théologien et l'Exégète*. Paris, 1907.

PRESTIGE, G. L. *Fathers and Heretics*. London, 1940.

RAUER, M. *Die Homilien zu Lukas in der Übersetzung des Hieronymus und die griechischen Reste der Homilien und des Lukas-Kommentars*. (Origenes, Vol. x, of *G.C.S.*) Introduction only. Leipzig, 1930.

SANDERS, J. N. *The Fourth Gospel in the Early Church*. Cambridge, 1942.

SWETE, H. B. *An Introduction to the Old Testament in Greek*. Cambridge, 1902; 2nd ed. 1914.

TOLLINTON, R. B. *Clement of Alexandria*. 2 vols. London, 1914.

—— *Selections from the Commentaries and Homilies of Origen*. Introductory Essay. London, 1929.

WILLIAMS, C. *The Descent of the Dove*. London, 1939.

WILLIAMS, N. P. *The Ideas of the Fall and of Original Sin*. Section on Origen, pp. 208–31. London, 1927.

B. Articles in Periodicals, Encyclopaedias, etc.

Arseniev, N. 'The Teaching of the Orthodox Church on the Relation between Scripture and Tradition.' Essay II in *The Eastern Churches Quarterly*, Vol. vii, 1947, Supplementary issue. Papers read at the *Eastern Churches Quarterly* Conference at Blackfriars, Oxford, Oct. 1946, and at a discussion group of Dominicans and members of the Mirfield Community, July 1946.

Balthasar, H. von. 'Le Mystérion d'Origène.' *Recherches de Science Religieuse*, tom. xxvii, 1936, pp. 513–62.

Bardy, G. 'La Règle de Foi d'Origène.' *Recherches de Science Religieuse*, tom. ix, 1919, pp. 162–96.

—— 'Les Traditions Juives dans l'Œuvre d'Origène.' *Revue Biblique*, 1925, tom. xxxiv, pp. 217–52.

Bouyer, L. 'Holy Scripture and Tradition as seen by the Fathers.' Essay I in *E.C.Q.* Vol. vii, 1947, Supplementary issue.

Cadiou, R. 'Dictionnaires Antiques dans l'Œuvre d'Origène.' *Revue des Études Grecques*, tom. 45, 1932, pp. 271–85.

Caspari, C. P. 'Hat die alexandrinische Kirche zur Zeit des Clemens ein Taufbekenntniss besessen, oder nicht?' *Zeitschrift für Kirchliche Wissenschaft und Kirchliches Leben*, tom. vii, 1886, pp. 352–75.

'Cassiodorus.' Article. *Dictionary of Christian Biography*. Edited by Smith and Wace. London, 1877.

Dix, G. 'The Ministry in the Early Church.' Essay IV in *The Apostolic Ministry*. Edited by K. E. Kirk. London, 1946.

Halévy, J. 'L'Origine de la Transcription du Texte Hébreu en Caractères Grecs dans les Hexaples d'Origène.' *Journal Asiatique*, 9me Série, tom. 17, Jan.–Juin 1901, pp. 335–41.

Hanson, R. P. C. 'Origen's Doctrine of Tradition.' *Journal of Theological Studies*, Vol. xlix (Jan.–April 1948), nos. 193–4, pp. 17–27.

Inge, W. R. Article, 'Alexandrian Theology'. *Encyclopaedia of Religion and Ethics*. Vol. i. Edinburgh, 1908.

Kehoe, R. 'The Scriptures as the Word of God.' Appendix II, in *E.C.Q.* Vol. vii, 1947, Supplementary issue.

Lebreton, J. 'Les Degrés de la Connaissance Religieuse d'après Origène.' *Recherches de Science Religieuse*, tom. xii (1922), pp. 265–96.

—— 'Le Désaccord de la Foi Populaire et de la Théologie Savante dans l'Église Chrétienne du IIIe Siècle.' *Revue d'Histoire Ecclésiastique*, 1923, tom. 19, pp. 481–506, and 1924, tom. 20, pp. 5–37.

'Longinus, Cassius.' Article. *Encyclopaedia Britannica* (Coronation ed. London, 1937).

Merk, A. 'Origenes und der Kanon des alten Testamentes.' *Biblica* (Commentarii editi a Pontificio Instituto Biblico), 1925, Vol. 6, pp. 200–5.

OPPEL, H. 'ΚΑΝΩΝ, zur Bedeutungsgeschichte des Wortes und seiner lateinischen Entsprechungen (Regula-Norma).' *Philologus*, Supplement-band xxx, Heft 4. Leipzig, 1937.

OULTON, J. E. L. 'Rufinus' Translation of the Church History of Eusebius.' *J.T.S.* Vol. xxx, no. 118 (for Jan. 1929).

SALMON, G. Article, 'Marcion'. *Dictionary of Christian Biography* (1882 edition).

SYMONDS, H. E. 'The Patristic Doctrine of the Relation of Scripture and Tradition.' Appendix I in *E.C.Q.* Vol. VII, 1947, Supplementary issue.

WESTCOTT, B. F. Article, 'Origen'. *Dictionary of Christian Biography* (1882 edition).

Also occasionally consulted:

Greek-English Lexicon. H. G. Liddell and R. Scott (8th edition, 1897).
Latin Dictionary. Lewis and Short (edition of 1890).
A Glossary of Later Latin to A.D. 600. A. Souter. Oxford, 1949.

INDEX OF
REFERENCES AND CITATIONS

I. BIBLICAL

(a) Old Testament and Apocrypha

(b) New Testament

II. PATRISTIC

(*a*) ORIGEN

(*b*) CLEMENT OF ALEXANDRIA

(c) Philo

(d) Eusebius

INDEX OF NAMES

Made in the USA
Middletown, DE
19 August 2018